Power Teaching

A Primary Role of the School Library Media Specialist

KAY E. VANDERGRIFT

American Library Association / Chicago and London 1994

School Media Centers: Focus on Trends and Issues

CULTURAL PLURALISM AND CHILDREN'S MEDIA by Ester Dyer

PROJECTING A POSITIVE IMAGE THROUGH PUBLIC RELATIONS by Cosette Kies

A STUDY OF COMBINED SCHOOL-PUBLIC LIBRARIES by Shirley Aaron

INSTRUCTIONAL DESIGN AND THE LIBRARY MEDIA SPECIALIST
by Margaret E. Chisholm and Donald P. Ely

continued by

School Library Media Programs: Focus on Trends and Issues,
edited by Eleanor Kulleseid

THE INSTRUCTIONAL CONSULTANT ROLE OF THE SCHOOL LIBRARY MEDIA SPECIALIST by Betty P. Cleaver and William D. Taylor

AT THE PIRATE ACADEMY by Gary Zingher

DESIGNING AND RENOVATING SCHOOL LIBRARY MEDIA CENTERS
by Jane D. Klasing

DEALING WITH DIVERSITY THROUGH MULTICULTURAL FICTION
by Lauri Johnson and Sally Smith

THE CHALLENGE OF TECHNOLOGY by Kieth Wright

POWER TEACHING by Kay E. Vandergrift

The paper used in this publication meets the minimum requirements of American National Standard for Information Sciences–Permanence of Paper for Printed Library Materials, ANSI Z39.48-1984. ∞

Vandergrift, Kay E.
  Power teaching : a primary role of the school library media specialist / by Kay E. Vandergrift.
      p. cm. — (School library media programs. Focus on trends and issues ; no. 14)
   Includes bibliographical references (p.) and index.
   ISBN 0-8389-3435-8
   1. School libraries—Activity programs. 2. Library orientation for school children. 3. Information retrieval—Study and teaching.
I. Title. II. Series.
Z675.S3V348 1993
027.8—dc20   93-35565

Copyright © 1994 by the American Library Association. All rights reserved except those which may be granted by Sections 107 and 108 of the Copyright Revision Act of 1976.

Printed in the United States of America.

98 97 96 95 94   5 4 3 2 1

For Jane

Contents

Figures *vii*
Lists *ix*
Introduction *xi*
Preface *xiii*

1 The Educational Context *1*
2 The School Library Media Specialist as Teacher *21*
3 The School Library Media Specialist: Teacher of Research Strategies *42*
4 Teaching Evaluation Strategies with Library Media Center Resources *58*
5 Webbing: Alternative Paths to Organizing Information and Ideas *77*
6 Staff Development and Workshop Initiatives *101*
7 Evaluation and the School Library Media Specialist *128*

Notes *147*
Appendix *161*
Index *169*

Figures

1. A Model of a Child's Meaning-Making Process in Response to a Literary Text   *14*
2. A Model of the Teaching Process   *26*
3. Selected List of Places for Students to Locate on Various Types of Maps or Atlases   *34*
4. Literary Settings for Map Project   *38–39*
5. Civil Rights for African-Americans   *52*
6. Web of Roald Dahl's Books   *84*
7. Web of *Strega Nona*   *86*
8. Food Web   *86*
9. *The Taken Girl* Web   *90*
10. *The Striped Ships* Web   *91*
11. Web of *Wait Till Helen Comes*   *94–95*
12. Management Control Schema   *105*
13. List of Challenged Materials and Typical Objections   *117–119*
14. Self-Evaluation Inventory: School–Public Library Cooperation   *133–136*
15. Photo-Analysis Diagram   *138*

Lists

1. Selected Books Useful in Map and Atlas Projects *31*
2. Selected Videocassettes on Maps and Mapping *35*
3. Selected Computer Software on Maps *36*
4. Selected Books on Columbus *61*
5. Selected Alternative Sources on Christopher Columbus *64*
6. Selected Books on Authors and Illustrators *67*
7. Selected Videocassettes on Authors and Illustrators *68*
8. Selected Videocassettes on Poets *70*
9. Selected Books of Poetry for Young People *70*
10. A Sample Exploration of Literature across the Science Curriculum *79*
11. Roald Dahl Materials: Focus of a Web *84*
12. Selected Books for Web on Food *85*
13. Voices of Female Protagonists in Selected Historical Fiction *91*
14. Selected Reviews of *Wait Till Helen Comes* *92*
15. Selected Articles on Ghosts in Literature *93*
16. List of Books Placed in the Web for *Wait Till Helen Comes* *98*
17. Selected Videocassettes to Stimulate Thought on Societal Issues *109*
18. Selected Books to Stimulate Thought on Societal Issues *110*
19. Selected List of Bibliographic Resources *112*
20. Selected Computer Software on Mathematics for Younger Children *113*
21. Selected Books on Mathematics for Younger Children *113*
22. Key Background Readings and Resources on Intellectual Freedom *115*
23. Supplementary Resources on Intellectual Freedom *115*
24. Selected Versions of *The Crane Wife* and Related Tales *121*
25. Selected Versions of *Beauty and the Beast* *122*
26. Selected Titles by Deborah Nourse Lattimore *123*
27. Feminist Theory *124*
28. Female Voices in Fiction, Biography, and Poetry *124*

Introduction

In the olden days teaching was regarded as a vocation to which individuals (mostly female) were called either by altruism or necessity. Today, as we brace ourselves for the coming millennium, teaching may be regarded as a high-risk professional enterprise with modest visible rewards and little awareness of its value on the part of those who must subsidize the enterprise—taxpayers. Educators are being challenged, more than ever before, to improve the quality of their "product"—a literate worker and socially responsible citizen—with fewer resources. As the wisdom of school administrators and teachers continues to be questioned, the literature of education will continue to elaborate themes of assessment and reform.

Kay Vandergrift's view of teaching is grounded in evaluation and in valuing an interactive and mutual teaching-learning process. She has worn many hats as an educator: elementary school teacher, curriculum specialist, school administrator, and professor in graduate programs of library and information science. Her teaching philosophy is as radical today, in an era of outcome-oriented accountability, as it was when John Dewey first articulated the so-called progressive model of education at the turn of the century. Besieged with requests to update an earlier work that appeared in the Trends and Issues series in 1979, Vandergrift has written a new tome which expands the scope of the teaching role and simultaneously refocuses it on the selection and use of print and nonprint media resources. New computer and telecommunications technologies are integrated with the familiar array of media, and practitioners are given numerous examples of curricular units in a number of subject areas, with specific multimedia titles recommended. Particularly useful are the examples of topic and book webs that suggest alternative methods of developing and elaborating concepts.

One of the most important aspects of this book is an implicit balance between efferent and aesthetic modes of making meaning described in the second chapter. Vandergrift has interwoven teaching/learning activities that call for the interplay of mind and heart, the active engagement of both the cognitive and affective domains of intelligence. This interplay is grounded in the author's vision of teaching as a creative compositional act. In her view, planning for a geography study with a group of seventh graders may be likened to an author's struggle with the draft of a novel in process, or to Beethoven's monumental struggle with the first draft of his fifth symphony. The actual performance of the works are also comparable, in that they are creative acts that may be repeated over time with different outcomes or results. This image of teaching as composition is uplifting, for it empowers the practitioner as an active shaper of events, rather than mere transmitter of a prescribed set of facts and skills. It is also challenging, for it demands the engagement of all capacities and a willingness to take chances, to risk failure. In this book school library media specialists will find ample concepts and content to implement the creative and proactive teaching role envisioned by the author. Her vision of teaching as composition will surely be an essential metaphor for professional survival in the coming decades.

ELEANOR R. KULLESEID
Series Editor

Preface

In one of the chapters that follows, I suggest pointing out to students that when authors put words on paper, their values show through to a greater or lesser degree. Certainly those who read this book will have little difficulty determining where my values lie. There are several assumptions that support every aspect of this work. First is the belief in young people as potentially creative and competent beings who, with the help of knowledgeable and caring adults, can change the world for the better. Second is the faith that this generation of young people will build a society for the twenty-first century that will truly celebrate a culturally diverse and gender-fair world. Third, school library media specialists are in an ideal position to act as those knowledgeable and caring adults who can help young people create this world. Fourth, school library media specialists can do their best work only as they work cooperatively and collegially with other teachers in the school. Fifth, there is no one "right" way to accomplish goals; all education should be a process in which learners are encouraged to choose from among many alternatives, and library media specialists are uniquely equipped to provide those alternatives. Finally, of all the roles library media specialists play, it is the teaching role that has the most powerful and profound influence on those with whom we work.

Information Power identifies the roles of the school library media specialist as information specialist, teacher, and instructional consultant. The particular view of teaching presented in this monograph emphasizes an in-depth knowledge of both informational and aesthetic resources, an understanding of teaching and learning, and the ability to match a variety of resources to educational activities in ways that expand, enrich, and provide alternatives to schooling practices. Thus, it encompasses, at least to some extent, both of the other roles. This perception of teaching goes hand in hand with the belief that each student is a unique maker of personal meanings in the world and that those meanings grow out of ever-expanding and more insightful encounters with information and ideas. These encounters come about through human interaction and in response to a wide variety of resources both within and beyond the school.

Chapter 1, "The Educational Context," presents an overview of the varied and rapidly changing efforts to restructure American education to meet the needs of the twenty-first century. Key aspects of the current dialogue about restructuring, such as the professionalization of teaching, national standards and assessment, the content of the curricular canon, the organizational approach to that canon, and parental choice in schooling, are considered. In addition, there is a concern with gender equity in education that is absent from much of the educational debate in spite of the results of the recent studies by the American Association of University Women. School-university partnerships are examined as one example of a model for incorporating some of the best thinking about educational innovation and change. This chapter posits a view of learning as meaning-making, drawing upon research on the human brain, and discusses how whole language programs, cooperative learning, and other approaches to schooling accommodate various learning styles. Most important for this audience, it presents the centrality of the school library media specialist in encouraging the use of multiple resources, multiple responses, and multiple technologies that will provide the richest and most supportive conditions for educational change.

Chapter 2, "The School Library Media Specialist as Teacher," presents a view of teaching as a compositional process in which the teacher plans for both efferent and aesthetic goals in creating environments for learning. The need for knowledge of many models of teaching in order to respond to personal needs and learning styles is discussed. The second part of this chapter actually demonstrates how a school library media specialist might work with classroom teachers to present many alternative learning opportunities and resources to teach particular subject content. The examples used are from the geography curriculum because that is a subject emphasized in the discussion of schools for the twenty-first century, because a knowledge of geography is necessary in global education and for our global economy, and because the use of many of the tools of geography study has long been taught by school library media specialists.

Chapter 3, "The School Library Media Specialist: Teacher of Research Strategies," refers to several of the excellent models for the teaching of the research process developed by others in our field and stresses the need for cooperative planning with classroom teachers in working through these strategies. The relationship of the research process to developing metacognitive awareness is considered, and special attention is given to the selection and design of specific research topics, especially within a teacher-given assignment. A form of semantic webbing is used as a way of organizing ideas, and there are demonstrations of ways to find a focus for research, either through an issue-centered approach or through a variety of materials-centered approaches. These examples also demonstrate one of the underlying tenets of the teaching role presented in this book—that school library media specialists must not only know about resources and how to find them, they must develop a thorough knowledge of the contents of those materials in order to match them appropriately to student and teacher needs.

Chapter 4, "Teaching Evaluation Strategies with Library Media Center Resources," is also materials-centered. This chapter is based on the premise that the process of education is one of developing critical abilities in evaluating information and ideas from all sources, recognizing that there is no absolutely objective source. Evaluation of biographical materials in various media is suggested as a means of developing such abilities, with a lengthy discussion of the recent materials about Christopher Columbus as an example of various interpretations of historical data over time and from different perspectives. Although the Columbus quincentennial is now past, the materials about his voyages to the Americas serve as what may be the most elaborate display of alternative views of the same events and thus as a useful model for the development of critical strategies for evaluating materials. This chapter also contains a section on biographical resources about authors and illustrators that should be useful in literature and whole language classrooms as well as of interest to library media center users who like to know more about those who create the books they enjoy. The chapter then focuses on docudrama as a popular contemporary form and the kind of critical awareness necessary in viewing these productions. It concludes with a discussion of media production as a means of increasing understanding of and developing evaluative strategies in the media.

Chapter 5, "Webbing: Alternative Paths to Organizing Information and Ideas," elaborates on an approach introduced in chapter 3. Here various approaches to webbing are demonstrated and webs shown at different stages of development. The first example, that of a series of complex and controversial topics in high school science, is actually a pre-web, that is, suggestions for an approach to content that would likely lead to a web and would certainly lead to enriched science study. The various stages of the literary webs that follow show the work of young children in response to *Strega Nona* and then samples of fairly complex webs that might be developed by teachers or students in the middle or high schools for the books *The Taken Girl* and *The Striped Ships*. The most complete web is that for *Wait Till Helen Comes*, which demonstrates how classroom teachers and library media specialists might begin with student interest in a popular novel to develop extensive learning activities while enhancing young readers' pleasure in the story itself.

Chapter 6 focuses on staff development and workshop initiatives. After a brief consideration of the many possibilities for informal staff development as a part of ongoing collegial activities in the school, readers are referred to a number of useful models for more formal staff development, an additional management control schema is provided, and teaching content for six different workshops is presented. These workshops represent a variety of topics and age and grade levels. With the exception of the mathematics workshop, which focuses on materials for young children, and Authentic Female Voices, which is designed for high school students, the workshops include sample materials that span the grade levels so that media specialists at various levels who wish to adapt these ideas to their own situations will have at least a few examples of the types of resources suggested. The chapter ends with a brief call for increased attention to some of the ways library media specialists might offer their expertise to parents and caregivers, perhaps in cooperation with others who share an interest in or responsibility for young people.

The final chapter, "Evaluation and the School Library Media Specialist," grows out of the belief that all human endeavor begins and ends with evaluation, with the question "What do I value?" After a brief overview of general types of evaluation, including problems with standardized tests, two instruments designed by the author are presented. The first of these collects information about time allocations and priorities in the overall activities of the school library media center. The second is a set of paired questionnaires to encourage professionals in the schools and public libraries to evaluate their working relationships. The next section combines some traditional forms of analysis of teaching with media technologies and assistance from the library media specialist. Finally, this chapter includes a consideration of some of the alternative forms of evaluation, such as aesthetic analysis based on the view of teaching as composition and portfolio evaluation designed in conjunction with newer strategies for changing education as we move toward the twenty-first century.

My understanding of the teaching process has been shaped by students and colleagues during thirty years in elementary and graduate school classrooms, the school library media center, and the principal's office. I have been fortunate over those years to have worked with many who share my enthusiasm and my beliefs and have been part of an ongoing dialogue about teaching. To all those who have enriched my professional life, l owe a debt of gratitude.

Special thanks are due to two friends and colleagues who have been directly involved with the production of this monograph. I wish to acknowledge the support of my editor Betty Kulleseid for her faith in this project, her gentle prodding, her suggestions, and her patience, and her patience, and her patience. Very special appreciation goes to Jane Anne Hannigan who has lived with this project from the very beginning and has served as a sounding board for every stage of its development. Her knowledge, her wisdom, and her caring are reflected throughout this volume, and our collaboration continues to be a source of insight and inspiration.

1

The Educational Context

Restructuring America's Schools

There has never been a more opportune time for school library media specialists to make themselves visible, in fact, indispensable, in American schools. Not since the late 1950s and 1960s, after the Soviet Union launched Sputnik, has there been so much public concern about education in this country. The often heated dialogue that has occurred since the publication of *A Nation at Risk* has altered the context in which teaching takes place. If library media specialists are to play a significant role in schooling, they must be cognizant of new theories and practices in education, participate in the dialogue, and work to improve their own teaching in light of new information and ideas.[1] *Libraries for the National Goals*[2] provides evidence of the roles of libraries in educational activities and programs that respond to the initiatives resulting from the six goals of *America 2000*.[3] It is this document expressing strategies for achieving the national goals, more than any other in recent memory, that has mobilized a variety of concerned educators, private citizens, and special interest groups to influence the future of education in the United States. School library media specialists have a vital role to play in the resulting educational drama.

The current discussion about restructuring American schools seems to have at least five foci:

Professionalization of teaching,
National standards and assessments,
Curriculum content,
Curriculum organization and approach to content,
Parental choice.

The Professionalization of Teaching

The professionalization of teaching recognizes that teachers can be, and should be, leaders in schools. For some time we have been hearing about master teachers

1

serving as coaches or mentors to novice teachers, teachers as researchers, and empowered teachers who seek to empower their students. Former President Bush, in his presentation of the national education strategy (The White House, April 18, 1991), supported this empowerment of teachers when he said, "It's time to turn things around—to focus on students, to set standards for our schools—and let teachers and principals figure out how best to meet them."[4]

Of course, standards set by agencies or individuals other than the professionals responsible for carrying them out may not be appropriate. Real professionalization of teaching would give teachers the power to challenge and ultimately to change not only national and state standards but traditional school structures, such as a district-imposed curriculum, classroom size and organization, allocation of at least some portion of educational funds, and both student and teacher evaluations. School-based management has, in some districts, given teachers this kind of decision-making authority and the responsibility that accompanies it. Often teachers choose to share that authority and responsibility with students, parents, and the community.[5]

Andrew Gitlin and Karen Price link teacher empowerment to voice, that is, "an articulation of one's critical opinions and a . . . challenge to domination and oppression."[6] The voice of teachers has almost always been merely a whisper in reaction to requirements imposed on them by others. Teaching has been considered a means to pass on to the next generation that which is valued by a particular society. Thus, power resides in whatever organizations or agencies act for society rather than with teachers. On the one hand, we speak of the profession of teaching while, on the other, we deny teachers the authority of their own work that defines a profession. The current discussion of the professionalization of teaching too often continues this practice. Allowing teachers some degree of self-determination in meeting someone else's predetermined standards neither empowers nor professionalizes teaching.

National Standards

The second focal point of educational debate may, in fact, also be read as a disempowerment of teachers and others involved in education at the local or regional level. The proposal of national standards is not new, but there has certainly been a renewed interest in such standards in recent years. According to *America 2000*, these standards are to be evaluated using "American Achievement Tests" for fourth, eighth and twelfth graders in five core subjects: English, mathematics, science, history, and geography. The National Council on Education Standards and Testing (NCEST), established in 1991, recommended the creation of voluntary national standards to be developed by major scholarly and professional associations.[7] In response to the confusion over the term "standards," NCEST recommended the adoption of three types of standards: (1) content standards to identify what students should know and be able to do, (2) student performance standards to assess the competence of individual learners, and (3) system performance standards to assess the success of all levels of schooling agencies, from the local to the national, in helping students attain their goals. In addition, NCEST calls on states to develop school delivery standards to monitor schools' delivery of educational opportunities.

The New Standards Project (NSP) is a consortium of seventeen states and a number of school districts representing almost half of America's schoolchildren. NSP is working to design and implement performance standards and authentic assessment and the staff development programs to make them work. The NSP content standards will be based on those developed by national professional associations but may be revised through impact with other groups and will be "internationally benchmarked." NSP will then collect actual samples of student performance from situations as close as possible to authentic work in authentic settings. Portfolios of work done over a period of time will include both that selected by student, teacher, or school and that prescribed by NSP. Finally, NSP will develop a network of training for educational trainers who will work with others on school reform.

NCEST and NSP are just two of many organizations and agencies working on national standards. National professional associations representing the various disciplines are developing standards for their content areas. The National Council of Teachers of Mathematics has already released its "Curriculum and Evaluation Standards for School Mathematics," and similar standards for English, science, social studies (including history, geography, and civics) and the arts are to be ready for classroom use for the 1994–95 school year.[8] The National Association for Sports and Physical Education published its "Outcomes of Quality Physical Education Programs" in 1992. This publication was not intended as a direct response to the call for national standards, but it serves the same purpose. The assessment tests that will follow these standards are to be voluntary, but colleges are expected to use them in admissions decisions and employers will probably pay attention to them in hiring. It is, therefore, not clear at what level the tests are to be voluntary. May individual students, teachers or schools decide not to participate in this program of testing, and what might be the consequences of such a choice? Even if "educational flexibility legislation," shifting more authority to local schools, is enacted, educators fear that national standards and the tests that measure progress toward those standards will inevitably lead to a national curriculum.

Few would deny the need for standards or the belief that they must change from time to time; but just a few years ago national standards and the assessment tests based on them would have been inconceivable to many Americans who have traditionally supported local control of schools. Recent accusations of the failures of schools in this country seem to have led to the acceptance of national standards as a kind of desperate, if simplistic, means of improving educational competence and performance. Higher standards are appropriate in many educational enterprises, but simply raising standards cannot and will not improve student achievement. Schools need additional resources to help students reach higher levels of achievement, and society needs to make more aggressive attacks on poverty, homelessness, substance abuse, poor nutrition, and other problems that effectively block the abilities of many young people in our schools.[9] A cautious optimism is now being felt by youth advocates who hope that the Clinton administration will attempt to deal with some of the problems of children in this country, many of whom fare worse than those in other industrialized nations.[10]

If national standards and assessments are to play a major role in restructuring American education, all those concerned must reexamine the history of testing in this country, paying special attention to the various biases built into most tests and to the cost and efficiency factors that have dominated decision-making in determining testing methods and procedures. In addition, educators must seriously examine such factors as the physical formatting of standardized "bubble" examinations, the ordering of questions, and even the color of the paper and ink as they influence test results. Most important, educators must find alternative ways to make student assessments more authentic. Curriculum reforms and innovative teaching strategies create a demand for new forms of assessment that really measure these new approaches to learning. To date, almost all attempts to assess student learning have been at least several steps behind what is actually happening in the best classrooms in this country and, therefore, do not really assess schooling. If educators can enlist parental, community, and institutional support for new combinations of a variety of developmentally appropriate assessment strategies, perhaps this current round of educational reforms will be able to demonstrate real progress. Just as important, schools and society must somehow provide a more level playing field so that all America's young people can, without the social and environmental problems that now inhibit student performances, achieve the same high standards.

Curriculum Content

The discussion of curriculum is the third focus of educational debate today. E. D. Hirsch, Jr., the author of *Cultural Literacy*, is best known for his concern with the lack of a core of common knowledge among young people. He has edited a series of grade-by-grade volumes beginning with *What Your First Grader Needs to Know!*[11] These books list specific content in various subject areas and add to the expectation of and pressure for a standardized national curriculum. In his *What Did You Learn in School Today?: A Parent's Guide for Evaluating Your Child's School*, Harlow G. Unger summarizes in fewer than fifty pages the content against which parents should measure their child's achievements from kindergarten through twelfth grade.[12] Unger's curriculum is based on former Secretary of Education William J. Bennett's curricula for English, social studies (including the *America 2000* core subjects of history and geography), mathematics, science, foreign language, fine arts, and physical education and health.[13] The inclusion of these last three subjects in the core curriculum would be encouraging to those concerned with expanding rather than narrowing the curriculum were it not for the fact that Bennett is no longer Secretary of Education and in any case his pronouncements about curriculum have been superseded by the five core subjects of *America 2000*. Many educators are concerned that national standards and the student examinations that assess progress in the five core subjects will lead to the neglect of the arts and other areas of the curriculum that may not be tested. Others, of course, fear a kind of deadening of the arts if subjected to traditional types of national assessments.

On the one hand, Hirsch and others are establishing a canon or body of specific information to be learned by all students. This core curriculum, combined with standardized testing, may lead less imaginative and less capable teachers to play a kind of trivial pursuit in which the primary objective is successful testing rather than the joy of learning. On the other hand, many educators are advocating more choice for both students and teachers with an emphasis on process rather than product. The debates between advocates of these two approaches are useful in keeping education on the national agenda, but there is a danger of entrenchment in a particular position rather than openness to necessary alternatives to provide the best possible education for all the nation's children. Even some who believe in the necessity for the mastery of a common core of cultural knowledge take issue with Hirsch's canon for its male and European bias. Rick Simonson and Scott Walker, editors of *The Graywolf Annual Five: Multi-Cultural Literacy*, have prepared a preliminary list of alternative items important to American culture but too often excluded from American education.[14]

The danger that arises when national leaders perceive of schooling based on a core curriculum and standardized testing is that students may be perceived of as containers for specific bits of information to be tested and teachers as those who provide that information. Content and evaluation procedures are predetermined by those outside the learning environment. Classroom organization and grouping, although not necessarily prescribed, tend to be selected as the most efficient means of reaching the specific goal which, unfortunately, is often interpreted as success on those tests used to measure educational progress. Certainly evidence, both from this country and from European and Asian countries with standardized examinations, indicates that test-driven curricula are the norm and that subjects or specific aspects of subjects that are not tested fall from the curriculum.[15] Obviously, this is of great concern to advocates of the arts, multiculturalism, physical education, languages, and other areas of schooling outside the five core areas, but equally important to an informed and enriched life.

Expanding the educational core to include subjects some consider "enrichments" or even "frills" does not necessarily mean a lack of concern with "basics." Most reasonable human beings might agree that students should leave school with some central core of knowledge, but it is difficult to reach agreement about what should be in that core or even about who should determine its content. In some instances, those calling for an expanded core in our yet-to-be-restructured schools seem to be referring more to expanded options or strategies and expanded time frames for greater numbers of students to meet basic requirements than to inclusion of additional or alternative content.

Another definition of an expanded core is a more representative multicultural view of content. Unfortunately, many educational critics seem to assume that multiculturalism can be equated with a lack of, or at least reduced, standards. Even those who advocate a more inclusive curriculum often find themselves in heated arguments about the relative values of what Catharine Stimpson calls "centricities," such as Afrocentrism, which focuses on one culture, and a truly multicultural approach showing the complex relationships among cultures.[16] One of the debates is whether attempting to include the accomplishments and cultures of women and minorities in the curriculum leads to fragmentation and fails to acknowledge the American spirit and a sense of national unity. Of course, all curricula are fragmented in a number of ways; and a serious look at global education, another concern of contemporary educators, would make it obvious that those we consider minorities in this country are actually the majority from a global perspective. One of the basic disputes here, although seldom stated, is the age-old question of whether a nation's schools should be more concerned with social control or social change.

Yet another form of the expanded core that leads to more "inclusive education" is the mainstreaming into regular classrooms of youngsters at risk because of mental or physical disabilities. In 1975, Public Law 94-142 was passed ensuring children with disabilities a "free, appropriate, public education" in the "least restrictive environment." Since the enactment of that law, little progress has been made. The fact is that much of public education is an inappropriate restrictive environment for all children, not just those with special disabilities. Parents and teachers of so-called typical children ought to get involved in their own cooperative ventures with groups such as the PEAK Parent Center to plan for the kinds of educational environments and resources that will enable all children to work and learn together and be responsive to every child's personal interests and special needs.[17]

Curriculum Organization and Approach to Content

Many proposals for changes in curricular content are so closely related to this fourth focus in the discussions of restructuring American schools that they might be considered as one. They are, however, separated here to ensure a focus on both aspects of curriculum, that is, content and approach. Interdisciplinary studies and depth rather than breath of coverage often are accompanied by an emphasis on higher-order thinking skills and student use of a variety and range of original documents and technological resources.[18]

One may posit the concept of integration of various technologies in schooling as an essential ingredient of educational success today and a major factor in the organization and approach to curricular content.[19] In addition, we must recognize all students as active learners who need to grasp academic content while demonstrating their ability to think and apply what they have learned to the solution of real problems. Karen Sheingold expresses an important philosophical principle when she writes, "By and large, tasks should not have one right answer, and problems should not have only one route to a solution."[20] David Cohen refers to adventurous teaching as the necessary companion to active or student-centered learning.[21] Of course, student-centered learning and adventurous teaching do not take place within tight structures of traditional schooling. In writing on privacy and children's rights, this author expressed a view that scheduling is one of the greatest invaders of privacy in schooling.[22] It is also one of the major impediments to real learning. Sheingold affirms that 40-minute periods "are too short to do justice to the kind of work students will be expected to do," and suggests that periods of 110 minutes might become the pattern.[23] This suggestion reminds us that authentic and integrated learning adventures need not be confined to the self-contained classroom of the elementary school. If such learning and teaching really work, we cannot afford to drop these practices after the first few years of schooling. Dramatic changes need to be made from preschool through post-graduate education. The concept of flexibility in the teaching environment and design is essential as we approach the task of restructuring our schools.

Sheingold also alerts us to the fact that " . . . some of the information resources that students will need for their work may not be found within the school but will instead be available in the larger community or through telecommunications networks."[24] We have already begun the process of telecommunications in schools in this country and around the world. Through "World Classroom" children in Hill View Elementary School in Salt Lake City, Utah, communicate directly with students in Moscow through an e-mail link.[25] The Indian Creek Elementary School in Indianapolis, Indiana, is a high-technology magnet school that uses an IBM computer-based multimedia tool called LinkWay that permits students and teachers to create multimedia presentations.[26] Students are able to take pictures, drawings, video images, text, and sound from various sources to create their own productions.

Mass LearnPike offers opportunities for specialized courses via telecommunications throughout the state of Massachusetts. This organization has produced and distributed various telecommunications teaching modules, such as courses in Japanese, that are useful in meeting needs that might be ignored if on-site classroom teachers were required. The state of Maine provides a statewide educational network via telecommunications to meet the needs of the citizens of that state.

The questions behind these ripples of educational change are numerous. Should schooling be subject-centered, teacher-centered, or student-centered? Is learning a private enterprise or a social phenomenon? Is knowledge external and objective or internal and subjective? Does schooling take place only within the traditional confines of the school building? These questions and some of the responses to them will be examined more closely from the perspective of the school library media specialist in chapter 3.

Parental Choice

A fifth and final focus is that of parental choice. In one sense there has always been parental choice for the more affluent in our society. Those who are financially able have traditionally selected the neighborhoods in which they live based, at least in part, on the quality of the schools their children will attend. Alternatively, they have chosen to send their children to any one of a variety of private or parochial schools. In recent years, many school districts have offered some degree of choice to all citizens in an effort to comply with desegregation mandates. To some extent magnet schools have attracted a racial mix of students, but there is still little evidence that such schools either desegregate or truly improve educational opportunities in a school district. It is also true that racial desegregation in special magnet schools often results in another kind of segregation based on intellect or a particular talent.

The Montgomery Blair High School in Silver Springs, Maryland, is a case in point. This school's nationally recognized science, math, and computer magnet program with its emphasis on research has drawn top students from all over Montgomery County to this predominantly African-American and Hispanic district. Unfortunately, however, few neighborhood students participate in the special, and especially well-funded and well-equipped, magnet offerings. (There are 377 students in the Blair magnet program, only 58 of them from Blair's own school district. African-American and Hispanic students make up less than 15 percent of those in the magnet program.) In fact, as Alvin Poussaint of Harvard University has indicated, magnet programs may send a very negative message to minority students. He says, "the image is, the fewer blacks and Latinos in it, the more elite the program."[27]

School choice is the focus of a heated political debate in the early 1990s.[28] Some believe that real choice would allow all parents, regardless of their ability to pay, to select from among both public and private schools for their children. They believe that the competition would weed out the weaker schools and encourage those that remain to provide the best possible education for students. Others, however, believe that such choice would lead to the erosion of the public school system and eventually leave already disadvantaged children with fewer educational opportunities than those available to them under the current system. It has always been those young people whose parents are unable or unwilling to be involved in their schooling who have been least served by our system of public education. It is doubtful whether increased power of choice for parents will benefit these students.

D. R. Moore and S. Davenport studied the results of choice of high schools in New York, Chicago, Boston, and Philadelphia and concluded that choice was a more efficient means of sorting by race, income, and achievement than previous schooling practices.[29] At-risk students were concentrated in schools where resources and expectations were extremely low and, as might be expected, so was performance. Of course, this need not be the result of school choice. Nevertheless, informed choice requires a great deal of information and counseling for parents and students. Clearly articulated options among schools, nondiscriminatory admission policies, available transportation, and a host of other factors must be available if this practice is to be an effective means of restructuring and improving education for our nation's children.

One thing is becoming clear, however; increasingly parents are expecting to have a greater voice in their children's schooling. Through vouchers, tax credits, or some other system, many parents want to be able to select the schools that best represent what they consider to be a quality education. Even, or perhaps especially, parents in busy two-career families, want to be welcome to participate in the decision-making that affects their children's schooling.

On the other hand, some parents who have experienced educational choice for their children are questioning its merits. Bonnie Blodgett, an author and social historian from St. Paul, Minnesota, where magnet schools have existed for more than a decade, compares school choice to supermarket shopping subject to the same kind of marketing and impulse-buying. Although the possibility of selecting from a variety of programs and teaching methods may sound ideal,

> I find it inconceivable that nobody out there really knows better than I do what sort of elementary education will work for my child. Has the teaching profession learned nothing worth keeping over the centuries?[30]

Many teachers who want to act with the authority of professionals believe they have learned something and, although they welcome parental involvement, are not ready to give control to nonprofessionals. If educated, informed, and affluent parents such as Blodgett are unable to make appropriate choices of schools for their children, how must less-advantaged parents deal with such choice? What happens to those students whose parents refuse to choose or to those who have no responsible adults in their lives to make the choice for them? Can society be assured that these children will be placed in the most appropriate learning environments rather than just dumped in the least-chosen schools? Finally, as we move to a form of schooling that empowers students and encourages them to assume greater responsibility for their own learning, at what point should the power of choice shift from the parent to the student?

Gender Equity in Education

One area of concern in American education that has not been addressed in the literature on restructuring is that of gender bias in schools. A 1992 report by the American Association of University Women (AAUW) documents the many ways that females are shortchanged in elementary and secondary education.[31] The research cited in *How Schools Shortchange Girls* indicates that females receive significantly less attention from teachers than do boys; and African-American girls receive less attention than Caucasian girls, even though they attempt to initiate more interactions. Socioeconomic status continues to be the key factor in school success, but poor minority girls suffer combined racial, sexist, and economic barriers in education. As a result of such treatment, girls suffer a loss of self-confidence and self-esteem over their years of schooling. Added to this are increasing incidences of sexual harassment of girls by boys in schools, noninclusion or marginalization of women and their concerns and accomplishments in what this report calls the "evaded" curriculum, as well as continued discouragement of females in the sciences and mathematics.

Gender-role expectations, including the assumption that girls adapt more easily to the culture of the school and, therefore, teachers must work harder to interest and involve boys, can be detrimental to female accomplishments. The competitive nature of many schooling activities and of grading practices may also disadvantage more females than males. It is interesting to note that even female teachers, some of whom consider themselves feminists and consciously wish to be strong role models for their female students, often exhibit classroom behaviors that favor male students. For instance, videotapes of their teaching revealed subtle favoritism of male students in various forms of encouragement such as eye contact, nonverbal acknowledgments of responses and actual verbal interactions.

School library media specialists also need to guard against such gender-role expectations and the inequities that may result. Materials selection and readers' advisory services, especially, may be subject to such expectations. How often have we heard that girls will read boys' books but boys will not read girls' books and built our collections or selected materials or topics for instruction with this in mind? What have we "evaded" in media center resources, in our own curricula, or in recommendations to teacher colleagues as a result? Are we shortchanging all our students, regardless of gender, if library media center materials and programs do not capture the full range of voices of all our peoples?

There has been some progress in federal legislation in the last twenty years to assure that the sexes receive equal education; however, much remains to be done. In 1972 Title IX added sex discrimination in education to other violations described in the Civil Rights Act of 1964. This was the first of a number of federal policies enacted to insure gender equity in education. The Women's Educational Equity Act of 1974 (WEEA) funds projects to help schools comply with Title IX and, in general, to improve educational opportunities for females. Other legislation that addresses gender equity includes the Vocational Education Act (VEA), which establishes permanent programs to promote gender equity, the Eisenhower Math and Science Education Act, which funds projects to improve instruction in math and science, and the U.S. Department of Education's Office of Educational Research and Improvement (OERI), which promotes research to improve educational equity. The Elementary and Secondary Education Act (ESEA), originally passed in 1965, must be reviewed and reauthorized by Congress in 1993, which will undoubtedly involve creating new programs as well as revising existing ones. The AAUW is recommending that Congress, in the process of reauthorizing ESEA, create an Office of Gender Equity that would "move from developing models and materials to the next steps: infusing gender equity policy throughout federal education programs and encouraging the implementation of effective gender equity programs at all levels of education."[32]

Although this legislation has been in force for more than twenty years—and great gains have been made in that time, especially in respect to access to educational opportunities—inequitable policies continue to exist. Moreover, long-established, inequitable practices are deeply ingrained in American education and remain untouched by federal policy statements. If the National Education Goals are to be achieved in restructured schools that will enable all students to realize their full potential, issues of gender equity will have to be addressed. Every student, regardless of gender, race, ethnicity, socioeconomic status, or special needs must be respected for his or her own personal and unique potential and own ways of making meaning in and about the world.

School-University Partnerships

If all of the discussions about restructuring and educational change are to have a significant impact on the nation's schools, there will have to be real cooperation among all the parties involved, from the national groups setting standards to parents fighting for the best possible education for their own children. Americans must acknowledge that a commitment to education is a commitment to the future and that we must begin to focus on the larger picture, from preschool programs through graduate school, to really make a difference. Piecemeal approaches have left too many children in jeopardy and have put our whole nation "at risk." On the other hand, cooperation and concern with the overall patterns of educational delivery cannot be interpreted as conformity. Communities of citizens, parents, teachers, and students must be free to design educational environments that work for them.

One approach that has gained impetus in the last decade is that of school-university partnerships in which local schools plan and work together as equal partners with universities to provide educational opportunities for students in both institutions.[33] They also work together on the research and experimentation that supports both that education and advances in the disciplines that are taught. The best of these partnerships create holistic and integrative learning environments that are flexible enough to adapt to the changes that will inevitably result from innovation and experimentation. The most important components in these partnerships are a nonhierarchical respect for all involved in the educational enterprise—from university administrators to elementary school students—and a shared commitment both to systematic and critical reflection upon personal and community goals and to working toward those goals. Such critical reflection is the very essence of education and, since most human learning takes place in collaborative inquiry, school-university partnerships may serve as one model for restructuring and improving our schools.

Learning As Meaning-Making

Brain-Based Learning

Any restructuring of education must begin with what is known about how human beings learn. Too often we have planned schooling as if students were information processing devices rather than thinking and feeling active meaning-makers.

Research on the human brain supports the premise that meaning-making is an innate activity of human beings, who continually extract patterns from the babel of confusing stimuli in their environments.[34] This research encourages teachers to think of students as naturally motivated, active learners who need complex real-life learning experiences rather than simplified step-by-step means to an end. The teacher then is one who respects students' abilities and creates a rich classroom environment in which those students may select authentic, ongoing projects that will enable them to expand their mental capabilities. An integrated thematic approach to content fosters this natural acquisition of knowledge and leads to a sense of joy and accomplishment in young learners. Cooperative ventures in a supportive learning community provide opportunities for students to make meaningful personal connections.[35] Early evaluations of brain-based teaching have not shown significant increases on standardized test scores, but alternative means of assessment indicate very promising results. This is, of course, not surprising since evaluation has ordinarily been perceived of as standardized measurement of the acquisition of specific content rather than the ability and willingness to learn from a broad base of content and the joy in doing so.

Whole Language Learning

Whole language approaches to language arts teaching such as literature-based reading programs, thematic studies, and process writing have made tremendous inroads in our schools and have spotlighted the need for extensive collections of fine children's books and other library media center materials.[36] The notion of language learning as being functional, meaningful, and naturally acquired in a relevant environment in which students have some degree of self-determination corresponds with what is known about how the brain works. Educators in New Zealand, acknowledged as among the world's best reading teachers and to whom many advocates of whole language teaching in this country turn, call their efforts natural language learning. These educational approaches focus on the integration of reading and writing with emphasis on learning to read by reading. Time is a critical factor in such teaching, with New Zealand teachers devoting as much as half a school day to reading and U.S. teachers integrating reading-writing activities in all aspects of the curriculum. Even more important, however, is the recognition that each person is a unique maker of meaning in an active and integrated learning environment.

Brian Cambourne's seven conditions for learning language identify some of the principles shared by whole language and brain-based teaching that should also be considered in our information skills and research process curricula in school library media centers.[37] The first is *immersion* into a holistic environment with purposeful and meaningful activities. Second is *demonstration* as those who are more skillful share experiences and expertise in real-life situations. Third, youngsters have the *expectation* that they will participate fully in the learning community and, fourth, they assume the *responsibility* for their own learning. The fifth condition is *approximation*, that is, learners work toward closer and closer approximations until fully competent performances are achieved. Sixth, there is *employment* of the learned behaviors in real situations and, finally, *feedback* from interested and supportive members of the learning community.

Human Differences in Learning

Recognition of differences among human beings begins, for educators, in the acknowledgment of different learning and teaching styles. In spite of all that is known about the varieties and importance of learning styles, most educational programs persist in presenting content as if there were only one right way to learn. We have concentrated on individualizing, rather than personalizing, learning and have often thought of individualization as the ability to pace oneself through prescribed learning activities with the option either of doing more of the same or engaging in other predetermined activities upon completion of the assigned task. In fact, when we talk about individuals in education, we generally define and distinguish among them according to certain quantifiable characteristics. We too often plan individualized instruction, if at all, for students according to age, grade level, IQ, and test scores as if such statistics were the most important, or the only, indicators of learning behavior. It is not that these indicators are not important but that there are other equally important factors to be considered. For instance, does one learn more easily working alone, with a peer, with a teacher, or in interaction with a group? Inductively or deductively? Through tactile, audio, printed, or other visual means or through multi-media productions? Through abstract or concrete experiences? In discrete bits or through integrated experiences? Is one's way of learning always the same for every kind of content?

These are but a few of the many differences in the way human beings construct and negotiate meaning, and discovering which way or combination of ways works best for each individual should be the primary goal of education: learning how to learn is the most necessary survival skill in today's society.[38] The model of a child's meaning-making process presented in figure 1 offers a means to study the phenomenon of meaning-making.[39] Although this model focuses on meanings made in response to a literary work, a similar process takes place as young people encounter other types of ideas and materials. It is important to note that the community meaning represented here exists only at a particular moment in time and is not necessarily ascribed to by all participants, even at that moment.

Many of the current rounds of curricular reforms do recognize, at least implicitly, the importance of this personal construction and negotiation of meaning. Whole language and brain-based education attempt to personalize learning in organic living environments in which one naturally negotiates meanings in concert with peers. Emphasis on multiculturalism or global education also encourages learners to consider alternative meanings in order to come to a deeper, more authentic understanding of our world. Concentration on critical thinking, learning to learn, and cooperative learning also emphasize that the process of negotiating

The Educational Context

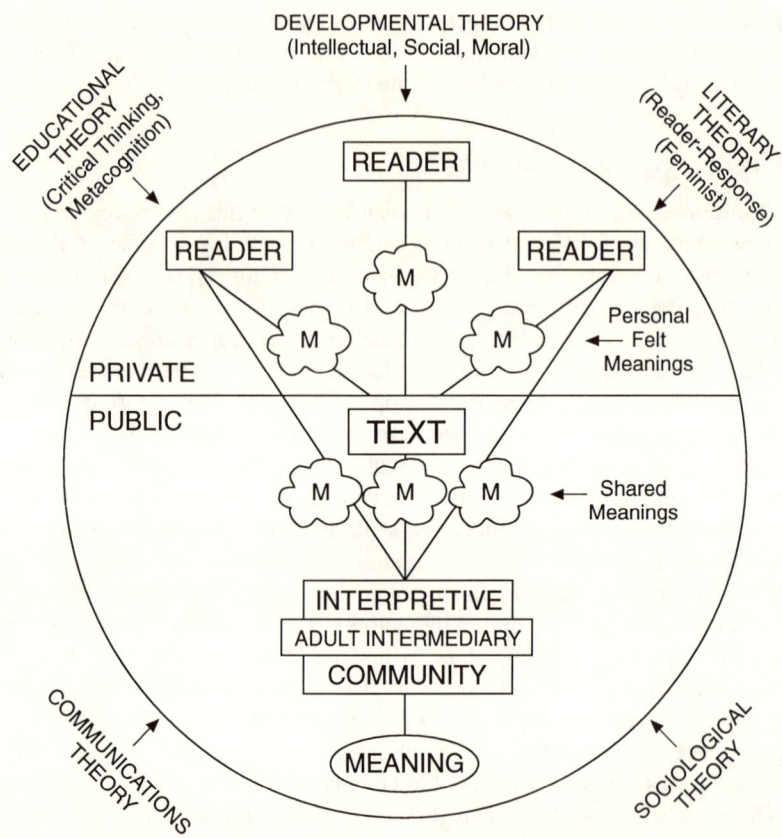

The following definitions are used:

TEXT: Story or metaphor which stimulates thought about feelings; assumed to be immediately comprehensible, even by the young child, but never fully comprehended.

READER: An active maker-of-meaning in the experience of responding to a text, that is, bringing meaning to and taking meaning from a symbolic form.

MEANING: An event in time, located in the consciousness of a reader so that the text disappears into the reader's experience of it just as the dancer cannot be separated from the dance or the musician from the music.

INTERPRETIVE COMMUNITY: A group of persons who share, exchange, and create meanings in response to a text.

ADULT INTERMEDIARY: The adult who shares symbolic experiences with young people and, at best, is both a member of their interpretive community and one who is responsible for encouraging and maintaining the process illustrated in this model.

Figure 1. A Model of a Child's Meaning-Making Process in Response to a Literary Text

meaning is at least as important as the specific knowledge acquired. Of course, supporters of more traditional education challenge that these curricular changes lower standards and fragment and politicize education by attempting to include too much internationalism and representation of women and minorities into a basic understanding of history and culture. Surely one can learn about and value the common ideals of American society, while respecting the contributions of the many individuals and groups who make up that whole society. Real learning and honest dialogue, which is what best defines us as human beings, cannot be reduced to simplistic either-or arguments.

The Role of the School Library Media Specialist in Meaning-Making

Multiple Resources

School library media specialists ought to be at the forefront of those advocating resource-based educational programs emphasizing personal learning styles and student evaluation, selection, and use of information in all media. What Lawrence Cremin said in 1965 of the role of the school in an age of mass media is equally true for all of us concerned with children and their metaphoric as well as intellectual connections to the world today. Our task "is to make youngsters aware of the constant bombardment of facts, opinions and values to which they are subjected; to help them question what they see and hear; and ultimately, to give them the intellectual resources they need to make judgments and assess significance."[40] A school with a strong library media center perceives of students as critical consumers of the prepackaged meanings provided by others in the process of making their own meanings and sharing them with others through dialogue and their own skillfully produced media packages. The very concept of the library media center is testimony to and celebration of the notion that personal meanings are made in the process of interacting with as many other ideas and positions as reasonable and possible.

Multiple Responses

Library media specialists are also involved in students' meaning-making through reader-response approaches to children's and young adult literature. Even those who have never studied reader-response critical theory are aware, at least intuitively, that many different meanings are evoked from the same text.[41] In their role as readers' advisors, they discuss books with students and try to match the meanings made from one work with those of another as students request "another book like this one." It is the dialogue resulting from such requests that really demonstrates that reading is a transaction in which the reader's personal meanings are stimulated by the text, resulting in a reshaping or recreation of meaning. Thus, opportunities abound for many levels of meaning, dependent upon what each reader brings to and takes from the work, that is, the way one fills in gaps or contextual voids in the text.[42] Often it is the library media specialist who helps young readers fill in these contextual voids or knowledge gaps. In most instances, this is accomplished through discussion, but this author and many others have also explored the possibility of hypermedia as a means of explicating a text.[43]

Any such efforts to enlighten readers or clarify aspects of a text must begin with a respect for the young reader's experiencing of literature and a willingness to acknowledge that personal meanings are to be appreciated even if they differ widely from those of other readers. "It is the joy children take from early experiences with literature that encourages them to continue reading and to read more deeply in order to increase that pleasure. Part of the pleasure for maturing readers is the intellectual excitement of looking more closely into a text, into the world represented by the text, and into their own responses to the text."[44] It is important to note that multiple responses are elicited from informational as well as aesthetic materials and that school library media specialists can help young information seekers consider and negotiate alternative meanings from such sources. This critical consideration of various responses in relation to the original text and in consultation with other resources provides a rich learning experience.

Multiple Technologies

One of the ways school library media specialists can exert their influence on the changing school is through their involvement with technology. Because of our expertise in and association with new media and technological advances, we need to develop the kind of sensitivity to students, teachers, and issues associated with technology that will enable us to ask appropriate teaching questions in a technological environment. Precisely because we are known as technical experts (or at least, as a group, library media specialists are often more committed to technology than other teachers), we should be better able to help others see not only the possibilities but the limitations of technology. We need to be in the vanguard of those who are advocating the use of technology in schools for the things that it is uniquely equipped to do; but, at the same time, we must discourage those who would embrace any technological invention as an end in itself with expectations beyond the capabilities of the particular medium.

In many situations in teaching, the critical content of a subject is not the logical, linear presentation of facts and characteristics but instead a series of humane judgments about the way it affects individuals and society. Many of us would not open a study of the Vietnam War or the Desert Storm conflict in the Middle East by listing important dates, military personnel, and battles. The contrasting mood of the sixties and the nineties and the various feelings about these conflicts might be a more appropriate, or at least an alternative, way to begin. To some extent these feelings can be conveyed through media packages containing film, recordings, and commentary; but a teacher with whom students have a personal relationship and who experienced both events can add depth and dimension and, most of all, concern not easily conveyed through any other medium. Teachers too young to remember the Vietnam era must familiarize themselves enough with the context to be able to evaluate and select the most appropriate materials to be integrated in the overall teaching design. Technology, including various instructional tools, can free teachers from the need to compile, organize, and present all the information desirable for students and, at the same time, allow them to spend more time in personalizing education through more interactive encounters with individuals and cooperative groups.

Stephen Kerr, reporting on research demonstrating the nature of teacher involvement with technology, writes, "Teachers accommodate slowly to the new possibilities that technology presents, but that accommodation, when it happens, may in fact lead to new perceptions about teaching and about their roles as instructors."[45] He further affirms that teacher time is a critical factor in the integration of technology into classroom practice. He writes, "How much time does it take for the teacher to learn how particular technologies work, to figure out how to integrate one technology (e.g., computers) with another (e.g., video), to develop an image of a classroom using technology, to communicate that image to students, and to evaluate the results?"[46] Significant in this regard is the move away from a "great expectations" mode, which attributes the incredible transformation of teaching and learning to the use of technology, to a more realistic view of technology as part of the restructuring process and as one means to achieve educational change. Karen Sheingold and Martha Hadley found similar characteristics and patterns in the interaction of technology with classroom practice reported in their national study.[47]

An interest in technology extends beyond the scientific to the aesthetic curriculum of the school. Virtual reality, a computer-generated artificial world that could have exciting applications in the student learning adventure, has already been incorporated into two young adult novels from Australia.[48] *Space Demons* and *Skymaze* both have plots that revolve around computer games that are quite close to a primitive form of virtual reality, and both have won children's book awards.[49] Using techniques of virtual reality in other subject areas, it is possible for a student to enter into an absorbing experience of the world of Ancient Egypt and to really sense the life and events that occurred there, or to experience flight and to test theories even as the Wright Brothers did. Thus, virtual reality is not only a part of the aesthetic curriculum through its presentation in literature but adds an aesthetic dimension to factual or scientific content.

Conditions for Educational Change

Those of us to whom these natural, whole language, brain-based, and technological approaches to education sound ideal must also be cognizant of the many difficulties in implementing such curricular changes in our schools. First, such changes cannot be mandated without a great deal of preparation for teachers. Several decades ago, what American educators called "open education" shared some of the same philosophical underpinnings with today's integrated, holistic approaches to learning. This movement failed when too many schools adopted the outward trappings without the essential strengthening of the inner core that supported them. For instance, some schools opened the physical environment to allow for greater flexibility without paying sufficient attention to the openness of mind and the attitudes and abilities required of both students and teachers as well as the support systems required to work in those spaces.

There are at least five variables that must be considered in implementing educational change. First, teachers expected to make fundamental changes in their work must be provided with a great deal of support to do so. Second, any educational approach that attempts to empower students, giving them increasing degrees of self-determination, must prepare them to assume that responsibility. We cannot expect young people who have had almost no personal authority or choice in schooling to assume such authority appropriately without both preparation and continuing support and guidance. Third, educational programs that move from a textbook-centered core require both rich and varied learning resources and students and teachers knowledgeable of and comfortable with their use. The school library media center and the professional librarian-educator who works there is central to the accomplishment of these three goals.

A fourth challenge to implementing such resource-saturated curricula is, of course, that of cost. It may be more expensive to provide a wide variety of materials to support different interests and learning styles than to support a basic textbook-dominated core curriculum. As the U.S. domination of the world market falters, there is little doubt that the impetus behind the federal government's call for educational change is economic. Nonetheless, educators are not encouraged that the financial resources to help support a real restructuring of American education will be forthcoming. *America 2000* calls for commitment from communities, teachers, and parents as if that commitment, without adequate allocations of material resources, is sufficient. Its rhetoric, including having all children come to drug and violence-free schools ready to learn, cannot help but remind educators of Cremin's characterization of American expectations of the public school as a solution to the nation's social problems. Only in the United States would people attempt to improve highway safety by emphasizing driver education courses in high schools rather than attempting to improve the national highway system or automobile design and construction. "It is a curious solution, requiring courses instead of seat belts, but typically American. . . . in other countries, when there is a profound social problem there is an uprising; in the United States, we organize a course!"[50]

Savage Inequalities chronicles Jonathan Kozol's visits to inner city schools and his conversations with the young people spending their lives in these frighteningly depressing racially and economically segregated environments. The voices of those he visited serve as dramatic evidence that, although money may not buy quality education, it is a necessary ingredient. Both politicians and educators should listen to the New Jersey student who said

> I have a friend. . . . She goes to school in Cherry Hill. I go to her house and I compare the work she's doing with the work I'm doing. Each class at her school in Cherry Hill, they have the books they're s'posed to have for their grade level. Here, I'm in eleventh grade. I take American history. I have an eighth grade book. So I have to ask, "Well, are they three years smarter? Am I stupid?" But it's not like that at all. Because we're kids like they are. We're no different. And, you know, there are *smart* people here. But then, you know, they have that money goin' to their schools. They have a nice *clean* school to go to. They have carpets on the floors and air-conditioned rooms and brand-new books. Their old books, when they're done with them, they ship them here to us.[51]

Along with money, there is a fifth factor needed to implement a holistic, student-centered curriculum or any real change in education—time. Americans are accustomed to seeking a "quick fix" to right educational wrongs and are impatient with remedies or changes with too much development or implementation time. We want results fast. As we approach the twenty-first century, politicians and educators are setting goals for the year 2000. Many of these goals may be impossible to accomplish in less than a decade. We must set goals, but we must be reasonable about those goals and be willing to reassess those goals in relation to changes that are bound to occur during this last decade of the twentieth century.

As this brief discussion reminds us, educational debate, reexamination, and reform of the curriculum and restructuring the schools are certainly not new phenomena in American education. In fact, one might posit that they are the very foundation of that education. The difficulty is that the debate is often posed as a dichotomy, an either-or situation, in which one must chose between educational standards and a *laissez-faire*, feel-good approach to schooling. Surely it is time for reasonable thinkers to find an intellectually authentic middle ground. Essential to the establishment of that intellectually authentic middle ground is, it seems to me, the acceptance of what we all know about human beings—they differ. Until we really acknowledge that difference where it counts, in the classroom, the continuing educational debate that ought to revitalize schooling will persist in pitting well-meaning reformers against each other rather than harnessing their combined intellectual energy toward the best possible education for all the nation's children. We *can* have empowered, joyful, self-determining learners in a rich, humanistic environment who are also culturally literate, and it is time all those concerned with education in this country work toward that goal. School library media specialists can and should be central to that work.

The availability of exciting learning resources and technological teaching tools provides increased opportunities for school library media specialists to fulfill the overall mission identified in *Information Power* : "to ensure that students and staff are effective users of ideas and information. This mission is accomplished (1) by providing intellectual and physical access to materials in all formats, (2) by providing instruction to foster competence and stimulate interest in reading, viewing and using information and ideas, and (3) by working with other educators to design learning strategies to meet the needs of individual students."[52] Obviously these three aspects of the mission statement correspond to the three primary roles of the school library media specialist as information specialist, teacher, and instructional consultant. All three of these roles are intertwined in the broader view of teaching posited here. When, as information specialists or educational consultants, we help students and teachers access, evaluate, and use information, we are doing so in the context of our teaching judgment about the appropriateness of the chosen information for the particular intellectual encounter and personal teaching and learning styles.

The next chapter posits a particular model of teaching encompassing the work of the school library media specialist. Subsequent chapters then explore various aspects of that model and present examples of both preactive and interactive teaching in our roles as teachers of information and research, as teachers of critical skills in all media, and as teachers of teachers. A final chapter explores the nature of evaluation, which can inform and improve our work in providing the best possible schooling for all the nation's children.

2

The School Library Media Specialist as Teacher

The school library media specialist is a teacher. Regardless of educational background, previous work experience, or our perceptions of ourselves, we are, according to certification procedures in most states and in actual practice, teachers.[1] The literature of the profession has, for a long time, included discussions of the teaching role of the school librarian, but in spite of those discussions some school library media specialists seem unconvinced that one of the most important aspects of our profession is that of teaching.[2] Perhaps the energies of school library media specialists have been so consumed with cutbacks and increased demands that we have allowed ourselves to push teaching concerns into the background. Perhaps it is that the word teaching refers as much to a separate professional group as it does to a particular interaction among people. Many practicing school library media specialists, however, do accept, even applaud, their roles as teachers. This commitment to teaching is one of the ways we distinguish our work from that of other librarians and other media professionals.

But what is the work we do? It may at times appear that school library media specialists are all things to all people, that we juggle a multitude of functions in a never-ending circus act. But if the arena in which we work can be compared to a circus, it must be clear that the center ring spotlight is always on the student, without whom there is no meaning to what we do. Even when we are working with classroom teachers or other adults, all of our efforts are ultimately for the benefit of young people; and many school library media specialists still consider the direct contact with students the most rewarding aspect of the job. Frequently, however, neither we nor others who observe us perceive of these experiences with students or our work with teachers as teaching.

Perceptions of the School Library Media Specialist

Each of us relates to others in a variety of personal and professional roles and is seen by others in many different ways. Students may perceive of the school library media specialist as a keeper and protector of materials, as a stern enforcer of silence and orderliness, or as a lively and responsive human being who knows how to find just the right book, computer program, video, or magazine article to excite interest or satisfy an informational need. Classroom teachers may see the library media specialist either as one who shares their rank and pay scale with greater autonomy and less accountability or as a valued colleague with a special knowledge of sources and materials useful for their work. Unfortunately, in many schools, classroom teachers value the library media specialist primarily as just one of several special area teachers who relieve them for a weekly prep period. Some school administrators and parents have very little real idea what we do. The research of Michael Bell and Herman Totten reveals a negative view of cooperation among teachers and library media specialists, but the ray of hope is in their finding that "evidence can be cited showing that the teachers most looked to for assistance by fellow teachers in instructional matters are also cooperating at slightly higher levels with the library media specialist."[3]

Of course, the most critical perceptions of the library media specialist are those we hold ourselves. The entire library profession has struggled with image for many years, and we continue to focus a great deal of attention on this topic.[4] Librarians who work in public schools have a special problem with image. We have, for many years, been unsure whether we owe our primary allegiance to the library profession or to schooling. Our own leaders, those who hold national offices and write for professional journals, are ordinarily part of the library establishment, while the primary collegial connection of most school library media specialists is with the teaching community. Our closeness with classroom teachers pulls us toward teaching while associations with other library professionals may emphasize the managerial, technological, or bibliographic aspects of our work.

It is not easy to call ourselves teachers these days. With both teaching and librarianship under fire, we have enough of our own library and information concerns without taking on those of the entire teaching profession. But if we are truly committed to a position that bridges two professions, education and librarianship, we must accept the problems as well as the rewards of each.

What Is Teaching?

One of the main problems of teaching is that of definition. Putting aside the question of whether teaching (or librarianship) is a profession or a quasi-profession, educators have for years been wrestling with the more general question, "What is teaching?"[5] This author agrees with those who believe that the act of teaching is that of creating environments in which students will be confronted with knowledge and ideas and presented with a mosaic of opportunities to achieve skillful performances. Such environments, however, are more than just the physical realities of the classroom or the school library media center. It is true that an experienced observer can usually detect many clues to the kind of teaching that takes place in a particular space by examining the physical facility, but that facility is merely the container for the multidimensional environment that is both the setting for and the result of teaching. When one defines teaching as creating special environments, the definition includes mental, emotional, social, aesthetic, and spiritual environments as well as physical ones. "Spiritual" is used here not for any narrow sectarian or specifically religious meaning, but in a larger sense concerned with the human spirit. Just as the furniture must "fit" the physical sizes of students, the learning environment must provide a space in which each child feels that he or she, as a person, "fits in." There must be ample territory for mental expansion and for all the other types of growth important to the work of teaching and learning. But what are the dimensions of these environments and how does one go about creating them? In other words, what is the nature of teaching? What is the role of the human intermediary (the teacher) within these environments?

Teaching as Composition

I propose that teaching is a compositional act, that the way a teacher composes schooling (the educational environment) is similar, in many ways, to an author's composition of a story.[6] I further propose that one of the many means of evaluating teaching is similar to the types of aesthetic criticism applied to literary compositions. Obviously this analogy can be carried only so far since an author sends a completed work out into the world alone and is unable to intervene between that work and those who encounter it. The teacher's composition, on the other hand, is a living, growing thing that can be shaped and reshaped through interaction with others. The teacher may try to entice students to reenact his or her dramatic composition, but the teacher's powers as director are limited and students as actors maintain control of the composed environment. This is both an advantage and a disadvantage of teaching. It can be disheartening to see something one had carefully planned and constructed be ignored or misused by those for whom it was composed, yet there is always the possibility of their reshaping and reforming the work to make it even more vital and useful. In spite of this breakdown in the analogy, we may draw some comparisons between the work of the literary artist and that of the teacher.

The reader sees only the finished form of the story and, ideally, is so caught up in the experience of the story that the work that went into its composition is not apparent. So too, the successful teacher's interaction with students will often appear effortless, not revealing the preparation that preceded it. This is true of any compositional act. There may be years of general preparation and long hours of specific work prior to a particular effort; but, to the outside observer and the recipient of that work, the best compositions appear to be effortless.

It may be useful here to make a distinction between two approaches to the teaching composition based on Louise Rosenblatt's definition of two approaches to reading, aesthetic and efferent.[7] Efferent readers approach a text expecting to take something from that text that can be used in the pragmatic, analytical world of public meanings; aesthetic readers enter into the text primarily for the pleasure of experiencing the playful, intuitive world of private meanings within the text. Comparably, efferent teaching may well be the more efficient means to help students arrive at specific behavioral objectives, that is, to gain access to certain information or develop specific skills. Often, however, a computer, a programmed text, or some other technological resource provides the most appropriate and efficient means of such instruction. Aesthetic teaching, on the other hand, is less concerned with cognitive knowledge and specific objectives than with overall goals, outcomes, and understandings. A computer can provide feedback to indicate to a student whether or not a given answer was correct, but a sensitive and talented human teacher is far better equipped to find out how the student arrived at that answer and to help him or her understand and appreciate its importance.

It is frequently noted that most teachers teach as they have been taught, and this is undoubtedly true, at least to some extent. Many of us remember those who taught us best and model our behaviors on a mentor's teaching practices to try to recreate that experience for our own students. We need to distinguish, however, between actual teaching performance and the student's feeling of having learned and to recognize that it is the latter that needs to be achieved. It is a student's excitement about ideas, the sense of empowerment, and the sense of wonder that leads one to care both about the specific content and about oneself as a learner. There is no one way to arrive at that essential and wonderful feeling of having learned, nor is there only one way to teach any specific content. As teachers then, we need to consider alternative approaches to content, available resources, our own strengths and weaknesses as teachers, and the differing learning styles of our students. The best teaching compositions blend efferent and aesthetic approaches into powerful learning environments and experiences.

The Teaching Process

The act of teaching is often described as unfolding in two phases, the preactive and the interactive. Sometimes a third or postactive phase is included.[8] Although the preactive phase is normally equated with the planning that a teacher does before a particular encounter with students, it may also be more broadly conceived of to include all that the teacher has thought and done in preparation for becoming a teacher. One aspect of the preactive stage of teaching is learning the craft of the teaching profession. As an author must acquire certain language skills and practice the craft of writing before composing a story worthy of publication, so too must the teacher acquire the skills and practice the craft of teaching. The basic skills and elements of crafting required for the composition of teaching are probably much less obvious and more encompassing than those for written composition.

The craft of teaching rests upon a basic knowledge of education and of the particular disciplines to be taught. It includes general language and social skills, specific skills integral to the teaching interaction, and the combination of those skills into strategies for teaching. The way in which a teacher selects, modifies, and uses a particular teaching strategy and appropriately practices teaching skills demonstrates that teacher's own personal teaching style, that is, his or her unique composition of teaching.

Thus, one who chooses to teach must develop those personal characteristics and interpersonal competencies that facilitate and enhance interactions with others in a learning environment. In addition, a teacher studies educational theory, learning theory, and the full range of developmental theories explaining the behaviors of the particular age or grade levels of students to be taught. Then the prospective teacher builds upon those bases by developing specific teaching competencies. Included among these competencies are understanding and using diagnostic tools; interpreting research and testing data; using motivational techniques; recognizing various learning styles; specifying goals and objectives; developing techniques for working with large and small groups and with individuals; establishing classroom rules, routines, and procedures; developing problem-solving strategies; stimulating higher order thinking skills; practicing questioning and feedback techniques; and developing competence in the use of educational technologies.

The interactive phase of teaching refers to what actually occurs in the living environment with students. These events in time cannot be totally planned for in the preactive phase because we cannot fully anticipate or control all the social, environmental, and personal variables that affect our work. As teachers, we are aware that our own physical or emotional well-being at a particular moment in time influences the teaching encounter in subtle or not-so-subtle ways. So, too, do the parallel feelings of students. A student who becomes physically ill in the middle of a lesson obviously causes dramatic changes in the educational environment, but more subtle changes occur when a normally cooperative student, still dwelling on a previous disagreement with a parent or friend, withdraws or does not cooperate with others in class activities. An overheated room or a sudden snowstorm can also disrupt the most carefully designed preactive teaching plan. We can anticipate some of these factors and revise preactive plans, and we can certainly evaluate the changes that occurred in the postactive phase once the actual interaction is completed, but we can never really control the interactive phase of teaching because of our limited control over the environment and over the human beings who participate in that encounter with us.

Thus, most of our discourse about teaching concerns the preactive phase. Even postactive reflections or evaluations are normally part of another preactive plan. Education has a long history of classroom interaction research studying verbal behaviors of students and teachers, but these too are means of capturing the content of particular fleeting moments primarily for the purpose of informing future preactive phases of teaching.[9]

Figure 2 presents a model of the teaching process showing various components of the preactive phase that contribute to both the efferent and aesthetic aspects of the interactive teaching composition. The actual interactive encounter with

Personal
  Awareness of one's own personal characteristics and interpersonal competencies and of those of faculty colleagues.
Professional
  Study of Education: theory, research, practice; developing teaching competencies
Instructional
  Planning (usually collaborative)
  • Setting goals and objectives (cognitive & affective)
  • Assessing student needs
    • Knowledge–skills–abilities
    • Interests, learning styles
  • Selecting content
  • Selecting a variety of resources for different needs
  • Designing teaching strategies
  • Determining alternative learning activities
  • Organizing the environment
  • Determining evaluative strategies

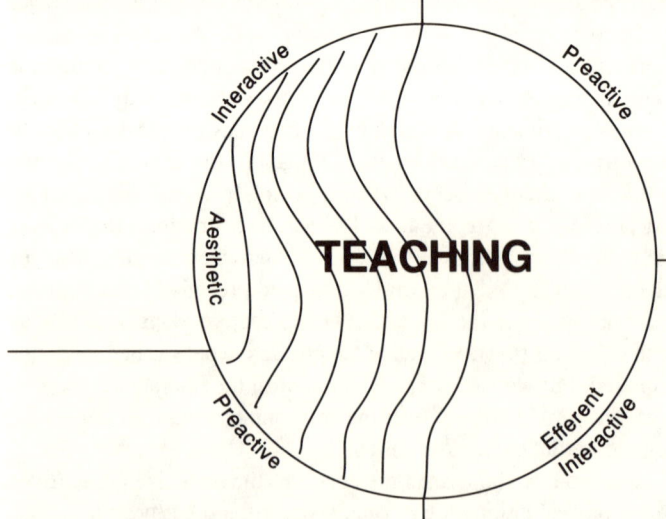

Personal and interpersonal encounters with the schooling environment that emphasize the enjoyment of the experience of learning and the sense of empowerment that enables students to perceive of themselves as lifelong learners.

TEACHING

Interactive / Preactive / Aesthetic / Preactive / Efferent Interactive

Planning emphasizes affective goals more than cognitive objectives, general abilities rather than specific skills, the living experience of schooling that is valued for itself and its aesthetic worth rather than for any practical applications.

Personal and interpersonal encounters with the schooling environment that emphasize the development of mastery over specific content, developing skills, or meeting immediate needs.

Figure 2. A Model of the Teaching Process

students occurs at elusive moments in time in which efferent and aesthetic aspects of teaching are intermingled. The postactive phase, not shown, is a reevaluation of all elements of both the preactive and interactive phases as a means of informing and improving future teaching compositions.

Models of Teaching

In the process of their preactive teaching, school library media specialists will join classroom teachers in sharing ideas about getting young people interested in and involved with learning activities. The very act of sharing will open up many possibilities, but the library media specialist might also take this opportunity to make a variety of professional materials available, both those that are content-specific and those that are more general. One very useful general resource for teaching is Bruce Joyce and Marsha Weil's *Models of Teaching*, which, since its first edition two decades ago, has encouraged teachers to imagine and try out new possibilities for their work.[10] The models presented in this book remind us that there is no one way to teach and that the richest and most useful educational environments will offer many alternatives to learning. Of course, thoughtful and accomplished teachers need not follow these models slavishly, but will adapt them to their own teaching strengths, to various learning styles, and to the particular teachable moment.

The models of teaching described by Joyce and Weil are derived from psychology, social psychology, therapy, the biological sciences, and other disciplines. Essentially each model consists of four basic operations: (1) the *Syntax*, or phases, of the model, (2) the *Social System* describing student and teacher roles and relationships, (3) the *Principles of Reaction* describing how the teacher responds to learners' behaviors, and (4) the *Support System*, that is, the conditions and resources required. These four operations are explained within the context of the particular theoretical assumptions and major concepts of the discipline from which the model is derived. The models are then classified into four families or basic approaches to teaching. Two of the four, Personal models and Social Interaction models, emphasize aesthetic aspects of the teaching composition. The other two, Information Processing models and Behavioral models, stress efferent aspects. Each of the families of models has much to contribute to current concerns about the restructuring of American schools.

Teachers focusing on the aesthetic to empower students by helping them increase their control over and direction of their own learning, for example, might select a synectic or a nondirective teaching model from the personal family. The use of these models helps to develop divergent thinking while enhancing the self-concepts of students. These student characteristics are also highly valued in recent emphases on cooperative learning, which are fostered by social interaction models of teaching. Teachers wishing to emphasize the efferent to help students become more competent critical thinkers, for example, may find help in some of the models from the information processing family. The behavioral family of models can make critical contributions to the design of both personal and technological means to achieve specific objectives for learners.

Developing a Repertoire for Teaching

Rather than relying only on those approaches to teaching that are natural or comfortable to us as teachers, we need to develop a repertoire of models or approaches that match the specific content to be taught and the various learning styles of students as well as the resources available to us. It is the professionals in classrooms and library media centers who should accommodate to the behaviors and needs of students rather than expecting all students to adapt their learning to a particular teacher's style. The models of teaching offer multiple considerations of ways to create educational environments and an organized structural approach to content. Although it is helpful to precisely follow the syntax of a model in the preactive phase while learning that model, one is rarely able to adhere to that syntax totally in the reality of interactive teaching. As teachers add more models to their personal repertoires, they become more versatile and more effective in their work with students. Accomplished teachers with many models available to them will probably modify or combine individual models in their preactive teaching and will also have a reservoir of strategies to draw upon in the immediacy of the interactive encounter. Each of the models also has both what Joyce and Weil call instructional or direct effects and nurturant or implicit effects on student achievement. These correspond to efferent and aesthetic effects, and both should be considered in selecting a model of teaching. For instance, specific instructional objectives may be met in either competitive or cooperative learning environments, but the student behaviors nurtured in these environments differ dramatically. Obviously, all of the approaches to teaching represented by these models can be combined to provide a rich, full educational environment for learners.

The essential thing to remember is that there is no one right or best way to teach any particular content. Caring teachers envision as many alternatives as possible in their preactive teaching so that students with different interests, abilities, and learning styles will encounter ideas and information in ways that will excite them and stimulate educational growth. The examples presented in the concluding section of this chapter demonstrate a number of approaches to the same basic content. Some of these approaches are drawn from more traditional materials-centered library lessons; others follow the structure of a particular model of teaching quite closely, but many combine aspects of several lessons or models, which is precisely what most teachers do as they attempt to accommodate the content and their own teaching preferences to the particular students to be taught. Obviously, these preactive teaching plans will be modified, at least to some extent, in the interactive phase when real learners encounter and act upon the educational environment.

Information Power: Guidelines for School Library Media Programs emphasizes the complementary roles of the library media specialist as information specialist, teacher, and instructional consultant.[11] Curriculum decisions, realized in the schools through the process of teaching, are made at a number of levels from national associations and commissions to the individual teacher preparing for the next day's work. School library media specialists should be represented on national and regional bodies concerned with schooling, and most certainly they should participate in district as well as local school decisions. In a system large enough and enlightened enough to have a district library media supervisor, the person holding that position is presumably a participant in all aspects of curriculum planning for the district. As a result of communication with library media specialists in each school, the library media supervisor is able to inform other planners of the availability of all kinds of resources in the various schools and then help building-level library media specialists prepare for and help implement any new curriculum developments.

The building-level library media specialist participates at many stages of the preactive teaching process. Some decisions are made at the school level, others by curriculum or subject-area committees, some by the informal dialogue among colleagues who share trust and teaching concerns, and many by individual teachers. Regardless of the level at which preactive decisions are made, the school library media specialist has input in various aspects of the process. At the very least, the library media specialist provides resources. These may be lists of what is already available in the library media center, a search for related professional materials for teachers, or a comprehensive plan for collection development listing materials to be bought, borrowed, and produced. Obviously, in order to select any of these resources wisely, the library media specialist must be knowledgeable and fully informed about the work of decision makers. Often the necessity for the kind of information required for the provision of resources can serve as an informal means of becoming a more active participant of the decision-making team when this has not been set up formally as it should be in schools.

Once accepted as a member of the preactive teaching team, the library media specialist must, like every other member, earn the respect of colleagues by demonstrating the value of his or her own professional expertise along with a working knowledge of the discipline to be taught and an understanding of the teaching process. Those who participate fully in the clarification of objectives and the identification of teaching strategies are really in the best position to match these decisions with appropriate resources. Such participation may also lead to the library media specialist being asked to participate in the interactive teaching process in an area of demonstrated interest or competence. One could easily become overextended in such activities, but a reasonable amount of participation in the teaching activities of colleagues helps to demonstrate the centrality of the library media center program in the school and wins the respect and the trust of other faculty members.

The knowledge that the library media specialist gains from working with various planning groups or with individuals can often be used to articulate one curriculum area or teacher to another, that is, to draw relationships and point out parallels that may be helpful to all. Such identification of common concerns by one who works with many different individuals and groups in the school may bring together people who would not ordinarily plan together and could eliminate unnecessary duplication of effort. The school library media specialist also works regularly with members of teaching teams to evaluate all aspects of the teaching composition and then uses the results of that evaluation as input into new educational planning and the process of change.

Again, a major problem is that of time. No matter how important one perceives the teaching role to be, it is still one of many roles. School library media specialists are not only responsible for the efficient organization and operation of the library media center (which certainly takes time), but are also on call to respond to immediate informational needs of students and teachers. These and other responsibilities draw them away from more sustained teaching efforts. Those who truly value their teaching responsibilities, however, will not allow this very important aspect of their work to be pushed aside or buried under the myriad details of day-to-day existence in the school library media center. Library media specialists must seek out teaching opportunities and emphasize the teaching components of all the work they do so that other professionals in the school will recognize and respect them as true colleagues in teaching.

The Library Media Specialist's Contributions to Teaching: Geography Studies

Since geographical studies and global education are important aspects of current educational reforms, let us look at different styles of teaching and learning geography through the study of atlases, maps, globes, and geographical reference tools as examples of alternative approaches to teaching particular content. This content is ordinarily a part of social studies instruction, often in fifth or sixth grade, but is also within the library media center curriculum. As library media specialists, we have traditionally been concerned that students are aware of the existence of these tools and able to use them effectively. The most common means of accomplishing this is to give young people a list of places to be located using the available resources. Such lists might be selected at random, located in published library media curricula, generated from known interests of students or coordinated with content of the classroom curriculum. Regardless of the source of the place names, this type of activity alone is unlikely to generate much interest in or knowledge of geography or geographical tools for most young people. The challenge for us as educators is to generate the kind of excitement that will bring this topic to life for our students, and we need to do so in ways that help students develop critical thinking skills.

Maps and Atlases

The basic contribution of the school library media specialist to the educational program of the school is still the provision of the best possible resources to students and teachers. The materials on List 1 are a sampling of different types of books available for that aspect of geographical study focusing on maps and atlases.[12] Library media specialists might use this list as a check against their own school's holdings and would obviously need to update it regularly.

List 1. Selected Books Useful in Map and Atlas Projects

Adams, Brian and others. *Atlas of the World in the Middle Ages*. New York: Warwick, 1981.

Adams, Simon and others. *Illustrated Atlas of World History: A Geographical Journey in Maps and Pictures from Prehistoric Times to the Present Day*. New York: Random House, 1992.

Allen, Phillip. *The Atlas of Atlases: The Map Maker's Vision of the World*. New York: Harry Abrams, 1992.

The Atlas of Mysterious Places. Ed. by Jennifer Westwood. New York: Weidenfeld & Nicolson, 1987.

Baynes, John. *How Maps Are Made*. New York: Facts on File, 1987.

Boeke, Kees. *Cosmic View: The Universe in 40 Jumps*. New York: John Day, 1957.

Contemporary Atlas of the United States. Ed. by Catherine M. Mattson. New York: Macmillan, 1990.

Couper, Heather, and Nigel Henbest. *The Space Atlas*. San Diego, Calif.: Harcourt Brace Jovanovich, 1992.

Davis, Kenneth C. *Don't Know Much about Geography: Everything You Need to Know about the World but Never Learned*. New York: Morrow, 1992.

Donnelly, Judy. *All around the World*. Illus. by True Kelley. New York: Putnam, 1991.

The Economist Atlas of the New Europe. New York: Henry Holt, 1992.

Exploring Your World: The Adventure of Geography. Washington, D.C.: National Geographic Society, 1989.

Fagg, Christopher, and Frances Halton. *Atlas of the Ancient World*. New York: Warwick, 1981.

Fargues, Philippe, and Rafic Boustani. *Atlas of the Arab World: Geopolitics and Society*. New York: Facts on File, 1991.

Ferrell, Robert H. *Atlas of American History*. New York: Facts on File, 1991.

Fuchs, Erich. *Looking at Maps*. New York: Abelard-Schuman, 1976.

Grant, Neil. *The Great Atlas of Discovery*. New York: Alfred Knopf, 1992.

Hammond Atlas of the World. Maplewood, N.J.: Hammond, Inc., 1992.

Knowlton, Jack. *Geography from A to Z: A Picture Glossary*. Illus. by Harriett Barton. New York: Thomas Crowell, 1988.

Knowlton, Jack. *Maps & Globes*. Illus. by Harriett Barton. New York: Harper & Row, 1985.

Lauber, Patricia. *Seeing Earth from Space*. New York: Orchard, 1990.
McVey, Vicki. *The Sierra Club Wayfinding Book*. Illus. by Martha Weston. Boston: Little, Brown, 1989.
Mango, Karin N. *Map-Making*. New York: Julian Messner, 1984.
Manguel, Alberto, and Gianni Guadalupi. *The Dictionary of Imaginary Places*. New York: Macmillan, 1980.
The New York Times Atlas of the World. 3d rev. ed. New York: Times/Random House, 1992.
Oxford Atlas of the World. New York: Oxford University, 1992.
Page, Michael, and Robert Ingpen. *Encyclopedia of Things That Never Were: Creatures, Places, and People*. New York: Viking, 1987.
Peck, Robert McCracken. *Land of the Eagle: A Natural History of North America*. New York: Summit, 1990.
Rand McNally Children's Atlas of the Universe. ed. by Elizabeth G. Fagan. Chicago: Rand McNally, 1990.
Rand McNally Children's Atlas of World Wildlife. ed. by Elizabeth G. Fagan. Chicago: Rand McNally, 1990.
Rand McNally Illustrated Atlas of the World. Chicago: Rand McNally, 1992.
Rhodes, Dorothy. *How to Read a Highway Map*. Illus. by Harry Garo. Chicago: Children's Press, 1970.
Rosenthal, Paul. *Where on Earth: A Geografunny Guide to the Globe*. Illus. by Marc Rosenthal. New York: Alfred Knopf, 1992.
Taylor, Barbara. *The Animal Atlas*. Illus. by Kenneth Lilly. New York: Alfred Knopf, 1992.
The Times Atlas of the World. 9th comp. ed. London: Times/Random House, 1992.
Townson, W. D. *Atlas of the World in the Age of Discovery 1453–1763*. New York: Warwick, 1981.
Weiss, Harvey. *Maps: Getting from Here to There*. Boston: Houghton Mifflin, 1991.

If a collection of such resources, selected for their interest, age-appropriateness, and the particular goals of the learning encounter, is made available, the library media specialist can provide a variety of learning encounters. Many students will undoubtedly be interested enough to examine these books on their own. Even in an informal student-centered perusal of these materials, the library media specialist or classroom teacher might provide cards with interesting map-related questions or specific places for students to locate. Then both faculty members will be available to provide assistance or new challenges and to observe and make informal diagnoses of student attitudes and abilities. At this time, it would be important to point out that even the most recently published maps and atlases will probably not reflect the current political boundaries in many parts of the world. Maps included in the latest newspapers or magazines might be compared to the newest atlases in their presentations of such places as the former Soviet Union, East Germany, and Eastern Europe. In the process of this activity, both the classroom teacher and the library media specialist could check on and assist students with their map-reading skills. Of course, globes, map puzzles, geographical games, and a variety of other library media center materials would also be available to students and teachers.

How to Lie with Maps is an adult book that would interest older students or good readers and stimulate interest in maps and mapping by raising provocative questions. This book begins, "Not only is it easy to lie with maps, it's essential. . . . to present a useful and truthful picture, an accurate map must tell white lies."[13] What better way to introduce a study of maps and encourage critical thinking! Mark Monmonier, the geography professor who wrote this book, reminds us that "maps, like speeches and paintings, are authored collections of information and also are subject to distortions arising from ignorance, greed, ideological blindness, or malice."[14] Many students, in fact, many teachers, may never have thought of maps in this way. It could be a very exciting learning experience to begin a lesson with the first quote above and encourage students to question:

Who might have said this? Why?
In what ways do maps lie?
Can we identify examples of maps that lie?
Do they all lie in the same way?
Are there "honest lies" and "dishonest lies" in mapping?

When the above discussion begins to lag, we might introduce Monmonier's second quotation above to add another dimension to the consideration of maps. Probably this will stimulate additional responses to the original set of questions, but it will also raise new questions about subjectivity and the creator's intent in mapmaking. A classroom teacher or library media specialist might then share maps such as the famous New Yorker's map of the United States originally published in *The New Yorker* and long available as a poster. Students could then create their own subjective maps of the classroom, library media center, school, neighborhood, or larger geographical area.

Students and teachers who enjoy creative or metaphoric learning experiences might begin a study of geographical reference materials through the use of various types of analogy in a synectics model.[15] This model, based on the work of William Gordon and Tony Poze is designed to encourage creativity and mental flexibility in generating alternative solutions to problem situations.[16] For instance, youngsters might begin a study of maps by thinking about a map as a human body, a rolltop desk, an erector set, a classroom, or a pinball machine and identify some of the commonalties that make the particular metaphor work. Such imagination-stretchers encourage students to think about content in ways that draw on previous knowledge and connect the topic of study with other areas of knowledge or interest. With this particular content, we might go even further to think about the relationship of a map to an atlas. Therefore, in probably the most obvious case, a map is to an atlas as a classroom is to a school. Students will undoubtedly be much more creative than most adults in this kind of metaphoric activity, which

Great Barrier Reef	Rings of Saturn
Local Public Library	Rice Fields
Troy	Lion Habitat
Amazon River	Native American Nations
Oregon Trail	Canary Islands
Garden of Olives	Middle Earth
Mississippi River	Paris
Trail of Johnny Appleseed	The United States prior to the Gold Rush
Little House on the Prairie	
Holy Roman Empire	

Figure 3. Selected List of Places for Students to Locate on Various Types of Maps or Atlases

is a joyful experience for most groups. It also introduces stimulating content and places it in perspective.

Another way of introducing these tools might be to use a form of Hilda Taba's inductive thinking or concept formation model, asking students to identify as many different kinds of maps and atlases as possible.[17] The initial list generated is likely to include a variety of both general and specific items such as maps of Narnia and Oz, and maps showing rivers and mountains. Then the class would group like things together and label or categorize each group. Such a student-initiated list of categories might include road maps, neighborhood maps, bus and subway maps, fantasy atlases, topographical atlases, weather maps, literary maps, aerial maps, product maps, space maps, historical atlases, and the like. Subsequently they might be given the following items (figure 3) and asked to determine which type of tool they would need to locate each item. The actual use of library media center resources to locate the items would naturally follow. Again, alternative locations might be used to highlight resources in a particular library media center or special interests of students.

Alternatively, students might be asked to create their own maps of the library media center, a classroom, the school, or the neighborhood, identifying traffic patterns or points of personal interest within those maps. In order to use such maps themselves or have classmates or friends use them, they would have to understand scale, the concept of x/y axis, symbols, and keys or legends. Again, this exercise encourages student-generated ideas and emphasizes the importance of maps in everyday life and then moves to specific skills of map reading. Map skills could also be developed using outline maps of the United States or the world and asking students to map their ideal vacation trip including at least five specific cities. City maps could then be used to plan activities at each stop on the trip.

Videotapes on Maps and Mapping

Another version of this learning activity would be to show a videotape such as *Touring America's National Parks* and have students locate those parks on a map. Other videos that might be appropriate for this type of activity are included below (see List 2). All of these works help to set the mood and get students interested and involved in exploring geography.

List 2. Selected Videocassettes on Maps and Mapping

As the Wind Rocks the Wagon: An American Odyssey. Color, 52 minutes. APL Educational Video, 1990.
Beautiful River: Rediscovering the Ohio. Color, 58 minutes. TV Image, 1991.
Geography: Five Themes for the Planet Earth. Color, 21 minutes. National Geographic, 1992.
A Magical Field Trip to the Mapmaker. Color, 15 minutes. Field Trip Videos. Distributed by AIMS.
Physical Geography of the Continents: Europe. Color, 25 minutes. National Geographic, 1991.
Shape of the World. 6 vols. Color, 60 minutes each. Granada TV and WNET. Distributed by Ambrose Video.
Touring America's National Parks. 2d ed. Color, 65 minutes. Encounter Productions, 1989. Distributed by Aylmer.
Visions of Adventure: 50 States 50 Capitals United States of America. 4 vols. Color, 25 minutes. Video Marketing, 1991.
Visions of Adventure: Understanding World Geography Using Maps and Globes. Vol. 1. Color, 25 minutes. Video Marketing, 1991.

A series of videotapes entitled *Visions of Adventure* includes a general tape that introduces the history of mapmaking and explains various kinds of projections used to make flat maps from a globe, longitude and latitude, the various types of maps, and how to read them. The next four videos present the four regions of the United States, with the same basic information about each state within the region. First the state is located within the map of the United States and its borders are identified. Economic information is given as a list of industries, agriculture, and products, and then the capital city, population, size and area, climate, geographic points of interest, and interesting notes of trivia are presented. The introductory tape is lively and fast-paced, but sometimes difficult to comprehend, especially for the intended audience of intermediate grade students. It could be used, however, with students who have a special interest in the topic, for whom it will open up a number of avenues for inquiry. The regions of the United States tapes, on the other hand, are clear and simple, but remind one of the kind of geography lessons that must have been taught since we first made maps of this country. Although many of us may not find these presentations exciting, they are probably more appealing than the same content in a printed text, and some young people do learn most easily from such readily digestible bits of information. A variety of materials and approaches to content are necessary to accommodate the differing learning styles of students.

Computer Software for Geography

A number of computer programs (List 3) are also available for the study of maps and mapping that could be used for independent study or for small group work. *International Inspirer* is a trip planner that might be either an alternative or an addition to the previous trip planning activity. The *Carmen Sandiego* programs, which are a great deal of fun, introduce specific geographical reference tools. *Bushbuck Charms* . . . shows early approaches to mapping the world, and *MECC Dataquest* obviously deals with a specific area of the world. Most of these can be used either in teams or as individual adventures.

List 3. Selected Computer Software on Maps

Bushbuck Charms, Viking Ships and Dodo Eggs. MS-DOS. PC Globe, 1991.
Discover Space. IBM. Broderbund, 1993.
Geographic Jigsaw. Apple II and Apple IIGS. Eclat MicroProducts, 1989.
The Great Solar System Rescue. Multimedia. Macintosh. Tom Snyder Productions, 1992.
GTV: Planetary Manager. Multimedia program. Apple IIGS, Macintosh, MS-DOS. National Geographic, 1992.
Hello World. MSDOS. Tom Snyder Productions, 1991.
International Inspirer. Apple II and MS-DOS. Tom Snyder Productions, 1989.
MECC Dataquest: The Middle East and North Africa. Apple II. Minnesota Educational Computing Corporation, 1989.
The Oregon Trail. Apple II, Apple IIGS, IBM. Minnesota Educational Computing Corporation, 1986.
Stars and Planets. Apple IIGS, Macintosh, IBM. Advanced Ideas, 1989.
STV: Solar Systems. Multimedia. Macintosh. National Geographic, 1992.
USA GeoGraph. Apple IIGS. Minnesota Educational Computing Corporation, 1989.
US ATLAS. MS-DOS. Software Toolworks, 1990.
Wagon Train 1848. AppleTalk. Minnesota Educational Computing Corporation, 1991.
Where in Europe Is Carmen Sandiego? Apple II, Macintosh, IBM. Broderbund, 1989.
Where in the USA Is Carmen Sandiego? Apple II, Macintosh, IBM. Broderbund, 1989. (available in CD-ROM)
World Geograph. Revised. Apple IIGS. Minnesota Educational Computing Corporation, 1991.

Schools with Macintosh computers and an AppleTalk-based network can apply social geography to a specific segment of American history with *Wagon Train 1848*, a cooperative learning program from MECC based on their award-winning simulation *Oregon Trail*. This interactive, interdisciplinary program is designed for students at different computers (wagons) who, after selecting an occupation and equipping themselves with appropriate supplies, make decisions similar to those made by the pioneers who actually traveled the Oregon Trail in the nineteenth century. The decisions made for each individual wagon affect the whole train, and cooperative learning is rewarded in this groupware. Using the talk feature of this program, students share information, ideas and decision-making for the common good. Critical thinking and cooperative learning skills are developed in content that combines geography, history, science, and language arts activities.

Another exciting resource for interdisciplinary study emphasizing geography is the National Geographic Society's videodisc program, *GTV: A Geographic Perspective on American History*.[18] With its IBM interactive computer software, students and teachers can access a large database of visual images, sound, and text from pre-Columbian times to the present. The teaching and learning potential of such resources are yet to be fully explored.

It is also possible to provide rich interdisciplinary learning programs with a strong geography component without complex or expensive hardware and software. Pat Brisson's award-winning "Kate" books are about a feisty and intellectually curious young heroine who travels around the United States and into Mexico, recording her observations of people and places in letters to family and friends, even her goldfish, back home.[19] Kate describes historical sites and natural and humanmade marvels, filling her letters and postcards with child-appealing factual tidbits as well as amusing family anecdotes. The cartoon-like illustrations by Rick Brown include maps on the endpapers and additional information in the form of sketches of state birds, flowers and trees and of various local artifacts representing the various places visited. Kate's enthusiasm for new places and new ideas will make these books welcome additions to almost every area of the elementary school curriculum. Social studies and language arts teachers will find them especially useful in resource-based and writing process classrooms. Calculations of mileage or estimates of travel costs could add a math component to the mix. Brisson's *Magic Carpet* introduces Elizabeth, another imaginative young female who takes imaginative trips to real-life places around the world with the help of Aunt Agatha's atlas.[20] Although these books are most appropriate for elementary school students, there are many similar stories for older readers that might stimulate similar mapping activities.[21]

Literary Maps

A favorite activity of library media specialists and of young readers is the creation of a storyland map. Using a bulletin board or mural paper with an outline map,

38　The School Library Media Specialist as Teacher

GRADE LEVEL	LITERARY WORK	SETTING
HS	Ashabranner, Brent. *Born to the Land, An American Portrait.*	Luna County, New Mexico
ES	Baker, Leslie. *Morning Beach.*	Martha's Vineyard, Massachusetts
ES	Bedard, Michael. *Emily.*	Amherst, Massachusetts
HS	Blume, Judy. *Tiger Eyes.*	Atlantic City, New Jersey, and Los Alamos, New Mexico
HS	Brooks, Bruce. *The Moves Make the Man.*	Wilmington, North Carolina
MS	Cameron, Eleanor. *The Court of the Stone Children.*	San Francisco, California
ES	Carlstrom, Nancy White. *Lullaby.*	Alaska
ES	Codye, Corinn. *Vilma Martinez.*	San Antonio, Texas
ES	De Angeli, Marguerite. *Thee, Hannah!*	Philadelphia, Pennsylvania
HS	Duncan, Lois. *Locked in Time.*	Baton Rouge, Louisiana
MS	Fitzhugh, Louise. *Harriet the Spy.*	New York, New York
MS	Fleischman, Paul. *The Borning Room.*	Lanseville, Ohio
MS	Forbes, Esther. *Johnny Tremain.*	Boston, Massachusetts
HS	Fritz, Jean. *Early Thunder.*	Salem, Massachusetts
MS	Greene, Bette. *Summer of My German Soldier.*	Jenkinsville, Arkansas
HS	Hall, Barbara. *Dixie Storms.*	Marston, Virginia
MS	Hamilton, Virginia. *The House of Dies Drear.*	Miami Valley, Ohio
HS	Harris, Mark Jonathan. *Come the Morning.*	Los Angeles, California
ES	Hendershot, Judith. *In Coal Country.*	Ohio River
ES	Hooks, William H. *The Ballad of Belle Dorcas.*	East Arcadia, North Carolina
MS	Konigsburg, Elaine L. *From the Mixed-Up Files of Mrs. Basil E. Frankweiler.*	New York, New York
ES	McCloskey, Robert. *Make Way for Ducklings.*	Boston, Massachusetts

Figure 4. Literary Settings for Map Project

either of the United States or of the world, youngsters locate the settings for favorite stories and place a character or other symbol of that story on the map. The citation for the story could be keyed to the symbol elsewhere on the display or in a separate card file. This could be a continuing activity, with students adding new books to the map as they read. Other students might enjoy trying to identify the stories from the symbols and locations on the map. Another version of the storyland map would be to prepare index cards with book titles such as those in figure 4 and have children select one or more for placement on the story map. Of course, one would suggest specific titles that either match the reading interests of

GRADE LEVEL	LITERARY WORK	SETTING
HS	McGowen, Tom. *The Great Monkey Trial: Science vs. Fundamentalism in America.*	Dayton, Tennessee
MS	Montgomery, Lucy Maud. *Anne of Green Gables.*	Prince Edward Island, Canada
HS	Myers, Walter Dean. *Scorpions.*	New York, New York
HS	Paterson, Katherine. *Lyddie.*	Lowell, Massachusetts
MS	Paulsen, Gary. *Canyons.*	El Paso, Texas, and Alamogordo Desert, Texas
MS	Paulsen, Gary. *The Monument.*	Bolton, Kansas
MS	Peck, Robert Newton. *A Day No Pigs Would Die.*	Rutland, Vermont
HS	Rinaldi, Ann. *Wolf by the Ear.*	Monticello, Virginia
MS	Rylant, Cynthia. *Missing May.*	Putnam County, West Virginia
HS	Seabrooke, Brenda. *Judy Scuppernong.*	Fitzgerald, Georgia
HS	Soto, Gary. *Baseball in April and Other Stories.*	Fresno, California
MS	Speare, Elizabeth George. *The Witch of Blackbird Pond.*	Wethersfield, Connecticut
MS	Taylor, Mildred. *The Road to Memphis.*	Jackson, Mississippi
ES	Turkle, Brinton. *Obadiah the Bold.*	Nantucket, Massachusetts
MS	Uchida, Yoshiko. *Journey to Topez.*	Berkeley, California, and Topez, Utah
HS	Voigt, Cynthia. *Dicey's Song.*	Crisfield, Maryland [Chesapeake Bay]
MS	Wilder, Laura Ingalls. *On the Banks of Plum Creek.*	North Hero Township, Redwood County, Minnesota [Walnut Creek]
HS	Willard, Barbara. *Beauty and the Beast.*	Rinebeck, Hudson River Valley, New York
MS	Yep, Laurence. *The Star Fisher.*	Clarksburg, West Virginia

students in the school or recall old favorites from earlier grades. The objectives of such a program might be to locate specific books and determine the setting and to locate the settings on the prepared map, with the help of an atlas. Figure 4 uses books set in the United States and Canada, but one might include a world view by having students place titles with wider settings on a world map.

Young people may need to be reminded that settings, even in realistic stories, may not be actual places that can be located on a map. Authors often keep settings somewhat vague such as Hendershot did for *In Coal Country*, set in CompanyRow on the Ohio River. Other authors set their stories in a large city or a rural area that readers can choose to identify with actual places they know. Informational writers are usually very specific in identifying places in their work.

Another activity integrating literary and cultural studies with geography could be an around-the-world storytelling program. Both students and teachers would read or tell stories that present various people and places, perhaps those of personal family origin. Listeners then locate the setting of the story on a map and identify characteristics of that setting or its inhabitants as revealed in the story. As these stories are shared, it may be of value to explore the commonalties as well as the differences among people and their stories. The importance of storytelling as a means of communication, of passing on the culture, and as a source of aesthetic pleasure might be another focus of this learning experience. Using his or her own expertise as a storyteller, the school library media specialist might work with young people to help them become more effective and affective storytellers. Thus, such activities combine aesthetic and efferent approaches to teaching.

Students might also enjoy and derive a great deal of benefit from creating maps of their own imaginary societies in a more expansive effort to understand how geography affects people. They might begin with a primitive society and explore how physical features help to determine the development of that society over time. For instance, if one chooses to establish an island society, the location of that island will be a predictor of physical features and climate that will, in turn, determine crops and influence other industry and transportation. Physical features also often lead to political boundaries and centers of population. As the population grows in this imaginary society, one must consider the resources necessary for the support of that population, a process that often leads to the realization that the inhabitants cannot be self-sufficient. This leads, in turn, to the establishment of trade routes both among different political and social groups on the island and to other societies beyond. Obviously this kind of playful activity can contain a great deal of depth when young people explore human interaction with the physical world and interdependence among groups of people as they develop more complex societies. The learning activity itself moves from personal effort to a collaborative venture as students explore how their various individual societies come together in a larger social system.

Conclusion

The use of exciting teaching materials as technological means of instruction is not a move away from our responsibilities as teachers. In fact, the orchestration of a range of materials to provide the best possible learning for students with various learning styles is a far more complex and more time-consuming form of teaching than our own presentation of content in a lecture or demonstration. School library media specialists, as instructional consultants and as vital members of the teaching faculty, participate at various levels and at various stages of the teaching process. They work directly with teachers in the preactive phase of teaching and may share responsibility for individuals, small cooperative teams, or class-size groups in many interactive learning activities. Regardless of the amount of involvement in interactive teaching, much of the work of school library media specialists as teachers takes place as partners in the preactive teaching carried on by others in the school. This is not a lesser aspect of teaching; rather it allows the teaching ideas and concerns of the library media specialist to exert far greater influence on schooling programs and on pupils than possible when planning only for one's own interactions with students.

The most powerful impact library media specialists can have on the educational program of the school is through the demonstration of commitment and expertise in their own work, either individually or in concert with others. As information specialists and as instructional consultants, they are actively involved in developing units such as the geographical studies described in this chapter. The teaching of media, information skills, and the research process to students and staff development activities for faculty as discussed in the chapters to follow are, directly and indirectly, dynamic evidence of the library media specialist's role as teacher and as change agent. As teachers, library media specialists join with other teachers to provide the best possible education and the best possible schooling for the students they will serve in the restructured schools of the twenty-first century.

3

The School Library Media Specialist: Teacher of Research Strategies

The primary role of the school library media specialist is, by definition, that of a teacher of media. Obviously, media includes all communications: print, non-print, and electronic. Library media specialists take it as their special prerogative to help students develop critical thinking skills in the access, evaluation, selection, and use of all forms of information, ideas, and materials.[1] *Information Power* clearly supports this in stating, "The mission of the library media program is to ensure that students and staff are effective users of ideas and information." The first objective is "to provide intellectual access to information through systematic learning activities which develop cognitive strategies for selecting, retrieving, analyzing, evaluating, synthesizing, and creating information at all age levels and in all curriculum content areas."[2]

Traditional Information Skills Instruction

Our response to this need for the development of informational or critical thinking skills has too often been very narrow and one-sided. The traditional forms of instruction in library media skills are often not very systematic and provide only the most rudimentary introduction to what is really needed. In fact, when placed in the much broader context of access, evaluation, selection, and informed use of all learning resources, we may question the value of teaching these skills at all. It is difficult, however, to shake some school administrators and library media specialists from their entrenched beliefs in the kinds of library instruction that have endured for many years, especially since some of the traditional library skills are now included in standardized achievement tests. How many of those who teach the Dewey Decimal System to all students have really considered whether it is important for them to know it? Once we have raised this question in regard to all aspects of our instruction, we may be able to figure out what really is of value in helping students develop critical abilities and personal learning strategies and then devise much more appropriate means of helping them deal with ideas and materials in their own meaning-making process.

Recent research on children's use of the card catalog and other library resources in their searches merits careful examination. Penelope Moore and Alison St. George studied the retrieval process of a sample of New Zealand sixth graders, exploring the cognitive difficulties encountered.[3] They reported that students had difficulty locating materials on library shelves because they did not fully comprehend the shelving process. The lack of understanding of the relationships among the card catalog, shelving systems, and the books themselves created a major problem in retrieving information. The authors alert us to the need for more research and better understanding of the range of skills needed in problem-solving tasks. For instance, children in the study did not always grasp the essential search terms in a given question. The example that best demonstrates this difficulty is the youngster who searched in the "W" drawer of the card catalog in addressing the question: "What is a bird?"[4] Such studies demonstrate the need for library instruction, but we need to consider whether traditional patterns and practices are providing the most appropriate instruction to meet student needs.

There is also a concern that much traditional instruction serves only habitual library media center users who learn most of the content through other experiences anyway, while simultaneously convincing reluctant users that it is just too much trouble to try to get materials from the library media center. Many of us have seen groups of youngsters enthusiastically involved in team games intended to teach them the use of the card catalog. It is good to see students enjoying themselves in this situation, but one might wonder how carefully the activity was planned and how much learning is actually retained. It is not unheard of for a child who has performed well on this form of game one week to have no idea how to find materials on a particular topic in a subsequent week. The question of instruction in the use of the card catalog is increasingly important in light of the proliferation of online catalogs in schools and public libraries.[5] We need to consider just what students find in their searches of these systems. Traditional instruction provides them with author, title, and subject term and requires them to demonstrate that they have located these items in the catalog. In reality, this is a test of their skill in alphabetization when what they really need to learn is how to figure out what search terms will lead them to the most appropriate information. Christine Borgman and others have been working for some time on new approaches to subject searching with young children using a database of science materials in a hypercard structure.[6] The research to date validates the ability of children to deal with hierarchical structure and to use terms that they recognize and understand.

If a primary goal is to provide access to a wide range of materials on a particular subject, followed by wise evaluation, selection, and use, then perhaps some students should be treated more as adults are in large research or reference collections, that is, have the materials brought to the student researcher for consideration. Most practitioners believe youngsters should acquire the basic skills that enable them to find materials in a public library or school library media center just as it is convenient for them to know the basic steps in multiplication and division in an age of calculators and computers. Some library media specialists, however, put the instruction of such skills between the user and the material. The student who runs enthusiastically into the library media center in search of an item recommended by a friend may decide it is not worth the effort if the library media specialist turns the search into a lengthy or tedious lesson in searching.

Library instruction has moved, in most cases, from a series of isolated lessons beginning with the "Parts of a Book" and "How to Find It in Our Library" through the "Use of the *Reader's Guide* and Special Reference Tools" to integrating such lessons with curricular content. This combination with other subject area content is logical and appropriate; however, we must also be aware that it may have the effect of turning students off to both. Those who are intrigued by the techniques used to teach reference skills may be put off by the association with their least favorite subject, while those absorbed with the subject matter may be impatient to get on with their work without what they perceive as interference.

What we have not done, in many instances, is really reconsider the whole idea of bibliographic or information skills instruction. In some schools the lessons have not changed very much over the years, except that we now are careful to have students practice the traditional library skills on subject matter related to classroom content. In so doing, however, some library media specialists seem to assume that strategies for teaching the various disciplines have not changed since the earliest days of library instruction in schools. Young people using modes of inquiry that are more student-centered and focused as much on process as on product will probably make very sophisticated use of the library media center and its resources, but lessons that are only superficially subject correlated do not necessarily relate to their assignments or the way students approach content.

It is essential to understand cognitive styles of learners in addressing how one might structure the teaching of research strategies.[7] There is a vast body of research on learning styles, but too often both classroom teachers and school library media specialists ignore the fact that people learn in different ways and continue to teach as if there were one right way.[8] We need to work with our colleagues in the preactive phase of teaching to identify both the cognitive and the affective style of each learner and then use that information in the interactive phase. This awareness of differences makes for a happier and more productive learning environment. It also requires the library media specialist as teacher to plan alternative strategies to teach the same content.

Developing a New Competency Base for Information Skills Instruction

Since library media specialists are experts in information science, it behooves us to take the lead and thoughtfully consider just what knowledge, skills, and attitudes we would have students acquire in this area. An obvious way of handling this is to develop some version of a scope and sequence chart similar to those used in other disciplines in the school. Many such charts or lists are available in library literature, from other school library media specialists, and even with commercial materials for bibliographic instruction and communication studies.[9] These could be shared and modified in cooperation with our classroom colleagues to eliminate traditional rote skills and bring these plans up-to-date with current technologies and educational knowledge. In examining or creating an overall curriculum development plan, it is essential for the teaching team to think through what today's students really need to know in order to decipher and deal with all the forms of information available to them, and to communicate their own ideas in various media. Increasingly the computer and other technological resources can be combined to personalize and make instructional content available on demand for a specific purpose at the point of use.

The prepared sources for bibliographic instruction can serve as a beginning, but library media specialists and classroom teachers should develop their own list of specific learning competencies for each student to best match the resources of a particular school's library media center and the needs of users. If this list is fully developed to include more complex means of acquiring and dealing with media and information, there should be a substantial degree of overlap with the work of other teachers.[10] If we are really concerned with the evaluation, selection, and use of information instead of merely locating it, we are inevitably dealing with content taught by others. If we are helping students formulate and give shape to their own thoughts in the medium that best conveys those thoughts, we will be dealing with ideas and information included in the sciences and the social sciences as well as the humanities. It would be wise, therefore, to identify these overlaps immediately by comparing the list of library media center competencies with those identified in curriculum materials or guides for other subject areas and in discussions with other teachers. It may be useful to duplicate this list of competencies in the form of a checklist on which the names of all the students in a particular homeroom or class can be placed for easy record keeping. With the computer, it is possible to store individual student records that would be useful in assessing progress in acquiring the identified competencies throughout one's school career. Students could even track their own skills acquisition on the computer and monitor their own learning. The teacher and library media specialist would also monitor these records of competencies and, in periodic negotiations, plan strategies for teaching. Thus, the work of the library media specialist can be presented as being integral to other disciplines rather than as extraneous or tacked on to someone else's work. It is at this point that questions such as the following are asked in relation to each competency identified.

Is It the Primary Responsibility of the Library Media Specialist or of the Classroom Teacher to Work with Students in the Development of a Particular Competency?

The decision making related to the first question assumes a trust in the competency of one's colleagues that may not exist on some school faculties. Most of us, whether library media specialists or classroom teachers, tend to think that if we really want it done and done right, we might as well do it ourselves. It is only when we really develop cooperative teams of library media specialists and other teachers working together for the good of students that we are able to provide the kind of instruction needed. Once we accept that the responsibility for students' development of information skills and research strategies is negotiated and shared, both students and faculty benefit. The library media specialist is in a unique position in the school to take the lead in organizing and nurturing such cooperative ventures. Even in schools in which the library class functions as a preparation period for teachers, the library media specialist should assume the responsibility of finding ways to cooperate with classroom teachers. Not only does this improve educational opportunities for students, it also demonstrates to teachers our investment in that process and enlists their support for our role as partners in the educational enterprise.

Is the Development of This Competency Better Achieved Individually, in Small Groups, or with the Total Class?

The second question assumes that we are not bound by traditional patterns of grouping for instruction in education. Decisions about grouping are always contingent upon such realities as curriculum, schedules, availability of resources, student learning styles and capacities, and individual teaching styles. Attitudes and traditions also influence decisions. Some library media specialists who say that they love their jobs because of the opportunity to work with individuals as well as with large groups have never seriously considered substituting some sort of individualized approach for group instruction in information skills. On the other hand, there are those who automatically eliminate group instruction without asking themselves if there are instances in which this form of learning might be economical and beneficial to students.

There is a danger here that has become increasingly apparent in our schools in recent years. Educators may decide that a particular form of instruction or grouping pattern is inherently better than others or that, given philosophical beliefs and economic factors, it is more appropriate in this time and place. There is no one way to provide a sound schooling program or even to teach a particular skill. We have all seen the results of programs based on groups of from twenty-five to thirty students and a single text for each subject, but sometimes even more invidious things have been done in the name of individualization. Some individualized programs do no more than allow each student to move at his own speed through prescribed sets of materials, much like the old textbooks except that they are divided into smaller units. Thus, students may have even less contact with the teacher who acts basically as a messenger and file clerk and with other students who might challenge, encourage, or stimulate ideas. In addition, there may be little or no recognition or accommodation of personal learning styles. The recent emphasis on cooperative learning is a positive response to research on how people learn, but we must also be aware that young people need to learn how to work effectively and efficiently in teams and that team projects may leave some students out or permit other inequalities. No single pattern of grouping is appropriate for all students or in all situations.

Similar concerns need to be considered in library media centers where students are expected to go through a series of individualized exercises in the use of the library media center. It is sensible to have available as many instructional materials as possible, but the important thing is the decision-making process, which determines what, when, where, how, and by whom these materials are used. A variety of approaches and alternatives for those who require them ought to be available for the development of library media center competencies, but it is even more important that the library media specialist, working with classroom teachers, makes sound teaching judgments in encouraging and helping students assess their own learning so that they will know when and how to best meet their information needs. Equally important is the quality of the materials available to students.[11]

Does the Development of This Competency Have a Natural Correlation with Other Subject Matter or Is This So Important That It Ought to Be Explored on Its Own?

Many competencies included in the information skills or research process curriculum are also included in language arts, science, or social science curricula. Here there is less concern with traditional library skills than with more complex abilities in the evaluation, selection, and use of materials and information. There is no question that it is essential for students in all subject areas to be critical in their encounters with ideas, information, and media. "Critical" is not used here as negative or as faultfinding but rather as a positive approach or a search for excellence. Higher-order thinking skills in relation to media and resources are essential to finding and using the best possible information and ideas in all disciplines. Such skills are acquired primarily within the context of subject area studies; but some, often the study of media themselves, may be included separately in the library media center curriculum as well. There is a tendency in our society to place value judgments on the various media of communication without really examining critically the content of those media. Many of us in library professions probably still tend to trust the printed word over television or motion picture coverage of the same topic. Others trust the eye of the camera more than the words of a particular individual. As library media specialists, we ought to help students value each medium for what it is uniquely equipped to do, identify the elements and means of composition in each, and develop the critical abilities to evaluate both accuracy and excellence in all media.

The Research Process: Developing Metacognitive Awareness

Library media skills were never intended to exist in isolation, either from other content in the curriculum or from each other in an ongoing informational project. Now there is a great deal of research available on the overall research process and how library media specialists can assist students in the process. Carol Kuhlthau has defined the information search process most clearly. "It is a complex learning process involving thoughts, actions, and feelings that takes place over an extended period of time, that involves developing a topic from information in a variety of sources, and that culminates in a presentation of the individual's new perspective of the topic."[12] Kuhlthau's model of the research process is probably the most useful of those currently available because it is grounded in theory and research and because it includes affective as well as cognitive behaviors.[13]

Kuhlthau refined and verified her model in a series of research studies, most of which concentrated on high school students; and, as she reports, the general reaction of library media specialists was "an intuitive recognition, an agreement with the results."[14] One might question, however, whether all aspects of this model are true for all researchers at all times. There is an assumption that the research process is in response to an assignment from a teacher, rather than a student-initiated project based on personal interest or need. When the students' task initiation stage is "characterized by feelings of uncertainty of *what is expected* and apprehension at the task ahead" [emphasis mine], one must wonder if there would be the same degree of uncertainty if these were self-initiated tasks to meet authentic personal needs rather than efforts to meet someone else's expectations.

At what Kuhlthau calls the Prefocus/Exploration Stage, one could hypothesize that the research process for empowered, self-determined learners might lead to exhilaration rather than frustration. Kuhlthau's research study, which included academic and public library researchers as well as high school students, gives some credence to this possibility. She reports that "public library users were more confident at initiation than the academic and school participants."[15] Surely, this has implications for further research addressing such questions as: Are public library users more accustomed to initiating their own research processes? Do they engage in the research process for their own pleasure and satisfaction as well as to meet some "imposed" obligation? If so, does this general attitude toward the search process carry over to externally imposed searches as well as to self-initiated ones? Do high school students who have been given greater personal authority and control over school assignments experience less confusion and frustration than those who must meet specific expectations in response to a teacher-initiated task? There is much yet to be learned from the Kuhlthau model as we examine the process of student learning in the varieties of restructured schools for the twenty-first century.

Michael Eisenberg and Michael Brown, reporting research evidence that skills instruction has a positive impact on achievement, agree with Kuhlthau and others that the emphasis should be on process rather than on specific sources.[16] If the process is dominant, it is useful to explore various means to translate that process into instructional units. It is clear that critical-thinking skills are a vital portion of the process approach. Therefore, if a student is assigned the task of locating information on Native Americans, it is important to decide in advance what thinking skills might be applied to this question. Often it is assumed that the simple act of locating any material on the subject will do the job, not recognizing that a student will probably need to identify specific subsets of the topic or types of information for the search. For example, some of the first distinctions a student needs to make are among Native American tribes and between fictional and fact-based content. It might prove helpful to have students keep a research journal or record of their thought process and of the investigations they undertake. Such journals may prove useful as retrospective tools and as evaluative portfolios as they progress through the grades. It is extremely important to discuss with students the strengths and weaknesses of the search strategies used in their investigations. How do students learn to select the appropriate sources and the relevant sections or segments of these sources. How do they learn to read, view, or listen critically to that content and then to think about what has been revealed about their specific topics? How does the library media specialist uncover, with the young person, the slips in logic or the incompleteness of an approach? At what point does the individual cease selecting, reading, and analyzing materials and begin to concentrate on the thought process that leads to writing or presentation?

Library media specialists can be most helpful in assisting students to synthesize information from various sources rather than merely copying segments from existing texts.[17] During the teaching of the research process the library media specialist might stress the meanings of key investigative words, such as *inferring, analyzing, sequencing, problem-solving, classifying, drawing relationships, organizing, predicting*, and *questioning*. By encouraging students to identify and practice these processes in their work, the library media specialist reinforces their understanding of the learning process and of their own learning styles.

Words or concepts such as *metaphor, imagination, creativity*, and *personal experience* are also essential in the grasp of critical thinking and add a dimension that is often overlooked in metacognitive awareness, that of aesthetic as well as scientific forms of knowing. As students think more precisely about what they are actually doing with the materials found in the search process and record this information in their research journals, both they and their teachers will be able to study their strategies and the sequence of decisions made to recognize strengths and diagnose needs.

Students should also be encouraged to use such techniques as a question log to help organize important portions of their research projects. For instance, the following questions could be asked in planning an assignment on bumper stickers.

1. What effect would I get if I opened my paper discussing bumper stickers in general and all the different kinds, giving examples?
2. Would this be too broad? Should I be more specific?
3. Maybe this would be too boring to the reader?
4. What type of audience would I write for?
5. Should I try to be broad enough for a variety of readers or should I get specific and center my paper on a specific group of people?
6. What about taking a specific type of bumper stickers like the "I ♡ . . . " stickers and developing a paper from those?
7. Would that give me enough to write about?
8. What about writing about the purpose of bumper stickers?

9. Would this be interesting?
10. Where could I find information?[18]

Such diagnostic tools provide the library media specialist, the classroom teacher, and students with a means to analyze and eventually enhance the metacognitive processes of learners. They also support the notion that the information and ideas in the proposed project might have a purpose beyond getting a grade and might appeal to an audience beyond the teachers giving the assignment. If students really want their work to be interesting to others, does this alter what might be selected from among a large array of materials? The posing of such questions is essential to the development of critical thinkers.

Arthur Applebee suggests questions that teachers might ask as they build instructional scaffolds, that is, temporary structures or models upon which students may build their own work. Library media specialists might use questions such as these to develop their own metacognitive awareness and evaluate their instruction.

1. Does the task permit students to develop their own meanings rather than simply following the dictates of the teacher or text? Do they have room to take ownership for what they are doing?
2. Is the task sufficiently difficult to permit new learning to occur, but not so difficult as to preclude new learning?
3. Is the instructional support structured in a manner that models appropriate approaches to the task and leads to a natural sequence of thought and language?
4. Is the teacher's role collaborative rather than evaluative?
5. Is the external scaffolding removed as the student internalizes the patterns and approaches needed?[19]

The various models and approaches designed to develop metacognitive awareness are of definite value in planning preactive teaching. Library media specialists, however, must avoid the tendency to devise such models and then proceed to teach a particular model rather than use that model to inform the teaching of content relevant to student needs.[20] One of the major criticisms of educators associated with critical or higher-order thinking skills in the curriculum has been that they sometimes seem to forget that such skills are to be used primarily to think about something other than the skills themselves. Too often teachers have used information about the metacognitive process as new content for study rather than as a means to inform and improve all teaching and learning activities.

Selecting and Developing the Research Topic

One of the most difficult aspects of the research process is deciding upon a specific topic for research. School library media specialists ought to identify both research strategies and materials that will help students explore various topics and the possible research paths related to those topics in ways that are enjoyable as well as enlightening. Even if a teacher has assigned the topic, students need to find their own slant on or subset of that topic in order to move successfully through that process.

Finding a Focus: Semantic Webbing

Semantic webbing is a very exciting way to help young people organize their ideas, see relationships, and develop a topic for research.[21] For instance, a group of students might begin brainstorming on a particular topic by placing that topic, or a question related to that topic, at the center of a web. As information or ideas related to the topic are elicited from students, they are depicted as strands of the web drawn out from that central focus. Additional information, supporting evidence, or subsets are again related and drawn on the web, and students are encouraged to explore relationships among all elements of that web. If one begins with the general topic "Civil Rights for African-Americans," for example, the initial web might look like figure 5. Individual students might then select a particular aspect of the original web or begin with a more specific question about the topic to create their own more focused webs for personal research.

It is important to remember that this technique is, at least at this point, practiced prior to any research as a way of getting student researchers to draw from their own interests and their own knowledge and, therefore, to invest some of themselves in the selection of a topic, that is, to help them claim ownership of their own work. Once some of the initial possibilities are explored in this manner, students can select a focus and move to general reference sources to examine coverage of the topic and to refine or expand their focus and perhaps the web. Then they reconsider what they already know, identify what they want to find out, and formulate specific research questions or hypotheses. Even if a teacher has assigned the broad topic, this activity can help students see possibilities within that topic, encourage their personal ownership of and involvement with the assigned task and, most importantly, get them excited both about what they already know and what is yet to be known.

Of course, we need to remember that webbing is just one way of mapping ideas. As an early stage in the research process, this visual form of organizing ideas is the equivalent of using language to organize and structure ideas in an outline. As such, webbing, can either be preliminary to or an alternative to the traditional numbered and lettered outline. In fact, we might present these alternative means of organization to students as examples and encourage them to share other approaches or strategies they use for the same purpose. Consequently, rather than attempting to force all students into a single mode, we could emphasize the importance of this initial stage of research while learning about and encouraging personal learning styles. Webbing is discussed further in chapter 5, and a variety of examples of ways of using this technique in teaching and learning are provided.

52   Teacher of Research Strategies

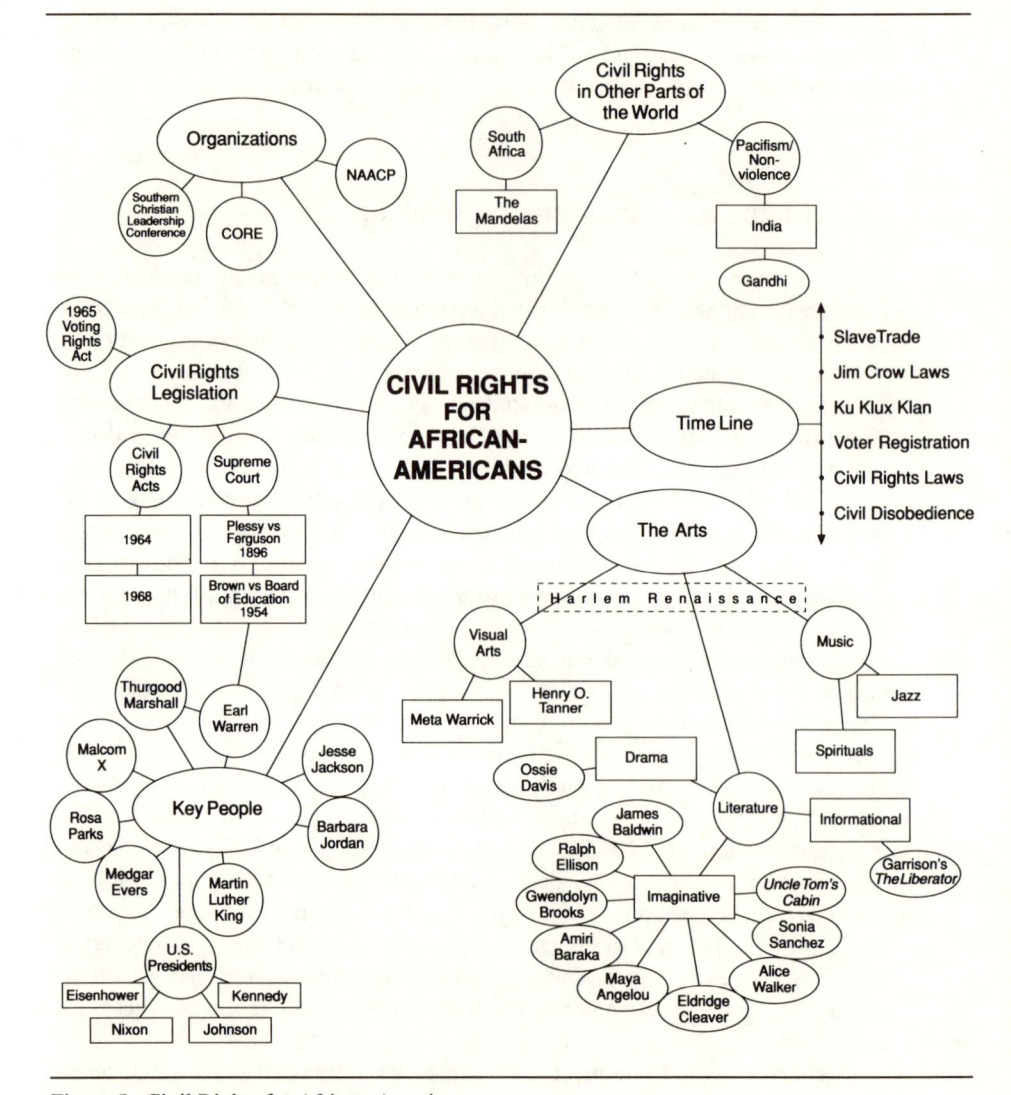

Figure 5. Civil Rights for African-Americans

Finding a Focus: An Issue-Centered Approach

Another approach to the development of critical thinking skills in the research process would be to begin a discussion of a current topic such as AIDS with the intent of helping students select key issues of concern. From those key issues and keywords it should be possible to set up a series of questions that might be searched. It may even be possible from such a discussion to determine a particular hypothesis that might be examined. At this point it would be useful to ask students where they might look for materials to answer their questions. One clear distinction will have to be made on the issue of timeliness as it relates to topics such as AIDS. Materials published several years ago are often superseded by newer research and information. Indeed some earlier information may even be dangerously in error. Having decided that recency is a major factor and having determined a series of terms for searching, one must decide what sources are most appropriate. The determination of periodical literature as a major resource is obvious although the availability of online data and listservs on Internet should be pointed out to students. Some discussion might follow on the value of different sources of articles, that is, the popular and the more scholarly. This topic offers an opportunity for the library media specialist to point out the importance of nontraditional sources, since much of the critical information about AIDS is found through telephone and computer hotlines of various agencies concerned with this problem. Especially if one chooses to study AIDS historically, an examination of various kinds of bias that influence the treatment of this topic would become obvious. Students in a school where this kind of research topic is encouraged would probably also be interested in the debate about whether, when, what, and how much information about AIDS should be allowed in the school curriculum, an issue that would lead to another consideration of values and biases. It would be useful to create a pathfinder to map an information search path to demonstrate how one moves through this process. A key objective is to have the student recognize the relative importance of various factors and resources in organizing and executing research on this topic.

Finding a Focus: Materials-Centered Approaches

Another interesting and enjoyable approach to helping students determine the focus of a project might be through the examination of such well-organized sources as the Eyewitness Books series.[22] For instance, *Arms and Armor* is a photo essay of weapons and armor from all over the world and spanning time from the Stone Age through the Wild West.[23] A student interested in this broad topic could, in browsing through this visually enticing work, select a photographic segment as a starting point for further study. Using both the index and the table of contents, one would see connections that are not at first apparent. A student who was considering a focus on pistols could turn to the table of contents and find headings for chapters entitled "Pistols," "Dueling Pistols," "The Percussion Revolver," and "Keeping Law and Order," all of which might contain useful information. The index would then lead to additional information on the topic. Using the chapter on "Pistols," a student might become fascinated with the small palm pistol or *lemon squeezer* used to assassinate William McKinley and, in the process, move from a focus on pistols to weapons of assassination. It would then be logical to look at the assassinations of Abraham Lincoln, John F. Kennedy, and Martin Luther King, Jr., which would, in the case of Kennedy, move beyond pistols to other weapons. Examining the chapter on "Keeping Law and Order" might lead a student to a very different focus on police through the ages or, even more specifically, on police in comic images or caricatures. An alternative path a student might select from examining these pages is an investigation of types of handcuffs.

Using this technique, students will recognize the wide range of foci that may be found under a broad or very general topic. What makes Eyewitness Books so elegant an approach in communicating this to students is the variety of topics included in this series as well as the balance of color illustrations and short texts that often address unusual or strange aspects of these topics. As a result of such a lesson, students should begin to see how a specific topic is ferreted out of a more general one. They will also recognize the importance of, as well as the similarities and differences between, the index and the table of contents in a single book. In this way students should be helped to select a specific topic of interest, one worth all the invested time to complete a full-scale presentation and, at the same time, take pleasure in the process.

There Once Was a Time is another example of a book that might prove useful in helping students consider alternative topics and informational paths.[24] Ventura's visual presentation of western civilization divides history into eight periods and then examines each through pictures of nine aspects of everyday life. This book is an excellent source to demonstrate to students how a large mural or time line of world history or of a specific period of history might be put together in an exciting fashion. The detailed illustrations reveal a significant amount of research and could be used to help students move off in a variety of directions in order to investigate items for their own mural.

The key here is to ask students who use the book to track the nature of the questions they formulate while reading and looking at various pages in this book. For instance, pages 44–45 contain pictures of many members of feudal society, both secular and religious, from the emperor and the pope to serfs and low clergy. Some obvious questions in response to these images will concern feudalism: How did this system function, and how could it be represented on a mural? What did various members in this social hierarchy do, and how might this be shown pictorially? Would you select dull colors or bright, lively ones as more appropriate to represent life in this time period? What role did women have in this early society? Then students might be asked to study a second set of pages, (54–55) which focus specifically on dress, fashion, and taste during the same "Before 1000" period. They will notice that the clothing of the various classes of society on these pages does not correspond with that of the previous pages representing "society, forms of government, institutions, economy." Since "Before 1000" includes a vast time span, students will need to be more precise in pinpointing the various costumes worn in these two sets of illustrations and could turn to additional material on costumes as well as more specific historical references.

A third set of pages (128–29) raises numerous questions about transportation and the industrialization of the world. Students might seek information on trains, trolleys, the stagecoach, the paddle steamer, and the first attempts at flying. In each set of pages selected, the object is to have the student learn to frame questions and determine key words for searching resources of the library media center and beyond in order to enrich their store of information, which will ultimately be pictured in their own mural. The overall question that needs to be repeated in each case is, "How will the answer to my question make a better visual presentation in the mural?"

Interest in early attempts to fly might lead some students to Russell Freedman's book about the invention of the airplane by the Wright Brothers.[25] If a student used this work as a starting point to explore the role of determination in invention, one possibility might be to prepare a divided list of "what I know" and "what I want to know." For instance, Wilbur and Orville Wright recorded their work through photography and thus the pictures contained in the book provide a history both of their lives and of this invention. Is it possible to identify what characteristics these two men possessed that permitted them to solve problems that others had attempted to solve for many years? If one studied the lives and works of other inventors, would it be possible to identify similar personal characteristics? If the initial question requires too difficult and too complex a search for this particular project, what other research directions might be explored? Would words like *aerodrome, glider, wind tunnel, ailerons, wing warping, propeller, lift, gusts*, and *ground crew* be useful as search terms for additional information? Helping students identify search terms is often accomplished using index terms as well as reading captions under photos. Who were the people surrounding the Wright Brothers during this period of their lives? How does the Wright Brothers' work relate to what others were doing in the early years of flying? For example, what did Otto Lilienthal, Samuel Langley, Octave Chanute, and Louis Bleriot accomplish? The Wright Brothers had a dream and managed to realize that dream, but what motivated them? Such questions might be recorded on a chart or in a research journal. Such record keeping helps students both to see what is contained in this wonderful book and to organize their work as researchers.

Another fascinating and very tightly focused work of history is Judith St. George's book about the Mason-Dixon Line.[26] The history of this line, drawn in 1763, was one of massacres, fights, wars, and rebellions that occurred for over two hundred years. Students can just enjoy this historical narrative, or they might use the index and illustrations to determine a focus for a paper or project. St. George, in all of her historical works, weaves into her primary focus the lives of many of the peoples who influenced or were influenced by, in this instance, the Mason-Dixon Line. William Penn, Lord Baltimore, Harriet Tubman, George Washington, Chief Pontiac, and Abraham Lincoln are just a few of those associated with that line. Through the study of works such as this, students begin to understand that a place, even an imaginary line, can have tremendous influence on the lives of both the famous and the common persons who pass through or live near that place. This book provides an opportunity for students to see the interdisciplinary nature of knowledge as they reach out from this narrative to clarify and embellish its contents. The use of Charles Mason's journal, original photographs, prints, maps, and other primary materials to recreate this place and time is a dramatic demonstration of the importance of such sources in studying and recreating history.

Still another interdisciplinary approach to understanding how particular phenomena occur can be explored using two videocassettes, *Pyramid* and *David Macaulay in His Studio*.[27] In the latter, Macaulay explains the research and creative process he used in drawing the pyramid for his book of that title. Students can begin to grasp what it might have been like to watch this massive structure being built at the same time that they see a contemporary artist at work. In addition to the videos, the opportunity to study Macaulay's book and to look at contemporary footage of the pyramids helps students discover many facets of this mighty historic achievement. Such a unit identifies a number of techniques that might help students think about their own research. First, students are exposed to the results of the author-illustrator's research. Second, special terms are defined and shown in these various media. Third, students hear about additional ideas, artifacts, and practices of the period that might be worth investigating, such as, mummification, the *Book of the Dead*, slaves, and various gods and goddesses. One overall issue that may be raised by students concerns the desire of human beings to create monuments. Is this characteristic of all peoples?

Given current concern for both environmental issues and for the protection of endangered species, Patricia Lauber's *Great Whales* is a good tool to use with third or fourth grades to trigger possible personal research projects.[28] This book presents a series of facts in a text that is lively and informed. It includes illustrations, photos, and an index that might be used to gain information, identify search terms, and pose research questions. This book also would be a natural connective to the music of whales and the history of whaling in the world and could be used to support a student-selected thesis in relation to whales or the environment. The idea of listing evidence from a source to support a personal position is significant even to elementary school children, who often learn only to record or memorize information rather than to use it. The school library media specialist can help young learners use a basic two-step approach: (1) determine the hypothesis and (2) select items from the text that offer support for the position selected or that modify that position. Of course, they would then go on to locate and use a variety of other sources to continue to test the hypothesis.

In those library media centers with computer access to CD-ROM or online databases, one needs to pay special attention to helping students with the process of recognizing appropriate search terms. If a student begins with a rather general term, the entries retrieved should be useful for demonstrating the broad range of content included within that topic. This may happen accidentally when a student retrieves a cluster of citations and begins to study them; an insight may occur, revealing connections that had never been seen using traditional print indexes. One of the explanations for this may be that computer printouts are easy to run whereas students often approach hard copies of the *Readers' Guide* or the like with the expectation of having to write out each citation. Thus, they are more likely to pay attention to only one item at a time and not see overall patterns and relationships. The use of a printout as a tool for study, therefore, may help students to see how ideas and issues are organized and interrelated. On the other hand, search terms that are too general do retrieve a large number of citations that are of no use for the particular topic or task. When the student recognizes this, the next phase of learning, that of examining, inferring, and evaluating the potential usefulness of the cited items, takes place.

Media other than print should also be used to teach information-gathering skills that have often been discussed only in the context of the book. Online searching and the use of CD-ROM databases offer time-saving aspects to students, but do not necessarily alter what we have traditionally taught and continue to teach in bibliographic instruction. With the use of such programs as Hypercard, students may see connections between the organization of ideas and the data needed to support those ideas as they compile evidence for a particular thesis. The intellectual structuring of stacks in a Hypercard array is, in itself, a revelation of analytical ability and higher-order thinking skills.[29]

The examples cited above are just a few of an almost infinite number of possibilities for using library media center resources to help students think about possibilities for their own research. Whether that research is self-initiated or students are attempting to find a personal topic of interest with a class assignment, it is the process that is stressed. Within that personal process, however, individual skills are learned and practiced and young people are empowered as learners. The attention to the analysis of library media center materials as a means of helping young people focus their research efforts emphasizes one of the traditional strengths of our profession, one that has too often been lost in efforts to embrace new ideas. Critical teaching of the information search process is essential, but that in no way devalues the need for library media professionals to concentrate on evaluation and selection of materials and to know their collections. It is only when one has a real knowledge of the specifics of the content of the collection that connections can be made that will really empower learners and encourage them to take joy in the process.

4

Teaching Evaluation Strategies with Library Media Center Resources

One of the most important roles of the school library media specialist is that of helping students develop critical skills in the evaluation of media. Of course, this is a part of both traditional information skills instruction and the more recent emphasis on teaching the research process. It is also, however, so important and potentially such an exciting learning adventure that it deserves to be considered on its own. We might begin by demonstrating that no writer, creator, or composer ever says all there is to say about a subject and that the creator's values always show through in whatever medium is used. These will be societal values of a particular time and place as well as the creator's own personal values. Further, young people need to realize that factual accuracy does not necessarily lead to *the truth*, that several *accurate* accounts of an incident or situation can present very different perspectives or *truths*. These are vital aspects of critical thinking and are easy to demonstrate in a well-stocked library media center.

One very basic exercise might be to compare entries on a given topic in different encyclopedias. Even though such entries will be very similar, one can begin to notice differences in the selection and omission of specific facts which develop certain emphases. If one uses such topics as *democracy* and *communism* or *AIDS* as examples, it will almost certainly become clear that even encyclopedia articles are not value-free. A historical look at the coverage of women, particularly women of color, or of the African nations through successive editions of the *Encyclopaedia Britannica* shows quite clearly that our perceptions of the world are bound by the time and place in which we live, that even "objective, scholarly" accounts of history are, in some ways, as revealing of the time in which they were written as of the time written about.[1]

Evaluation of Print Biographical Materials: Changing Perspectives

School library media specialists might well plan a program that directly addresses this need for students to make more critical and more knowledgeable judgments about the sources of information on which they rely. One fascinating way to approach the development of critical abilities in selecting and using media in the research process is through the study of famous individuals. A quick overview would confirm the perception that we have historically lived in a white, Eurocentric, male-dominated world, a view many groups have been trying to remedy for several decades. As we focus in on particular individuals about whom a great deal of material has been produced for young people, we find that these figures often come across as plaster saints rather than as living, breathing, feeling human beings.

Abraham Lincoln

Abraham Lincoln is a good example, since there is probably more material for students available about him than about any other person in U.S. history. Most library media centers will contain at least a dozen, probably many more, items relating to his life, including biographies, fictional accounts, photographs, documents, filmstrips, recordings, motion pictures, and other materials. If there were only four to six books available, it would still be possible, in most instances, to demonstrate different points of view and different perceptions of the man, even if they all treat him as a role model.[2] Many biographies for young children concern themselves primarily with the childhood of the individual. These, too, may vary in approach from a portrait of a normal, fun-loving youngster to a kind of foreshadowing of the future by depicting a saintly and wise young child predestined for statesmanship who, in his early years, resolved childhood squabbles with thoughtful and convincing statements of the issues involved.

Some biographies for children may deal with Lincoln as the great emancipator or Lincoln as president. Still others may focus on the importance of reading in his life, on his relationship with animals, on his family life or just about any other theme or gimmick an author or publisher can imagine. While comparing the variety of approaches to biographical presentations of Lincoln's life in print, youngsters might also look at fictional and poetic accounts. Students often find it amazing to discover that a poem or a work of fiction with Lincoln as a character or even one that merely refers to the man may have as many actual facts about the person's life as some of those works classified as biographies. They may become intrigued with uncovering the exact number of verifiable facts in a particular work and then inventing alternative interpretations of those facts.

One might also demonstrate the possibility of alternative interpretations of facts by giving each student the identical brief chronology of the life of an unidentified person, either one they would know if named (perhaps even Lincoln) or an imaginary person, and asking them to prepare a biographical sketch of that person. Ordinarily, interpretations will vary widely. Thus, it becomes obvious that facts do not always point to the truth, and that a biographer is not necessarily an objective recorder of the facts of another's life.

Students of any age who are encouraged to look critically at biographies will soon begin to ask how authors could possibly know what a historical figure such as Lincoln had done and even what he had said at a particular moment in his childhood. This opens up the fascinating question of the legitimacy of fictionalization in biography. High school students will still find evidences of unrealistic foreshadowing and of invented conversations and events in the biographies they read. They will also become increasingly aware of another form of fictionalization, that of psychological speculation attributing motives to the person and meanings to the events of that person's life. Young adults are also more likely to be reading biographies of a *debunking* nature or those that establish a totally different, negative perspective from which to view the person written about. In Lincoln's case, this might be the view of some African-American historians on the misrepresentation of him as the great emancipator or a psychologist's view of him as a greatly disturbed personality.

Christopher Columbus

Christopher Columbus is another historical figure about whom there has been a great deal of speculation in recent years. Throughout the history of education in the United States, both textbooks and trade books have taught youngsters to pay tribute to Columbus as *discoverer* of the new world. Now, five hundred years after his voyage to America, he has become a major subject of inquiry. A study of what has been said about Columbus in textbooks and trade books over the years, along with recent reassessments of his accomplishments, will demonstrate that what is firmly established in print, even in many reference books, is not necessarily the truth. To illustrate this point one might read the official statement of the National Council for the Social Studies for historical context and the contemporary relevance of the Columbian Quincentenary. This statement includes seven basic points of knowledge about the historical setting and effects of Columbus's voyages beginning with the fact that "Columbus did not discover a new world and, thus, initiate American history."[3]

This reassessment of Columbus and his work may cause some to question whether children need heroes and whether those who have made key contributions to our history ought to be represented to them as such, regardless of less heroic aspects of their lives. If so, at what point should we introduce this more realistic, less heroic perspective to young people? It is all too easy to glamorize individuals and to convey to children a false impression of the real person. Young people need opportunities to explore the concept of historical accuracy. For instance, in reference to Columbus, it is important to recognize the position of Native Americans with regard to his explorations, including the acts of violence he committed against native peoples. *Newsweek* magazine, in cooperation with the Smithsonian's Natural History Exhibit "Seeds of Change," prepared a special Columbus issue that will prove useful to students in the process of their research on this topic.[4]

An interesting product of research concerning the events surrounding the famous voyage of 1492 might be the creation of imaginative alternative histories as they might have been recorded by different Native American or African peoples of the time. Jane Yolen's *Encounter* tells of the meeting of the Taino people with Columbus from the point of view of a young Taino boy. The account is brief but utterly poignant, both verbally and visually. Although this is a picture book, it would make a very exciting discussion item for older children as well. The refrain, "No one listened to me, for I was but a child," carries a strong message as the tale unfolds. *Morning Girl* by Michael Dorris is a beautifully written account of Taino family life at the time of Columbus' initial voyage. The fact that the arrival of the Spanish ships, as seen from a young girl's perspective, comes in the last chapter leaves readers with a sense of dread for the family they have come to care about throughout the book. Francine Jacobs's *The Tainos* elaborates on the lives of these Native Americans for older children. Jean Fritz and others in *The World in 1492* explore the state of a number of civilizations throughout the world, including that of Native Americans, putting Columbus's voyage in a more universal context.

Using the list of titles provided in List 4, along with entries from textbooks and traditional reference sources produced at different times, should lead to an exciting discussion of facts, fictions, errors, and alternative interpretations of the explorations of Columbus. Such discussions will also help young people think more critically about the general subjectivity of history. Although the interest in Christopher Columbus may have waned after the 1992 quincentenary, the kind of historical reassessment this event stimulated stands as an exemplar of the need for critical analysis of information presented to young people. Using material on Columbus, it is possible to demonstrate that reports of history are as dependent on the social and cultural context of the times in which those reports are written as on the known facts of historical events. Such revisionist views of history point out that there are almost always alternative views of a situation or event and that what is considered history in a particular time and place is the result of the perspectives of the people in power. Young people might examine the materials in List 4 for alternative interpretations of the events of 1492 and inquire into how much the time and political climate in which a work was written determine its view of historical content.

List 4. Selected Books on Columbus

Adler, David A. *A Picture Book of Christopher Columbus*. Illus. by John and Alexandra Wallner. New York: Holiday House, 1991.

Asimov, Isaac. *Isaac Asimov's Pioneers of Science and Exploration: Christopher Columbus, Navigator to the New World*. Milwaukee, Wisc.: Garth Stevens, 1991.

Baker, Nina Brown. *The Story of Christopher Columbus*. New York: Grosset & Dunlap, 1952.

Brenner, Barbara. *If You Were There in 1492*. New York: Bradbury, 1991.

Conrad, Pam. *Pedro's Journal: A Voyage with Christopher Columbus, August 3, 1492–February 14, 1493*. Illus. by Peter Koeppen. Homesdale, Penn.: Caroline House, 1991.

Dalgliesh, Alice. *The Columbus Story.* Illus. by Leo Politi. New York: Scribner's, 1955.

D'Aulaire, Ingri, and Edgar D'Aulaire. *Columbus.* Garden City, N.Y.: Doubleday, 1955.

Davis, Jim. *Garfield Discovers America.* Illus. by Mike Fentz. New York: Grosset & Dunlap, 1992.

Dodge, Stephen C. *Christopher Columbus and the First Voyages to the New World.* New York: Chelsea House, 1990.

Dor-Ner, Zvi. *Columbus and the Age of Discovery.* New York: Morrow, 1991. (Companion Volume to the PBS Series)

Dorris, Michael. *Morning Girl.* New York: Hyperion, 1992.

Duvoisin, Roger. *And There Was America.* New York: Alfred Knopf, 1938.

Dyson, John. *Westward with Columbus.* Photos by Peter Christopher. New York: Scholastic/Madison, 1991.

Erdrich, Louise, and Michael Dorris. *The Crown of Columbus.* New York: Harper Collins, 1991.

Faber, Harold. *The Discoverers of America.* New York: Scribner's, 1992.

Finkelstein, Norman H. *The Other 1492: Jewish Settlement in the New World.* New York: Scribner's, 1989.

Fritz, Jean. *The Great Adventure of Christopher Columbus.* Illus. by Tomie dePaola. New York: Putnam & Grosset, 1992. (Pop-up Book)

Fritz, Jean. *Where Do You Think You're Going, Christopher Columbus?* Illus. by Margot Tomes. New York: Putnam, 1980.

Fritz, Jean and others. *The World in 1492.* Illus. by Stefano Vitale. New York: Holt, 1992.

Gross, Ruth Belov. *A Book about Christopher Columbus.* Illus. by Syd Hoff. New York: Scholastic, 1974.

Hill, Ken. *Voyages of Columbus.* Illus. by Paul Wright and others. New York: Random House, 1991.

Humble, Richard. *The Voyages of Columbus.* Illus. by Richard Hook. New York: Watts, 1991.

I, Columbus: My Journal 1492–3. Ed. by Peter and Connie Roop. Illus. by Peter E. Hanson. New York: Walker and Co., 1990.

Jacobs, Francine. *The Tainos: The People Who Welcomed Columbus.* New York: G. P. Putnam's, 1992.

Krensky, Stephen. *Christopher Columbus.* Illus. by Norman Green. New York: Random House, 1991.

Lauber, Patricia. *Who Discovered America? Mysteries and Puzzles of the New World.* Illus. by Mike Eagle. New York: HarperCollins, 1992.

Lawson, Robert. *I Discover Columbus: A True History of the Great Admiral by One Who Sailed with Him.* Boston: Little, Brown, 1941.

Levinson, Nancy Smiler. *Christopher Columbus: Voyager to the Unknown.* New York: Lodestar Books, 1990.

The Log of Christopher Columbus. Selected by Steve Lowe. Illus. by Robert Sabuda. New York: Philomel, 1992.

The Log of Christopher Columbus' First Voyage to America. Illus. by J. O'H. Cosgrave, II. Hamden, Conn.: Linnet, 1989.

McGovern, Ann. *The Story of Christopher Columbus.* New York: Random House, 1963.

Maestro, Betsy, and Guilo Maestro. *The Discovery of the Americas.* New York: Lothrop, Lee & Shepard, 1991.

Martin, Susan. *I Sailed with Columbus.* Illus. by Tom La Padula. Woodstock, N.Y.: Overlook, 1991.

Marzollo, Jean. *In 1492.* Illus. by Steve Bjorkman. New York: Scholastic, 1991.

Meltzer, Milton. *Columbus and the World around Him.* New York: Franklin Watts, 1990.

Pelta, Kathy. *Discovering Christopher Columbus: How History Is Invented.* Minneapolis, Minn.: Lerner Publications. 1991.

Schlein, Miriam. *I Sailed with Columbus.* Illus. by Tom Newsom. New York: HarperCollins, 1991.

Sis, Peter. *Follow the Dream: The Story of Christopher Columbus.* New York: Alfred Knopf, 1991.

Sperry, Armstrong. *Voyages of Christopher Columbus.* New York: Random House, 1950.

Syme, Ronald. *Columbus: Finder of the New World.* Illus. by William Stobbs. New York: Morrow, 1952.

Tallarico, Anthony. *Where's Columbus?* New York: Smithmark, 1992.

Ventura, Piero. *1492: The Year of the New World.* New York: G. P. Putnam's, 1992.

The Voyages of Christopher Columbus. Ed. by John D. Clare. San Diego, Calif.: Harcourt Brace Jovanovich, 1992.

Weil, Lisl. *I, Christopher Columbus.* New York: Atheneum, 1983.

Weisman, JoAnne B., and Kenneth M. Deitch. *Christopher Columbus and the Great Voyage of Discovery.* New York: Discovery Enterprises, 1990.

West, Delno C., and Jean M. West. *Christopher Columbus: The Great Adventure and How We Know about It.* New York: Atheneum, 1991.

Yolen, Jane. *Encounter.* Illus. by David Shannon. San Diego, Calif.: Harcourt Brace Jovanovich, 1992.

Yue, Charlotte, and David Yue. *Christopher Columbus: How He Did It.* Boston: Houghton Mifflin, 1992.

The works cited in List 5 are adult books and other source materials against which teachers and library media specialists might check their own understandings and interpretations of the accomplishments of Christopher Columbus. They may also be used by capable students to verify the views of Columbus presented in their textbooks and other library media center resources.

List 5. Selected Alternative Sources on Christopher Columbus

Allis, S. and others. "Whose America?" *Time* 138, no. 1 (July 8, 1991): 12–17.

Bigelow, William. "Once upon a Genocide. Christopher Columbus in Children's Literature." *Language Arts* 69, no. 2 (February 1992): 112–20.

"Christopher Columbus: Encounters with the Americas." *Ohio Media Spectrum* 44, no. 2 (Summer 1992): 5–85.

The Christopher Columbus Encyclopedia. Ed. by S. A. Bedini. New York: Simon & Schuster, 1991.

Elleman, Barbara. "Classroom Connections: The Columbus Encounter." *Book Links* 1, no. 1 (September 1991): 6–13.

Elleman, Barbara. "Classroom Connections: The Columbus Encounter—Update." *Book Links* 2, no. 1 (September 1992): 31–34.

Foote, Timothy. "Where Columbus Was Coming From." *Smithsonian* 22, no. 9 (December 1991): 28–41.

Gardner, Susan. "My First Rhetoric of Domination: The Columbus Encounter in Children's Biographies." *Children's Literature in Education* 22, no. 4 (December 1991): 275–90.

Ingber, Bonnie Verburg. "The Writing of *Encounter* : The Editor's Perspective." *The New Advocate* 5, no. 4 (Fall 1992): 241–45.

Jackson, Donald Dale. "Who the Heck Did 'Discover' the New World?" *Smithsonian* 22, no. 6 (September 1991): 76–85.

Juhnke, James C., and Jane Yolen. "An Exchange on *Encounter.*" *The New Advocate* 6, no. 2 (Spring 1993): 93–96.

MacLeish, William H. "From Sea to Shining Sea: 1492." *Smithsonian* 22, no. 8 (November 1991): 34–48.

Manning, Patricia. "The World of 1492: In Company with Columbus." *School Library Journal* 38, no.2 (February 1992): 27–30.

Meltzer, Milton. "Selected Forgetfulness: Christopher Columbus Reconsidered." *The New Advocate* 5, no.1 (Winter 1992): 1–9.

Pena-Ramos, Alfonso. "An Encounter with History." *Millersville Review* 105, no.3 (Spring 1992): 15–17.

Sale, Kilpatrick. *Conquest of Paradise: Christopher Columbus and the Columbian Legacy.* New York: Alfred Knopf, 1990.

Seeds of Change: A Quincentennial Commemoration. Ed. by Herman J. Viola. Washington, D.C.: Smithsonian Institution, 1991.

Taxel, Joel. "The Politics of Children's Literature: Reflections of Multiculturalism, Political Correctness, and Christopher Columbus." In *Teaching Multicultural Literature in Grades K-8,* ed. by Violet J. Harris. Norwood, Mass.: Christopher-Gordon, 1992.

West, Jane and others. "Expectations and Evocations: Encountering Columbus through Literature." *The New Advocate* 5, no. 4 (Fall 1992): 247–63.

"When Worlds Collide: How Columbus's Voyages Transformed Both East and

West." Columbus Special Issue: *Newsweek* (Fall/Winter 1991):82 pages. (A Joint Project with the Smithsonian's natural history exhibit "Seeds of Change.")

Without Discovery: A Native Response to Columbus. Ed. by Ray Gonzalez. Seattle, Wash.: Broken Moon, 1992.

Yolen, Jane. "Past Time: The Writing of the Picture Book *Encounter.*" *The New Advocate* 5, no. 4 (Fall 1992): 235–39.

Alternative Subjects for Biographical Study

Other people who might make excellent topics for explorations are Amelia Erhardt, Tituba, Matthew Henson, Eleanor Roosevelt, Marian Anderson, Thomas Edison, Caesar Chavez, Gandhi, Margaret Sanger, Zora Neale Hurston, Georgia O'Keeffe, James Baldwin, Margaret Mead, Benito Juarez, Martin Luther King, Jr., Barbara Jordan, and Winston Churchill. Or consider a study of Louisa May Alcott, taking into account the newer scholarship and feminist studies that have emerged in recent years.[5] Compare, for example, the older award-winning biography by Cornelia Meigs, *Invincible Louisa*, with the newer *Louisa May: The World and Works of Louisa May Alcott* by Norma Johnston. How does each author deal with facts and fiction? Note that Johnston makes extensive use of Alcott's writings as well as the latest research on her life and work.

Evaluation of Biographical Materials in Media Other than Print

Inquiry into what was recorded about historical figures during their own lifetimes can be very revealing and, for contemporary figures, will often include information in a variety of media. We have only to look at the biographies of President John F. Kennedy to see again how the perspective of time changes our views of individuals, and that a period of mourning for an untimely death is only a temporary respite from the critic's pen. Certainly, views of both his public and private lives have changed over the years since his death. The 1991 film *JFK*, directed by Oliver Stone, rekindled national interest and concern over the accuracy of the Warren Commission Report. Although public perceptions of Kennedy have generally become more critical, figures such as Harry S. Truman have been viewed much more positively after their deaths than they were during their own lifetimes. Current periodical articles about people in today's world are bound to be colored by specific concerns at a particular moment in time. For instance, during the 1992 presidential election most articles about President Bush were influenced, in some way, by the economic recession and the belief by many, even members of his own political party, that he was more concerned with foreign policies than with domestic issues. In 1991 he was basking in the glory of a victory in Desert Storm; in 1992 Americans questioned the motives, the results, and even the reporting and interpretation of actual events in that conflict. By the time this is published and read, these issues along with the Los Angeles riots, the humanitarian mission to Somalia, and the pardoning of those involved in the Iran-Contra affair may be perceived as having little or no historical significance in evaluating George Bush's role as U.S. president. It will be equally interesting to follow the written perceptions and photographic records of Bill and Hillary Clinton over their years in public life.

Recognition of the impact of multiple perspectives and changing views of the historical record can certainly be supported by a study of the dissolution of communism in Russia and East Germany. Television has given us a close-up view of the power of individuals to command people in their struggle for freedom. Boris Yeltsin is a classic example of charismatic power at its fullest, but he too began to slip from the pedestal of perceived greatness very quickly as his people suffered from the lack of basic necessities. Only time will tell what his place in history will be, whether he is a primary force or only a footnote.[6]

Obviously information about individuals conveyed in media other than print also must be examined critically. One might begin by comparing still photographs, drawings, or cartoon caricatures of a particular individual. Note the achievement in this regard of Russell Freedman in his Newbery Award–winning *Lincoln: A Photobiography*.[7] This kind of study may be more interesting and more revealing if a contemporary character is chosen because, over time, many such graphic views of a historical figure may disappear until we have what might almost be called *authorized* pictorial versions. Cases in point are the Sargeant portrait of Lincoln or the all-too-familiar silhouette that shows up on bulletin boards each February. James Daughtery, author of *Abraham Lincoln*, provides a brief exploration of this concern from an alternative perspective in his video presentation for Weston Woods Studios.[8]

A collection of pictorial depictions of a current or recent political figure would provide a fertile field for such a critical study. Different shots taken almost simultaneously at the same news conference or event can, both literally and figuratively, show the character in a totally different light. Camera angles, focus, and the background included, as well as variations in lighting, may portray many images of a person. A photographer will, of course, select the one or two photos from the many taken to convey precisely what he or she wants others to see in the person. When we add motion to a series of pictures, as in films, videos, or television, a viewer must also be aware of additional film factors such as editing, sequencing, the use of cuts and splices, and sound-tracking. Political speeches and press conferences are obvious sources for different visual interpretations of an event, but students might also want to demonstrate this themselves by attempting to shape opinions by filming a classroom or school activity to present alternative views or by working with a taped interview of a political candidate or other person of prominence.

Authors and Illustrators: Biographical Resources

With the increased use of whole language approaches in schooling, it is important to recognize that the reading-writing connection might be encouraged through having students see how authors and illustrators talk about the relationships between their lives and their work in autobiographies. In reading about the childhood of a favorite author, potential writers may begin to see connections and possibilities for their own work. List 6 offers a sample of such works. Beverly Cleary has presented a warm picture of her early days, and Michael Forman captures, in both illustrations and text, a sense of what the world was like in his boyhood years and some of the influences that led him to write and illustrate as he does. Certainly Bill Peet shares his infectious humor through his autobiography. Biographies, as well as autobiographies, provide insights into a creator's work; and, where both are available, it could be informative to compare the two. A parallel writing activity for young people might be to interview each other about a specific incident in each student's own life and then compare the subject's own written autobiographical account with that of his or her student biographer.

List 6. Selected Books on Authors and Illustrators

Anderson, William. *A Biography of Laura Ingalls Wilder.* New York: Harper Collins, 1992.
Angelou, Maya. *I Know Why the Caged Bird Sings.* New York: Random House, 1970.
Boston, Lucy M. *Perverse and Foolish: A Memoir of Childhood and Youth.* New York: Atheneum, 1979.
Bruce, Harry. *Maud: The Life of L. M. Montgomery.* New York: Seal Bantam, 1992.
Byars, Betsy. *In My Own Words: The Moon and I.* Englewood Cliffs, N.J.: Julian Messner, 1992.
Carpenter, Angelica Shirley, and Jean Shirley. *Frances Hodgson Burnett: Beyond the Secret Garden.* Minneapolis, Minn.: Lerner Publications, 1990.
Carpenter, Angelica Shirley, and Jean Shirley. *L. Frank Baum: Royal Historian of Oz.* Minneapolis, Minn.: Lerner Publications, 1992.
Cleary, Beverly. *A Girl from Yamhill: A Memoir.* New York: Morrow, 1988.
Dahl, Roald. *Boy.* New York: Farrar, Straus & Giroux, 1984.
Daly, Jay. *Presenting S. E. Hinton.* Boston: G. K. Hall, 1987.
Duncan, Lois. *Chapters: My Growth as a Writer.* Boston: Little, Brown, 1982.
Duncan, Lois. *Who Killed My Daughter?* New York: Delacorte, 1992.
Forman, Jack Jacob. *Presenting Paul Zindel.* Boston: Twayne, 1988.
Forman, Michael. *War Boy: A Country Childhood.* New York: Arcade Books, 1989.
Hurston, Zora Neal. *Dust Tracks on the Road.* New York: Lippincott, 1942.
Hyman, Trina Schart. *Self-Protrait: Trina Schart Hyman.* Reading, Mass.: Addison-Wesley, 1981.

Johnston, Norma. *Louisa May: The World and Works of Louisa May Alcott.* New York: Four Winds, 1992.
Kamen, Gloria. *Edward Lear: King of Nonsense.* New York: Atheneum, 1990.
Kerr, M. E. *Me, Me, Me, Me, Me: Not a Novel.* New York: Harper & Row, 1983.
Little, Jean. *Stars Come Out Within.* New York: Viking, 1990.
Marcus, Leonard S. *Margaret Wise Brown: Awakened by the Moon.* Boston: Beacon, 1992.
Meltzer, Milton. *Starting from Home: A Writer's Beginnings.* New York: Viking, 1988.
Nilsen, Alleen Pace. *Presenting M. E. Kerr.* Boston: G. K. Hall, 1986.
Peck, Richard. *Anonymously Yours.* New York: Julian Messner, 1992.
Peet, Bill. *Bill Peet: An Autobiography.* Boston: Houghton Mifflin, 1989.
Rylant, Cynthia. *But I'll Be Back Again.* New York: Orchard Books, 1989.
Sufrin, Mark. *Stephen Crane.* New York: Atheneum, 1992.
Yep, Laurence. *In My Own Words: The Lost Garden.* Englewood Cliffs, N.J.: Julian Messner, 1991.
Zindel, Paul. *The Pigman and Me.* New York: HarperCollins, 1991.

Along with the biographies and autobiographies mentioned above, there are now a number of videocassettes that bring authors and illustrators into the classroom or library media center as in List 7. To see and hear how individual creators have struggled in their work is an encouraging demonstration for young people. Students might also consider how actually seeing the person and hearing his or her voice adds to or changes the impression one receives from a print source.[9]

Meet the Author: Martin Godfrey is unusual in its technical delights, and Godfrey is a dynamic character who captures the viewer with his bursts of energy and obvious caring for young people. Although many children may not be familiar with this Canadian author, this videotape will serve as a real enticement to his work. Other videos serve as a friendly visit to one previously known only through his or her work and provide some insight into how that work came to be.

The videotape *William Golding: The Man and His Myth* would be a fascinating beginning to a unit on Golding's work. Although only fifteen minutes in length, this is an exciting visual experience for students since it draws not only upon Golding's own life, but also upon the film *Lord of the Flies.*

List 7. Selected Videocassettes on Authors and Illustrators

Good Conversations! A Talk with Paula Fox. Color, 20 minutes. Tim Podell Productions, 1992.
Good Conversations! A Talk with Phyllis Reynolds Naylor. Color, 26 minutes. Tim Podell Productions, 1991.
Her Side of the Mountain: A Conversation with Jean Craighead George. Color, 27 minutes. Tim Podell Productions, 1989.
Madeleine L'Engle: Star*Gazer. Color, 29.5 minutes. Ishtar Films, 1989.

The Making of a Storybook: Mary Calhoun–Storyteller. Color, 18 minutes. Chip Taylor Communications, 1991.
Maurice Sendak. Color, 15 minutes. Weston Woods, 1986.
Meet Leo Lionni. Color, 19 minutes. American School Publishers, 1992.
Meet Marc Brown. Color, 20 minutes. American School Publishers, 1991.
Meet the Author: Gordon Korman. Color, 19:32 minutes. Produced by School Services of Canada, 1991. Distributed by Educational Audio Visual.
Meet the Author: Martin Godfrey. Color, 15:35 minutes. School Services of Canada, 1991.
Meet the Caldecott Illustrator: Jerry Pinkney. Color, 21 minutes. American School Publishers, 1991.
Meet the Newbery Author: Mildred Taylor. Color, 21 minutes. Produced by Miller-Brody, 1991. Distributed by American School Publishers.
Meet the Picture Book Author: Cynthia Rylant. Color, 10 minutes. Produced by Miller-Brody, 1990. Distributed by American School Publishers.
Meet Valerie Tripp. Color, 18 minutes. Pleasant Company, 1991.
Trumpet Video Visits Donald Crews. Color, 19 minutes. The Trumpet Club, 1992.
Trumpet Video Visits Gary Paulsen. Color, 24 minutes. The Trumpet Club, 1993.
Trumpet Video Visits Mem Fox. Color, 18 minutes. The Trumpet Club, 1992.
A Visit with Eve Bunting. Color, 19:20 minutes. Houghton Mifflin-Clarion, 1991.
William Golding: The Man and His Myth. Color, 15 minutes. Sunburst, 1990.
The Writing Process: A Conversation with Marvis Jukes. Color, 8:45 minutes. Produced by Disney Educational Productions, 1989. Distributed by Coronet/MTI. 1989.

Some of these productions are not as strong technically as they might be, but the content is of tremendous interest and importance. The inclusion of young people and their responses to the author's works in some of the videos is a charming addition and often makes the tape more appealing to students. The library media specialist might use these presentations in a series of celebrations of authors and illustrators throughout the school year.

The use of videotapes also serves as a means of sharing poetry with children. The videotape *Meet Jack Prelutsky* (Meet the Author series) is a wonderfully humorous introduction to sound and rhythm and the music of very child-appealing poetry. The poet's performance of *"The Ballad of the Boneless Chicken"* is Prelutsky at his most comical. He shares his author's notebook with viewers, showing how he collects ideas and words to be shaped into new poems.

To accompany this cluster of videos (see List 8), a collection of poetry books should be introduced to students. Since poetry is so often either neglected or ignored in schooling, this is a wonderful opportunity for the library media specialist to offer children an exciting journey through language and metaphor. List 9 contains just a few samples of the wide range of poetry collections available to young people.

List 8. Selected Videocassettes on Poets

Good Conversation! A Talk with Karla Kuskin. Color, 22 minutes. Tim Podell Productions, 1991.
Good Conversation! A Talk with Lee Bennett Hopkins. Color, 18 minutes. Tim Podell Productions, 1990.
Good Conversation! A Talk with Nancy Willard. Color, 18 minutes. Tim Podell Productions, 1991.
Meet Ashley Bryan: Storyteller, Artist, Writer. Color, 23 minutes. American School Publishers, 1992.
Meet Jack Prelutsky. Color, 24 minutes. Miller-Brody Productions, American School Publishers, 1992.
The Poetry Book: Nonsense Verse. Color, 15:29 minutes. Thames Films, 1991. Distributed by Films for the Humanities & Sciences, 1991.
Poetry for Children—The Symposium. Color, 26 minutes. Tim Podell Productions 1991.

List 9. Selected Books of Poetry for Young People

Good Books, Good Times! Selected by Lee Bennett Hopkins. Illus. by Harvey Stevenson. New York: Harper & Row, 1990.
Hearne, Betsy. *Polaroid and Other Poems of View.* Photos by Peter Kiar. New York: McElderry, 1991.
Imaginary Gardens: American Poetry and Art for Young People. Charles Sullivan, ed. New York: Harry Abrams, 1989.
Kendrick, Dolores. *The Women of Plums: Poems in the Voices of Slave Women.* New York: Morrow, 1989.
Kuskin, Karla. *Near the Window Tree: Poems and Notes.* San Diego, Calif.: Harcourt Brace Jovanovich, 1975.
Larrick, Nancy. *Cats Are Cats.* Illus. by Ed Young. New York: Philomel, 1988.
Madgett, Naomi Long. *Octavia and Other Poems.* Chicago: Third World Press, 1988.
The Place My Words Are Looking For. Selected by Paul B. Janeczko. New York: Bradbury, 1990.
Prelutsky, Jack. *Something BIG Has Been Here.* Illus. by James Stevenson. New York: Greenwillow, 1990.
Read-Aloud Rhymes: For the Very Young. Selected by Jack Prelutsky. Illus. by Marc Brown. New York: Alfred Knopf, 1986.
Reflections on a Gift of Watermelon Pickle . . . And Other Modern Verses. Comp. by Stephen Dunning and others. New York: Scholastic, 1974.
Sing a Song of Popcorn. Selected by Beatrice Schenk de Regniers and others. Illus. by Nine Caldecott Artists. New York: Scholastic, 1988.

Talking to the Sun: An Illustrated Anthology of Poems for Young People. Selected by Kenneth Koch and Kate Farrell. New York: The Metropolitan Museum of Art and John Holt, 1985.
Time Is the Longest Distance. Selected by Ruth Gordon. New York: HarperCollins, 1991.
Walk Together Children: Black American Spirituals. Selected and illus. by Ashley Bryan. New York: Atheneum, 1974.
Walker, Alice. *Horses Make a Landscape Look More Beautiful.* San Diego, Calif.: Harcourt Brace Jovanovich, 1984.
Willard, Nancy. *Pish, Posh, Said Hieronymus Bosch.* Illus. by the Dillons. San Diego, Calif.: Harcourt Brace Jovanovich, 1991.
Willard, Nancy. *A Visit to William Blake's Inn.* Illus. by Martin Provensen and Alice Provensen. San Diego, Calif.: Harcourt Brace Jovanovich, 1981.
Yolen, Jane. *Bird Watch.* Illus. by Ted Lewin. New York: Philomel, 1990.

Docudrama

Docudrama, or fact-based drama, seems to have come into its own on television as a form of quasi-documentary and may provide fascinating opportunities for students to sharpen their evaluative skills.[10] In the late 1970s, a student pursuing an interest in Abraham Lincoln might have watched a miniseries reenacting parts of his life on network television. Many other fact-based dramas about key figures or major events in history were also appearing on prime time television during this period. Some of these, such as the three-part special about Martin Luther King, Jr., did not obviously stray from the truth and used many actual film clips from the subject's life in the dramatization. Other docudramas have taken greater liberties with historical facts and have even rewritten history to their own ends. The current controversy surrounding Stone's film *JFK*, mentioned above, reminds one of an earlier docudrama about Lee Harvey Oswald in which the producers stopped Ruby's bullet from killing Oswald and brought him to trial for President Kennedy's assassination as a way of reexamining the facts contained in the Warren Report. At the end of the docudrama, viewers were asked to serve as the jury and indicate whether or not they were convinced that Oswald was responsible for Kennedy's death, either alone or as a part of a conspiracy. A similar device was used to dramatize a trial of General George Custer that might have taken place had he survived Little Big Horn.

Thus, docudrama, either because of deliberate intent or the nature of the medium, can become a distortion as much as a reenactment of history. *The Economist* comments: "By providing the flow of action and dialogue that viewers associate with 'real' life, extra 'reality' might be imparted to the story. It is no longer enough, perhaps, to lay facts baldly out. Still photography, after all, was once supposed to be the last word in reality; but now the posing and touching-up of photographs is virtually taken for granted. So too television, once the all-seeing and unaltering eye, now feels an increasing need to dress up the facts it has to deal with."[11] Albert Auster provides a case study of docudrama that offers additional insight into how this form of television drama focuses on individuals and presents a version of history to a popular audience.[12]

A contemporary emphasis on fact-based television dramas seems to have shifted the focus from exploring facts about important historical persons and events to attempting to understand the minds of criminals who have perpetrated the most heinous and irrational crimes. The fact that all three major networks rushed to present prime time movies based on the Amy Fisher/Buttafuoco case, in which a teenage girl shoots the wife of the man with whom she was supposedly having an affair, proves this point. It is interesting to note that, within a week, three two-hour versions of these events were presented from three different points of view, that of Amy Fisher, of the Buttafuocos, and of a reporter who covered the case.[13] Our national fascination with mass murderers and the like has led to a series of docudramas and outright fictional accounts trying to provide a viewing audience with rationales for such behavior. Even prime time shows such as "Law and Order" use actual criminal cases to develop fictional accounts of the events. Case after case presented is recognized as being closely akin to recent news accounts. At the same time, although perhaps not as popular, television stories continue to be based on real-life heroes and heroines, such as Mary Lindell, who helped allied servicemen escape from France during the Nazi occupation.[14] Another form of popular fictionalized history is represented by "Quantum Leap," the television series in which the hero travels back in time each week to participate in historical events.

Such works present special opportunities to help students respond more critically to all types of media and messages. Even in productions or reenactments that attempt to adhere absolutely to the facts, there is a question of how much the drama controls the documents, of how much the selection of documentary information is skewed for dramatic purposes. There are other questions: How authentically can a television crew recreate all the details of the time and place in which a historical figure lived? Was the fact-based drama produced purely to preserve a dramatic incident or personality or was it set up in a way that forced us to rethink the past in the light of the present? What is the effect of having actors play the part of well-known figures?

Photographic records and docudramas of historical events are not the only sources of materials for the critical study of the effect of the media in the actual shaping of history. Consider the teaching potential of video replays of such political events as the Nixon-Kennedy debates or the anti-Dukakis commercial on the furlowing of Willy Horton, a known murderer who, when released from prison on furlow, killed again. Consideration of how such television productions may have influenced past presidential elections could provide a foundation for the study and evaluation of media use in current political campaigns.[15] Using all of these strategies, and others, students will continue to develop their critical abilities in the evaluation of media and information.

Media Evaluation through Production

Just as students develop critical abilities and become more appreciative of good written composition through their own attempts to communicate in writing, they learn to be more astute consumers of any other medium as they better understand its elements and means of composition. If students are really to develop a literacy in all media, the library media specialist should take the lead and provide experiences for students as producers as well as consumers of various media. These should not be separate and distinct programs and not just for older students. Any child old enough to be in school is old enough to begin. Videotaping and filmmaking, both live action and animation, are natural avenues for students' handling of ideas and information and for their own imaginative creations. In many schools, students produce their own local newscasts, complete with commercials paid for by community merchants, or sponsor festivals of award-winning student-made films. The key ingredient is, of course, understanding both the content and the language of the particular medium, which enables one to encode and decode ideas efficiently and effectively in that format. Beyond that, students exercise all their critical thinking and organizational abilities to select content and then plan, produce, and exhibit their work.

The skills and abilities necessary for both the criticism and the production of various media are developed gradually as a child progresses through school and responds to the media-saturated world in which we live. Even very young children can be quite adept in their responses to film and are quick to visualize their own ideas in this medium. However, it takes time and practice as well as fully developed hands and muscular coordination to be able to handle video or motion picture equipment skillfully enough to communicate effectively with others. What we must do is match the appropriate activities in media production with the maturation of the child and enable the two to grow together. As more and more schools make computers available for student use, it is logical to assume that computer graphics may be a more appropriate way for youngsters to begin to develop their command of visual forms of composition.[16]

Unfortunately, in too many schools, filmmaking and videotaping, even computer use, are seen as gimmicks, catchy means of rewarding bright students or something that will motivate slower or more reluctant students to get involved in a school-sponsored activity. These compositional media should be as intrinsic to the school curriculum as is written composition. All are means of organizing ideas for presentation in ways that inform and affect others. In some schools students are developing visual essays as class projects or reports, combining personal photography, video work, and downloading of visual images from laser products.[17] Such visual essays are often a tangible symbol of pride in one's work, something that students value far more than traditional essays or test scores and also a more informative evaluative portfolio for teachers to assess accomplishment. It is the responsibility of the school library media specialist to help students determine if particular images and music are appropriate for the message they seek to convey.

It is the task of the library media specialist to communicate to others in and about various media, to help both students and teachers realize the possibilities and limitations of all media, and to help them develop the skills necessary to communicate in each. Filmmaking, videotaping, computer graphics, and other media activities may someday be such natural forms of communication that they will permeate all areas of the curriculum, just as reading and writing do, and will no longer be considered the special province of media teachers. The language arts will then be expanded to include the languages of all media and we will be able to focus our attention on the content rather than the format of the medium employed and on the critical thinking abilities and the research process of learners.

If this equality of media is ever to come about, library media specialists must help it along in two ways. First, they must encourage students and teachers to de-emphasize the medium and concentrate more on the message when compiling information for their research. In order to do so, all members of the learning community must be convinced that there is no hierarchy of media in which print information is inherently better than that contained in other formats. On the other hand, library media specialists must, as discussed above, explore with others in the school the special properties and possibilities of various media. It is for this reason that the discussion about the evaluation of biographical materials included all kinds of nonprint as well as print materials. Although it is becoming more common and acceptable to integrate all media into the materials available to students to meet their informational needs, we rarely do this in our discussions and evaluations of nondiscursive or aesthetic forms. Most schools do acknowledge the value of helping students become more critical and more appreciative of various kinds of story and poetic forms. However, seldom do we include other media in our study of aesthetic forms. It seems reasonable to explore story compositions on film, and perhaps in other media, as well as in print. Let us consider for a moment how this might be done.

Students can develop critical skills in the comparative analysis of a story on film and in print by identifying compositional elements common to both and by exploring the ways they are handled in each medium. Many students have learned to look at such elements as character, plot, setting, mood, symbol, and point of view in written stories. The library media specialist may even have discussed these elements with them, at least informally, as a means of helping students evaluate and make more appropriate selections from the world of imaginative literature. As we evaluate filmed stories with young people, it seems reasonable to make use of what they already know about the elements of a story and determine how these compositional elements work in other media.

Students can examine the possibilities and the limitations inherent in each medium prior to their own productions through a comparison of two or more different media presentations of the same basic content. Weston Woods Studio has, for many years, provided a rich resource for such study with their filmstrips, records or tapes, and videos and motion pictures of children's books. With their materials, it is possible to move from the original book to a recording, to a sound filmstrip, and then to an iconographic, animated, or live-action video or film. In some instances, other filmmakers have also produced versions of the same book. Examining many versions of a single work may suggest to students possibilities for their own use of media and show that one cannot merely transcribe works from one medium to another, but must really transform them to match the new form of communication.

A number of companies have produced videos drawn from the stories that are mainstays of children's or young adult literature.[18] For example, Wonderworks has provided young people with video versions of Katherine Paterson's stories *Bridge to Terabithia* and *Jacob Have I Loved*. Many of Beverly Cleary's books, such as *Runaway Ralph, Ralph S. Mouse, Ramona: The Great Hair Argument*, and *Ramona: Rainy Sunday*, have been made into videos by Churchill Films. *Ramona* has also been available to children as a television series. Classic stories, such as Franco Zeffirelli's *Romeo and Juliet* (Paramount Home Video), Washington Irving's *The Legend of Sleepy Hollow* (Playhouse Video), Ray Bradbury's *The Martian Chronicles* (Fries Home Video) and Jane Austen's *Pride and Prejudice* (CBS Fox Video) are available in video versions. Even stories that might not attract the contemporary reader in their print versions, prove very appealing as video presentations. For instance, *The Girl of the Limberlost* is an example of an older story that might otherwise be lost to or inappropriate for most young people today.[19] Students viewing this film might compare and contrast print and film versions in an attempt to determine why the film is likely to be more appealing to young audiences today. These and many other films adapted from children's books are ordinarily viewed for their aesthetic enjoyment, which is, of course, their primary purpose; but they can also be studied as examples of a filmmaker's art.

Since critical thinking is a primary objective in education, it is useful to explore how one retains a focus on basic skills or established curricula while fostering such thinking, especially since real thought on the part of students often leads them beyond the bounds of a planned instructional program. Obviously, the use of various thinking processes such as inference, organization, analysis, imagination, classification, questioning, prediction, problem solving, sequencing, evaluating, and perceiving relationships are essential in the development of student skills in the disciplines. The library media specialist can work with subject area teachers to plan ways of developing critical thinkers in the context of various disciplines. In addition, the library media specialist can also help students practice critical thinking playfully and independently in evaluating library media center resources. In addition, it might prove useful for the library media center to display an ongoing *thought-starter* board, either on a computer network or an actual bulletin board in the center. Such a board would pose a variety of problems, questions, inquiries or images that students would respond to with subsequent students responding both to the original thought-starter and to previous responses. For instance, a board might include mathematical sequences of numbers; matching of classical gods and goddesses; words to be defined; visual puzzles to be identified; or just a provocative statement to elicit responses.

Conclusion

The development of critical thinking skills in the evaluation, selection, and use of the wide varieties of materials in the library media center collection is a primary teaching responsibility and one that is frequently part of a collaborative effort with classroom teachers. Even when library media specialists share this responsibility with others, they will often agree to take the lead in this aspect of the work because of their special expertise and the fact they are likely to be more informed about available resources. It is also true, however, that the kinds of exploration of materials described in this chapter are so important in our media-saturated world and often so much fun for students that they may be carried on independently in the library media center. If students can, through such activities, experience the joy of discovery and the sense of control over the flood of information and ideas in their world, they will have made a giant step toward being concerned and committed lifelong learners.

5

Webbing: Alternative Paths to Organizing Information and Ideas

One organizational schema associated with the whole language movement that has gained a great impetus in recent years is the use of webbing.[1] There are many different versions of webbing, and the library media specialist can have significant impact on the development of different types of webs as a way of helping students organize information and ideas for research or presentation. Webbing may be a simple graphic representation of various subsets of a single topic, or of works in different genres or media that can be related to that topic. As such, it may be based on a curricular topic that leads to alternative paths of interest for student work such as the civil rights web in chapter 3. Webbing may also be designed with a specific book at the center, from which the paths of reading are drawn. Webs that represent different interests or reading paths leading from a book may also serve as graphic representations of possible responses to that regular request from children: "I want another book like this one." Most of the following are just the beginnings of webs to demonstrate some of the ways this technique might be useful in teaching and some of the forms a web might take. The final web in the chapter is the most complete, including a variety of resources and suggestions for teaching.

Literature across the Science Curriculum

Resource-based education and a concern with aesthetic as well as efferent learning have encouraged teachers to enhance subject area studies with imaginative literature as well as with alternative forms of informational narratives. Such approaches to particular curricular content may be considered a first step toward webbing. Since it is often more difficult, both for school library media specialists and for science teachers, to make connections between the required curriculum and a range of resources than it is for social studies or language arts teachers, it is important to focus on this area. What follows are various stages of the very beginning of an effort to explore alternative information and ideas related to some secondary school science topics that have a great potential interest for young adults. List 10 includes the first stages of attempts to define topics and focus attention on resources related to seven topics that might be placed in a high school science curriculum: AIDS; Artificial Intelligence and Neural Memory Transfer; Chaos Theory; Ecology and Environment; Mutation and Genetic Engineering; the Search for Extraterrestrial Intelligence and Alien Communication; and Virtual Reality. Overall, the intent is to gain insight into how a subject can be explored through informational narratives and through fiction and to find ways to use those resources to enhance teaching in the content area. The library media specialist might develop initial lists such as the following and, using the pattern below, suggest that classroom teachers and students expand upon them by

1. Providing definitions of terminology.
2. Reading preliminary sources provided.
3. Providing rationale for including these materials in a study of the particular topic.
4. Providing additional resources that expand the depth or the scope of this topic.
5. Analyzing the items selected and providing annotations connecting them to the particular curricular content.
6. Being as selective as possible; it is more important to provide close connections than to provide large numbers of resources.

As resources are examined in these ways, science study moves from dependence on textbooks and curriculum guides to informational trade materials and then to fiction. What ordinarily happens in this process is the increase of the number of points of access to this content so that students who do not perceive of themselves as "good in science" may find new ways of thinking about scientific ideas and, therefore, new interest in science study. The most dramatic difference is the move from "hard science" to science fiction, which speculates on the results of that science in human life. For instance, although some textbooks and many trade books consider social and moral issues of genetic engineering, environmental planning, and artificial intelligence, stories that actually present created worlds in which scientific principles have been carried to their logical conclusions force readers to consider the consequences on human life. In fact, the best science fiction pushes the barriers of the mind to consider the biggest question of all: What is it to be human? In reading *Eva* and *The Ship Who Sang* trilogy, for example, one is faced with questions about human consciousness implanted in non-human forms such as Kelly, the Chimpanzee, in *Eva* or the space ship or space station in McCaffrey's stories. Young readers, in their emotional and aesthetic responses to such stories, also begin to understand and come to grips with the meaning of what they are studying in science. The cold, crisp language of the textbook may or may not have impact, but the emotional involvement with characters and situations in a story definitely will.

One thing classroom teachers and library media specialists need to be aware of in contemporary science fiction for young adults is the acceptance of all types of sexuality as an incidental and natural part of life. In general, however, sexual passages are brief and almost never the focus of the novel.

In examining the list of topics in List 10, it is obvious that many different linkages could be made both among these topics and to other areas of interest. For instance, artificial intelligence might be connected to genetic engineering and virtual reality. Thus, webs might be developed demonstrating these relationships or individual webs for each topic might be expanded. In either case, such webs would include strands from other disciplines such as art, music, and mathematics.

List 10. A Sample Exploration of Literature across the Science Curriculum

AIDS

ADULT RESOURCES

"Sexuality Education in the Age of AIDS." *Independent School* 51, no. 3 (Spring 1992): 11–43.
What Kids Need to Know about AIDS: Resources and Life Skills Exercises for Education K-6. Planned Parenthood of Northeast Pennsylvania, 112 N. 13th Street, Allentown, PA 18102.

INFORMATIONAL NARRATIVES

Blake, Jeanne. *Risky Times: How to Be AIDS-Smart and Stay Healthy*. New York: Workman, 1990.
Condoms: A Responsible Option. 10 minutes. Falls Church, Va.: Landmark Films, 1991.
Johnson, Earvin. "Magic." *What You Can Do to Avoid AIDS*. New York: Time, 1992.
Kettridge, Mary. *Teens with AIDS Speak Out*. New York: Messner, 1991.
Madaras, Lynda. *Lynda Madaras Talks to Teens about AIDS: An Essential Guide for Parents, Teachers, and Young People*. New York: Newmarket, 1988.
Nourse, Alan E. *Teen Guide to AIDS Prevention*. New York: Watts, 1990.
100 Questions and Answers about AIDS: A Guide for Young People. New York: New Discovery, 1992.

FICTION

Arrick, Fran. *What You Don't Know Can Kill You*. New York: Bantam, 1992.
Durant, Penny Raife. *When Heroes Die*. New York: Atheneum, 1992.
Hoffman, Alice. *At Risk*. New York: Putnam, 1989.
Kerr, M. E. *Night Kites*. New York: Harper & Row, 1986.
Miklowitz, Gloria. *Goodbye Tomorrow*. New York: Delacorte, 1987.
Simmons, Dan. *Children of the Night*. New York: Putnam, 1992.

ARTIFICIAL INTELLIGENCE, NEURON MEMORY TRANSFER, NEURAL NETWORKING AND BIOCHIP TERMINOLOGY

Artificial Intelligence: "The relation of artificial intelligence to the study of cognitive and linguistic processes in humans is especially important. . . . The psychological theories of problem solving, long-term memory structure, and the organization of knowledge are essentially the theories from artificial intelligence." Parker, Sybil P., ed. *McGraw-Hill Dictionary of Scientific and Technical Terms*, 4th ed. (New York: McGraw-Hill, 1992):123.

Biochip Technology: "An experimental type of integrated circuit whose basic components are organic molecules." Ibid., 215.

Neural Network: "A type of information processing system whose architecture is inspired by the structure of biological neural systems. In particular, neural networks attempt to mimic the functions of the central nervous system and some of the sensory organs attached to it." Caudill, Maureen, and Charles Butler. *Naturally Intelligent Systems* (Cambridge: MIT, 1990):5.

INFORMATIONAL NARRATIVES

The Brain Machine. Videocassette. Color, 26 minutes. Princeton, N.J.: Films for the Humanities and Science, 1991.

Caudill, Maureen. *In Our Own Image: Building an Artificial Man.* New York: Oxford University, 1992.

Caudill, Maureen, and Charles Butler. *Naturally Intelligent Systems.* Cambridge: MIT, 1990.

Ferris, Timothy. *The Mind's Sky: Human Intelligence in a Cosmic Context.* New York: Bantam, 1992.

Fjermedal, Grant. *The Tomorrow Makers: A Brave New World of Living-Brain Machines.* New York: Macmillan, 1986.

Hofstadter, Douglas R. *Gödel, Escher, Bach: An Eternal Golden Braid.* New York: Vintage, 1989.

Johnson, George. *Machinery of the Mind: Inside the New Science of Artificial Intelligence.* New York: Times, 1986.

Jubak, Jim. *In the Image of the Brain: Breaking the Barrier between the Human Mind and Intelligent Machines.* Boston: Little, Brown, 1992.

Levy, Steven. *Artificial Life: The Quest for a New Creation.* New York: Pantheon, 1992.

FICTION

Card, Orsen Scott. *The Memory of Earth.* New York: TOR, 1991.
Dickinson, Peter. *Eva.* New York: Delacorte, 1989.
Fisk, Nicolas. *Grinny.* New York: Nelson, 1975.
Lawrence, Louise. *Andra.* New York: HarperCollins, 1991.
McCaffrey, Anne. *The Ship Who Sang.* New York: Walker, 1969.

McCaffrey, Anne. *All the Weyrs of Pern.* New York: Ballantine, 1991.
McCaffrey, Anne, and Margaret Ball. *Partnership.* New York: Baen, 1992.
McCaffrey, Anne, and Mercedes Lackey. *The Ship Who Searched.* New York: Baen, 1992.
Mayhar, Ardath. *A Place of Silver Silence.* New York: Walker, 1988.
Sargent, Pamela. *Earthseed.* New York: Harper & Row, 1983.
Sleator, William. *The Duplicate.* New York: Dutton, 1988.

CHAOS THEORY

INFORMATIONAL NARRATIVES

Briggs, John, and F. David Peat. *Turbulent Mirror: An Illustrated Guide to Chaos Theory and the Science of Wholeness.* New York: Harper & Row, 1989.
Gleick, James. *Chaos: Making a New Science.* New York: Viking, 1987.
Tsonis, Anastasios A. *Chaos: From Theory to Application.* New York: Plenum, 1992.

FICTION

Card, Orson Scott. *The Memory of Earth.* New York: TOR, 1991.
Crichton, Michael. *Jurassic Park.* New York: Alfred Knopf, 1990.
Sleator, William. *Strange Attractors.* New York: Dutton, 1990.

ECOLOGY AND ENVIRONMENT

INFORMATIONAL NARRATIVES

Attenborough, David. *The Atlas of the Living World.* Boston: Houghton Mifflin, 1989.
Gore, Albert. *Earth in Balance: Ecology and the Human Spirit.* Boston: Houghton Mifflin, 1992.
Henricksson, John. *Rachel Carson: The Environmental Movement.* New York: Millbrook, 1991.
Langone, John. *Our Endangered Earth.* Boston: Little, Brown, 1992.
Rain Forests: Proving Their Worth. Videocassette. Color with B/W sequences, 28 minutes. Jonathan Schwartz, director. Oakland, Calif.: The Video Project, 1990.

FICTION

Baird, Thomas. *Smart Rats.* New York: Harper & Row, 1990.
Barnes, John. *Orbital Resonance.* New York: Tor, 1991.
Lindholm, Magan. *Alien Earth.* New York: Bantam, 1992.
Rider, Julie. *Space Traders Unlimited.* New York: Atheneum, 1988.
Stevermer, Caroline. *River Rats.* San Diego, Calif.: Harcourt Brace Jovanovich, 1992.

Wilhelm, Kate. *Where Late the Sweet Birds Sang.* New York: Harper & Row, 1976.
Zebrowski, George. *Macro Life.* London: Futura, 1979.
Zebrowski, George. *Sunspacer.* New York: Harper & Row, 1984.

MUTATION AND GENETIC ENGINEERING

INFORMATIONAL NARRATIVES

The Genetic Revolution: Scientific Prospects and Publications. Ed. by Bernard D. Davis. Baltimore, Md.: Johns Hopkins University, 1991.
Orlica, Karl. *Understanding DNA and Gene Cloning.* 2d ed. New York: Wiley, 1992.

FICTION

Bujold, Lois McMaster. *Falling Free.* Riverdale, N.Y.: Baen, 1988.
Carmody, Isobelle. *The Farseekers.* New York: Viking, 1990.
Carmody, Isobelle. *Obernewtyn.* New York: Penguin, 1988.
Hughes, Monica. *Keeper of the Isis Light.* New York: Atheneum, 1981.
Jones, Diana Wynne. *Dogsbody.* New York: Alfred Knopf, 1975.
Kagan, Janet. *Mirabile.* New York: Tor, 1991.
Lawrence, Louise. *Children of the Dust.* New York: Harper & Row, 1985.
Norton, Andre. *Exiles to the Stars.* New York: Viking, 1971.
Yep, Laurence. *Monster Makers, Inc.* New York: Morrow, 1986.

SEARCH FOR EXTRATERRESTRIAL INTELLIGENCE
AND ALIEN COMMUNICATION

The Seti Institute   A research and data collection agency in the
2035 Landings Drive search for extraterrestrial intelligence.
Mountain View, CA 94043

INFORMATIONAL NARRATIVES

Blum, Howard. *Out There.* New York: Simon & Schuster, 1990.
Drake, Frank, and Dava Sobel. *Is Anyone Out There? The Scientific Search for Extraterrestrial Intelligence.* New York: Delacorte, 1992.
First Contact. Ben Bova and Byron Preiss, eds. New York: New American Library, 1990.
Overbye, Dennis. *Lonely Hearts of the Cosmos.* New York: HarperCollins, 1991.
Sagan, Carl. *Contact.* New York: Simon & Schuster, 1985.
White, Frank. *The Seti Factor.* New York: Walker, 1990.

FICTION

Bear, Greg. *Anvil of the Stars.* New York: Warner, 1992.
Bova, Ben. *Mars.* New York: Bantam, 1992.

Lindholm, Magan. *Alien Earth.* New York: Bantam, 1992.
McCaffrey, Anne, and Jodie Nye. *Crisis in Doona.* New York: Ace, 1992.
Rubinstein, Gillian. *Beyond the Labyrinth.* New York: Orchard, 1990.
Zebrowski, George. *The Stars Will Speak.* New York: Harper & Row, 1985.

VIRTUAL REALITY

INFORMATIONAL NARRATIVES

Presence: Teleoperators and Virtual Environments. Periodical. Cambridge: MIT, 1992–.
Rheingold, Howard. *Virtual Reality.* New York: Summit, 1991.

FICTION

Card, Orson Scott. *Ender's Game.* New York: Tor, 1991.
Crispin, A. C., and Deborah A. Marshall. *Serpent's Gift.* New York: Ace, 1992.
Hughes, Monica. *Invitation to the Game.* New York: Simon & Schuster, 1991.
McCrumb, Sharyn. *Bimbos of the Death Sun.* Lake Geneva, Wisc.: TSR, 1988.
Rubinstein, Gillian. *Skymaze.* New York: Orchard, 1991.
Rubinstein, Gillian. *Space Demons.* New York: Pocket, 1986.
Sleator, William. *Interstellar Pig.* New York: Bantam, 1986.
Velde, Vivian Vande. *User Unfriendly.* San Diego, Calif.: Harcourt Brace Jovanovich, 1991.

Author Webs

Another approach to webbing is to organize all the works of a particular author to show the relationships among those works. The cleverness in Roald Dahl's plots and characters contributes to his enormous popularity with young people and may encourage them to explore webbing as a means of showing relationships among his books and with those of other authors. The Author's Eye series includes a videocassette of Dahl commenting on his books and on his writing process. Dahl has also written a number of autobiographical works that add dimension to a student's interest in the author of some of their favorite works. Dahl's notion of writing "as a long walk" presents an interesting metaphoric approach to writing that a teacher or library media specialist might use with young people. One might begin thinking about the various works produced by Dahl by dividing them basically into those for children and those for adults as in figure 6. Each of Dahl's children's books included in List 11 might then be analyzed and a web designed showing the relationships among these works and to other related works of interest to children.

84 Webbing

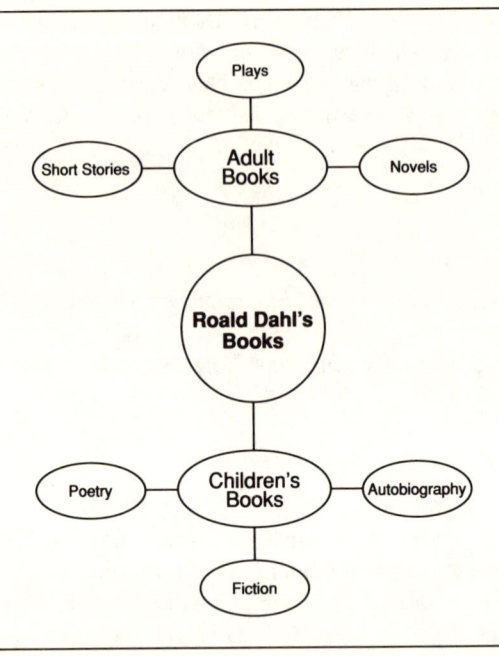

Figure 6. Web of Roald Dahl's Books

List 11. Roald Dahl Materials: Focus of a Web

The BFG. Illus. by Quentin Blake. New York: Farrar, Straus & Giroux, 1982.
Charlie and the Chocolate Factory. Illus. by Joseph Schindelman. New York: Alfred Knopf, 1964.
Charlie and the Great Glass Elevator. Illus. by Joseph Schindelman. New York: Alfred Knopf, 1973.
Danny the Champion of the World. Illus. by Jill Bennett. New York: Alfred Knopf, 1975.
Dirty Beasts. Illus. by Quentin Blake. New York: Farrar, Straus & Giroux, 1983.
The Enormous Crocodile. Illus. by Quentin Blake. New York: Alfred Knopf, 1978.
Esio Trot. Illus. by Quentin Blake. New York: Viking, 1990.
Fantastic Mr. Fox. Illus. by Donald Chaffin. New York: Alfred Knopf, 1970.
George's Marvelous Medicine. Illus. by Quentin Blake. New York: Alfred Knopf, 1981.
The Giraffe and the Pelly and Me. Illus. by Quentin Blake. New York: Farrar, Straus & Giroux, 1987.
The Gremlins. New York: Random House, 1944.
James and the Giant Peach. Illus. by Nancy Ekholm Burkert. New York: Alfred Knopf, 1961.
The Magic Finger. Illus. by William Pene duBois. New York: Harper & Row, 1966.

Matilda. Illus. by Quentin Blake. New York: Viking Kestral, 1988.
The Minipins. Illus. by Patrick Benson. New York: Viking, 1991.
Revolting Rhymes. Illus. by Quentin Blake. New York: Alfred Knopf, 1982.
The Twits. Illus. by Quentin Blake. New York: Alfred Knopf, 1980.
The Vicar of Nibbleswicke. Illus. by Quentin Blake. New York: Viking, 1991.
The Witches. Illus. by Quentin Blake. New York: Farrar, Straus & Giroux, 1984.
The Wonderful World of Henry Sugar and Six More. New York: Alfred Knopf, 1977.

AUTOBIOGRAPHICAL

The Author's Eye: Roald Dahl. Videocassette. Color, 23:16 minutes. Random House Video, American School Publishers, 1988.
Boy. New York: Farrar, Straus & Giroux, 1984.
Going Solo. New York: Farrar, Straus & Giroux, 1986.

Book Webs

Strega Nona

Still another approach to webbing is to use a specific book as a starting point. A very simple web created by young children from the story *Strega Nona* is presented in figure 7. Discussion of this initial *Strega Nona* web revealed that it was the food topic that most interested young readers, and so the focus shifted from the specific book to the general topic as represented in books for young children. At another time or with another group, interest might have focused on witches or tall tales or magic. List 12 includes books that could be used to create a secondary web on food. Obviously, this is a long and varied list representing the importance of food in the lives of young children and in the books created for them. Such a list might be placed on a bulletin board for children to explore or in a database for children to use in various projects. In this instance, the list of books was explored and categorized to create the beginnings of the new web pictured in figure 8. Thus, what began as a strand in the *Strega Nona* web led to an additional, and much more complex, web on one aspect of the web from the original book.

List 12. Selected Books for Web on Food

Addy, Sharon Hart. *A Visit with Great-Grandma.* Illus. by Lydia Halverson. Niles, Ill.: Albert Whitman, 1989.
Aliki. *A Medieval Feast.* New York: Thomas Y. Crowell, 1984.
Ancona, George. *Bananas: From Manolo to Margie.* New York: Clarion, 1982.
Asch, Frank. *Milk and Cookies.* New York: Parents Magazine, 1982.

86   Webbing

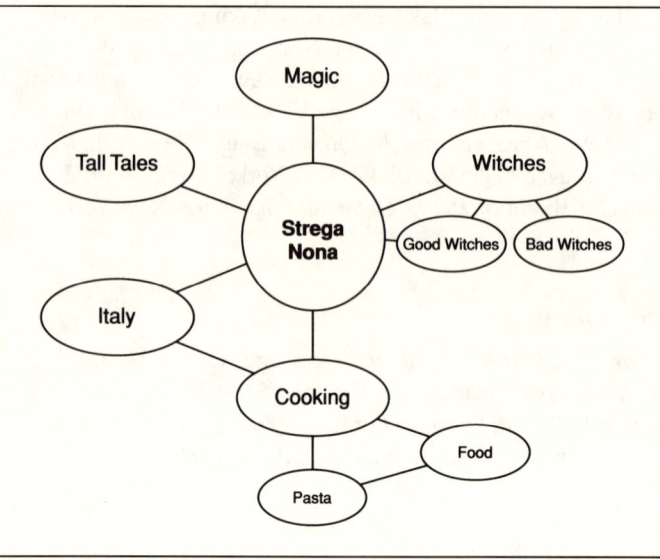

Figure 7. Web of *Strega Nona*

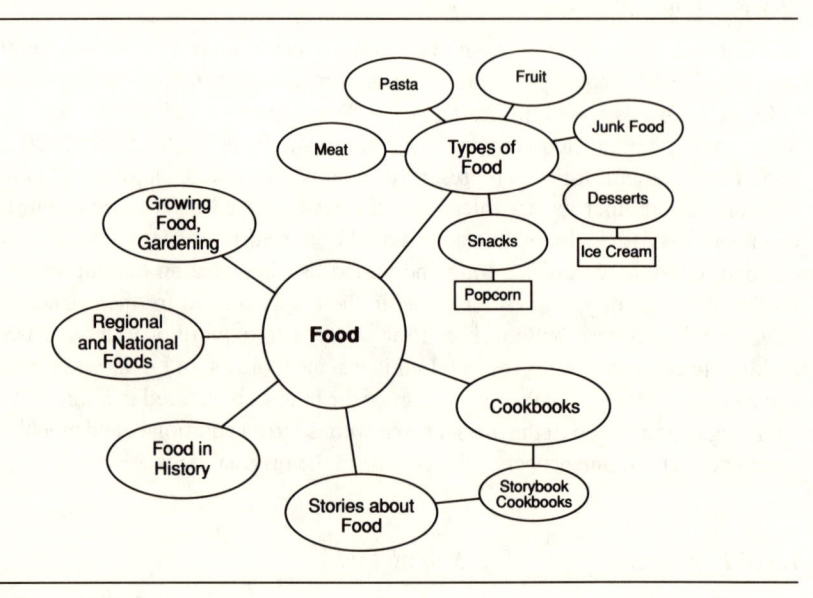

Figure 8. Food Web

Back, Christine. *Bean and Plant.* Photographs by Barrie Watts. Morristown, N.J.: Silver Burdett, 1984.

Bastyra, Judy. *Busy Little Cook.* Illus. by Nicola Smee. New York: Jelly Bean, 1990.

Bayley, Monica. *The Wonderful Wizard of Oz Cookbook.* New York: Macmillan, 1981.

Better Homes and Gardens New Junior Cook Book. Des Moines, Iowa: Meredith, n.d.

Biucchi, Edwina. *Italian Food and Drink.* New York: The Bookwright, 1987.

Bjork, Christina. *Elliot's Extraordinary Cookbook.* Illus. by Lena Anderson. Trans. by Joan Sandin. New York: R & S Farrar, Straus and Giroux, 1990.

Blain, Diane. *Better Homes and Gardens Step-by-Step Kids' Cook Book.* Des Moines, Iowa: Meredith, 1985.

The Boxcar Children Cookbook. Morton Grove, Ill.: Albert Whitman, 1991.

Brown, Marcia. *The Bun: Tale from Russia.* New York: Harcourt Brace Jovanovich, 1972.

Brown, Marcia. *Stone Soup.* New York: Scribner, 1947.

Burningham, John. *Avocado Baby.* New York: Thomas Y. Crowell, 1982.

Carle, Eric. *Pancakes, Pancakes!* New York: Pantheon, 1975.

Carle, Eric. *The Very Hungry Caterpillar.* New York: World, 1970.

Cauley, Lorinda Bryan. *The Bake-Off.* New York: G. P. Putnam's Sons, 1978.

Cauley, Lorinda Bryan. *Pease-Porridge Hot: A Mother Goose Cookbook.* New York: G. P. Putnam's Sons, 1977.

Clark, Elizabeth. *Meat.* Illus. by John Yates. Minneapolis, Minn.: Carolrhoda, 1990.

Cobb, Vicki. *The Scoop on Ice Cream.* Illus. by G. Brian Karas. Boston: Little, Brown, 1985.

Cole, William, comp. *Poem Stew.* Illus. by Karen Ann Weinhaus. New York: Lippincott, 1981.

Degen, Bruce. *Jamberry.* New York: Harper & Row, 1983.

de Paola, Tomie. *The Popcorn Book.* New York: Holiday House, 1978.

de Paola, Tomie. *Strega Nona.* Englewood Cliffs, N.J.: Prentice Hall, 1975. *See also Strega Nona.* Videocassette. Color. Weston Woods, 1985.

de Paola, Tomie. *Strega Nona's Magic Lessons.* San Diego, Calif.: Harcourt Brace Jovanovich, 1982.

Dobrini, Arnold. *Peter Rabbit's Natural Foods Cookbook.* New York: Warne, 1977.

Douglass, Barbara. *The Chocolate Chip Cookie Contest.* Illus. by Eric Jon Nones. New York: Lothrop Lee & Shephard, 1985.

Ehlert, Lois. *Growing Vegetable Soup.* San Diego, Calif.: Harcourt Brace Jovanovich, 1987.

Ellison, Virginia H. *The Pooh Cook Book.* New York: Dell, 1975.

Felix, Monique. *Yum Yum!: I'll Be My Own Cook.* La Jolla, Calif.: Star & Elephant, Green Tiger, 1982.

Galdone, Paul. *The Gingerbread Boy.* New York: Clarion, 1975.
Galdone, Paul. *The Little Red Hen.* New York: Seabury, 1973.
Galdone, Paul. *The Magic Porridge Pot.* New York: Clarion, 1976.
Gibbons, Gail. *The Milk Makers.* New York: Macmillan, 1985.
Green, Melinda. *Bembelman's Bakery.* Illus. by Barbara Seuling. New York: Parents Magazine Press, 1978.
Greene, Karen. *Once Upon a Recipe.* New Hope, Penn.: New Hope, 1987.
Hazelton, Niki. *Raggedy Ann & Andy's Cookbook.* New York: Bobbs, 1975.
Hoban, Russell. *Bread and Jam for Frances.* New York: Harper & Row, 1964.
Hopkins, Lee Bennett, comp. *Munching: Poems about Eating.* Illus. by Nelle Davis. Boston: Little, Brown, 1985.
Janice. *Little Bear's Pancake Party.* Illus. by Mariana. New York: Lothrop Lee & Shephard, 1960.
Jaspersohn, William. *Cranberries.* Boston: Houghton Mifflin, 1991.
Jones, Judith, and Evan Jones. *Knead It, Punch It, Bake It!* Illus. by Lauren Jarrett. New York: Thomas Y. Crowell, 1981.
Joosse, Barbara M. *Jam Day.* Illus. by Emily Arnold McCully. New York: Harper & Row, 1987.
Kahl, Virginia. *The Dutchess Bakes a Cake.* New York: Scribner, 1955.
Khalsa, Dayal Kaur. *How Pizza Came to Queens.* New York: Clarkson N. Potter, 1989.
Kovalski, Maryann. *Pizza for Breakfast.* New York: Morrow, 1990.
Krauss, Ruth. *The Carrot Seed.* Illus. by Crockett Johnson. New York: Harper & Row, 1945.
Krensky, Stephen. *Scoop after Scoop: A History of Ice Cream.* Illus. by Richard Rosenblum. New York: Atheneum, 1986.
Lane, Margaret. *The Beatrix Potter Country Cookery Book.* New York: Warne, 1981.
MacGregor, Carol. *The Fairy Tale Cookbook.* Illus. by Debby L. Carter. New York: Macmillan, 1982.
Mahy, Margaret. *Jam: A True Story.* Illus. by Helen Craig. Boston: Atlantic Monthly, 1985.
Mitgutsch, Ali. *From Seed to Pear.* Minneapolis, Minn.: Carolrhoda, 1981.
Morgan, Pierr. *The Turnip: An Old Russian Folktale.* New York: Philomel, 1990.
Morris, Ann. *Bread-Bread-Bread.* New York: Lothrop Lee & Shephard, 1989.
Neimark, Jill. *Ice Cream!* Illus. by Karen Milone-Dugan. New York: Hastings House, 1986.
Ontario Science Centre. *Foodworks: Over 100 Science Activities and Fascinating Facts That Explore the Magic of Food.* Reading, Mass.: Addison-Wesley, 1987.
Phillips, Louis. *The Million Dollar Potato.* Illus. by George Ulrich. New York: Simon & Schuster, 1991.
Pillar, Marjorie. *Pizza Man.* New York: Thomas Y. Crowell, 1990.
Rayner, Mary. *Mrs. Pig's Bulk Buy.* New York: Atheneum, 1981.
Rey, Margaret and Allan J. Shalbeck, Jr., eds. *Curious George and the Pizza.*

Boston: Houghton Mifflin, 1985.

Rice, Karen. *Does Candy Grow on Trees?* Illus. by Sharon Adler Cohen. New York: Walker, 1984.

Sawyer, Ruth. *Journey Cake, Ho!* Illus. by Robert McCloskey. New York: Viking, 1953.

Seixas, Judith S. *Junk Food—What It Is, What It Does.* Illus. by Tom Huffman. New York: Greenwillow, 1984.

Wake, Susan. *Citrus Fruits.* Minneapolis, Minn.: Carolrhoda, 1990.

Watson, N. Cameron. *The Little Pigs' First Cookbook.* Boston: Little, Brown, 1987.

Williams, Vera. *It's a Gingerbread House: Bake It! Build It! Eat It!* New York: Greenwillow, 1978.

Woodside, Dave. *What Makes Popcorn Pop!* New York: Atheneum, 1980.

Yoda, Junichi. *The Rolling Rice Ball.* Illus. by Saburo Watanabe. English version by Alvin Tresselt. New York: Parents Magazine, 1969.

Young, Robert. *The Chewing Gum Book.* Minneapolis, Minn.: Dillon, 1989.

Among the general questions that might be asked in creating or using such a web with or for young children are the following:

> For a given topic or unit, such as food, are resources available in sufficient variety to meet the needs of students at different age, ability, and interest levels?
>
> Do these resources include a variety of fictional and informational materials? Print and other media?
>
> Does the collection present alternative views about topics of concern to children and young people?
>
> What variations in webbing might be set up to help young people in completing an investigation of this topic either in their lives or in literature?

The Taken Girl

The Taken Girl by Elizabeth Gray Vining is a historical novel concerned with the nature and development of political protest and the use of violence as a means of action. Figure 9 provides one approach to the webbing of this book that extends the discussion of the abolitionist movement and the role of Quakers in that movement.[2] The inclusion of John Greenleaf Whittier and his poetry leads to a discussion of real personages in fiction. The idea of bound children and orphan children are natural extensions of this story that arise from conjecture about its title.

The Striped Ships

The Striped Ships by Eloise McGraw is a story focusing on the challenges facing young Juliana who lost her home at the invasion of the Normans and became involved in the creation of the Bayeux Tapestry.[3] Figure 10 depicts some of the

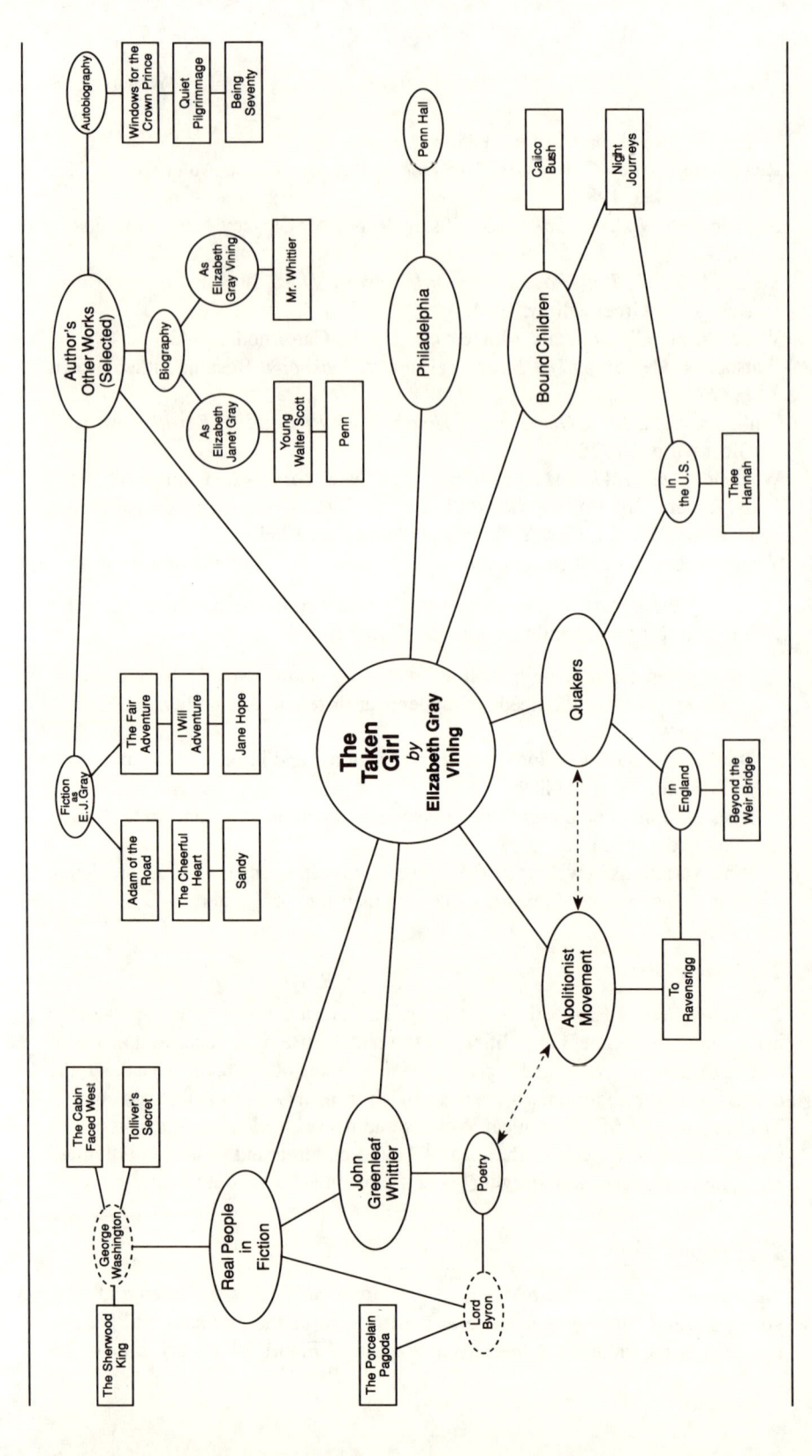

Figure 9. *The Taken Girl* Web. Reprinted from *School Library Journal*. Copyright by Reed Publishing, USA.

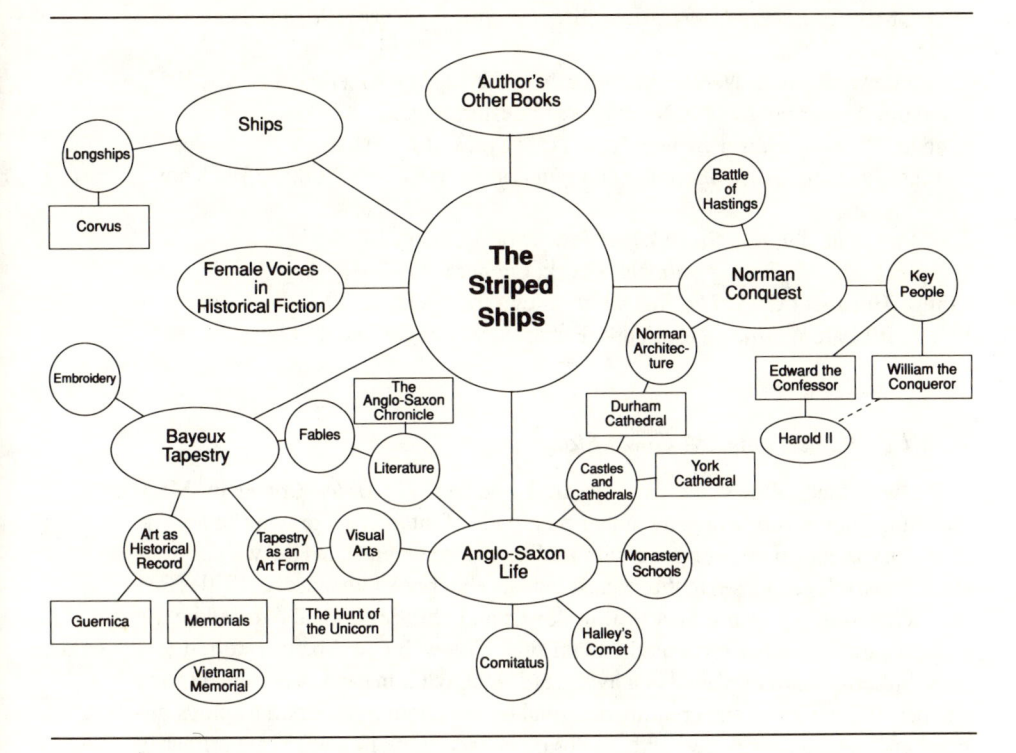

Figure 10. *The Striped Ships* Web

directions or paths of interest to which this work might lead readers. Each strand in the web could, in turn, lead to additional information and ideas and perhaps even become the focus of a new and connecting web. One aspect of a web based on this book might be the feminist, since Juliana is a strong female protagonist. This strand of interest might lead to selecting a group of books that portray similar heroines with strong female voices such as those in List 13.

List 13. Voices of Female Protagonists in Selected Historical Fiction

Avi. *The True Confessions of Charlotte Doyle*. New York: Orchard, 1990.
Beatty, Patricia. *Turn Homeward, Hannalee*. New York: Morrow, 1984.
Clapp, Patricia. *I'm Deborah Sampson: Soldier in the War of the Revolution*. New York: Lothrop, Lee & Shepard, 1977.
Conrad, Pam. *Prairie Song*. New York: Harper & Row, 1985.
Field, Rachel. *Calico Bush*. New York: Macmillan, 1987.
Hendry, Frances Mary. *Quest for a Maid*. New York: Farrar, Straus & Giroux, 1990.
Lasky, Kathryn. *Beyond the Divide*. New York: Macmillan, 1983.
Levitin, Sonia. *The Return*. New York: Ballantine, 1990.

Lyons, Mary E. *Letters from a Slave Girl: The Story of Harriet Jacobs.* New York: Scribners, 1992.
Markandaya, Kamala. *Nectar in a Sieve.* New York: New American Library, 1956.
Paterson, Katherine. *Lyddie.* New York: Lodestar, 1991.
Shange, Ntozake. *Betsey Brown.* New York: St. Martin's, 1986.
Staples, Suzanne Fisher. *Shabanu: Daughter of the Wind.* New York: Alfred Knopf, 1991.
Tan, Amy. *The Kitchen God's Wife.* New York: Putnam, 1991.
Temple, Frances. *Taste of Salt.* New York: Orchard, 1992.
Vining, Elizabeth Gray. *The Taken Girl.* New York: Viking, 1972.
Walsh, Jill Paton. *Grace.* New York: Farrar, Straus & Giroux, 1992.

Wait Till Helen Comes: A Ghost Story

In the web that follows, the focus is the book *Wait Till Helen Comes* by Mary Downing Hahn, from which a number of strands of interest are drawn (figure 11). This story is enormously popular with middle grade students, and the web demonstrates possible responses to the request for "another book like that one." Titles that are included in the web reflect reading levels and abilities both above and below as well as at the same level as the main title. The web could be transferred to a large bulletin board or placed in a hypercard stack with, in each case, students and teachers adding items and creating marginal notes for other readers. The plot summary and the lists of reviews and articles on ghosts (Lists 14 and 15) are primarily for teachers although more able students might also find them useful. One of the activities suggested in relation to this web emphasizes various ways for students to explore the elements of a story with titles on the web.

PLOT SUMMARY OF *Wait Till Helen Comes*

When their mother remarries, Molly and Michael have to cope with a new house, a new father, a new sister, and a ghost who lives in the cemetery on their property. To make matters worse, the stepsister (Heather) clings to her father and tells lies about the other children. She is drawn into a relationship with a ghost child, Helen, who wants to claim her as a permanent friend. Molly struggles with her fears and dislike and confronts Helen and Heather in order to protect her new family from evil.

List 14. Selected Reviews of *Wait Till Helen Comes*

Bulletin of the Center for Children's Books 40 (October 1986): 27.
Horn Book 62 (November/December 1986): 744.
School Library Journal 33 (October 1986): 176.

List 15. Selected Articles on Ghosts in Literature

Armstrong, Judith. "Ghosts as Rhetorical Devices in Children's Fiction." *Children's Literature in Education* 9, no. 2 (1978): 59–66.

Armstrong, Judith. "Ghost Stories: Exploiting the Convention." *Children's Literature in Education* 11, no. 3 (1980): 117–23.

KEY LITERARY ELEMENT: SETTING

A key literary element in ghost stories is setting—the place and time in which a ghostly character comes to life. In *Wait Till Helen Comes*, the hidden grave in the cemetery near their house frightens Molly and draws her new stepsister, Heather, to it. This helps to create a sense of impending doom for readers who feel the power of the ghost, Helen. We expect to find ghosts in graveyards and haunted houses, but different types of ghosts appear in different settings. Sometimes a ghost joins a real character in everyday adventures in our modern world. Many times ghosts take contemporary characters back into history and help us understand past events. As we read ghost stories, it is fun to think about the connections between a ghost and the time and place in which it appears. How are the type of ghost and activities of that ghost related to setting? Does the setting also help to create the mood? Are humorous ghost stories likely to be set in very different places and times than those that are horrible or frightening? Is there a fitting habitat for a ghost?

OTHER LITERARY ELEMENTS

CHARACTER

As you read the ghost stories in this web, think about how the authors make the ghosts believable. Are there certain types of human characters to whom a ghost is more likely to reveal itself? Is there a special link between the ghost and the real character in these stories? In most of the stories, the ghost is seen only by young characters; why do you think this is so? Does the protagonist have to be vulnerable to be reached by a ghost? Are lonely and unhappy protagonists predisposed to ghostly visitations? Are ghosts of the same age as the protagonist more believable? Does the ghost seek its own likeness? Some human characters such as in *The Ghost Squad and the Ghoul of Grünberg* invite ghostly participation in their lives while others are reluctant to admit that they have special receptive powers and attempt to resist. Troy and Barney in *The Haunting* and Cassie in *The Haunting of Cassie Palmer* are examples of such reluctance.

POINT OF VIEW

In *Wait Till Helen Comes*, the story is told by Molly rather than by Heather, who sees Helen's ghost. How might the story have changed if Heather had told it? What if we heard this story from the ghost's point of view? Choose an event from *Wait Till Helen Comes* and retell it as Heather, the ghost, Michael, the mother or the

94   Webbing

"Talking of ghosts . . . it is undecided whether or not there has ever been an instance of the spirit of any

Hahn's Other Books

- The Sara Summer
- The Time of the Witch
- Daphne's Book
- Tallahassee Higgins
- The Jellyfish Season
- Stepping on the Cracks

- Following the Mystery Man
- December Stillness
- Doll in the Garden: A Ghost Story
- The Dead Man in Indian Creek
- The Spanish Kidnapping Disaster
- The Wind Blows Backward

WAIT TILL HELEN COMES
A Ghost Story
(Mary Downing Hahn)

Ghosts

Setting — Time / Place — *Literary Element*

Nonfiction Ghosts

Ghosts in History
- Ghosts: An Illustrated History (Haining)
- Haunted Houses (Roberts)
- The Haunted Realm (Marsden)

Unexplained Phenomena
- How to Find a Ghost (Deem)
- Ghosts & Poltergeists (Williams)

Folklore Ghosts
- Scary Stories to Tell in the Dark (Schwartz)
- Ghosts Go Haunting (Nic Leodhas)

Haunted Buildings
- Ghost Abbey (Westall)

Graveyards
- Wait Till Helen Comes (Hahn)

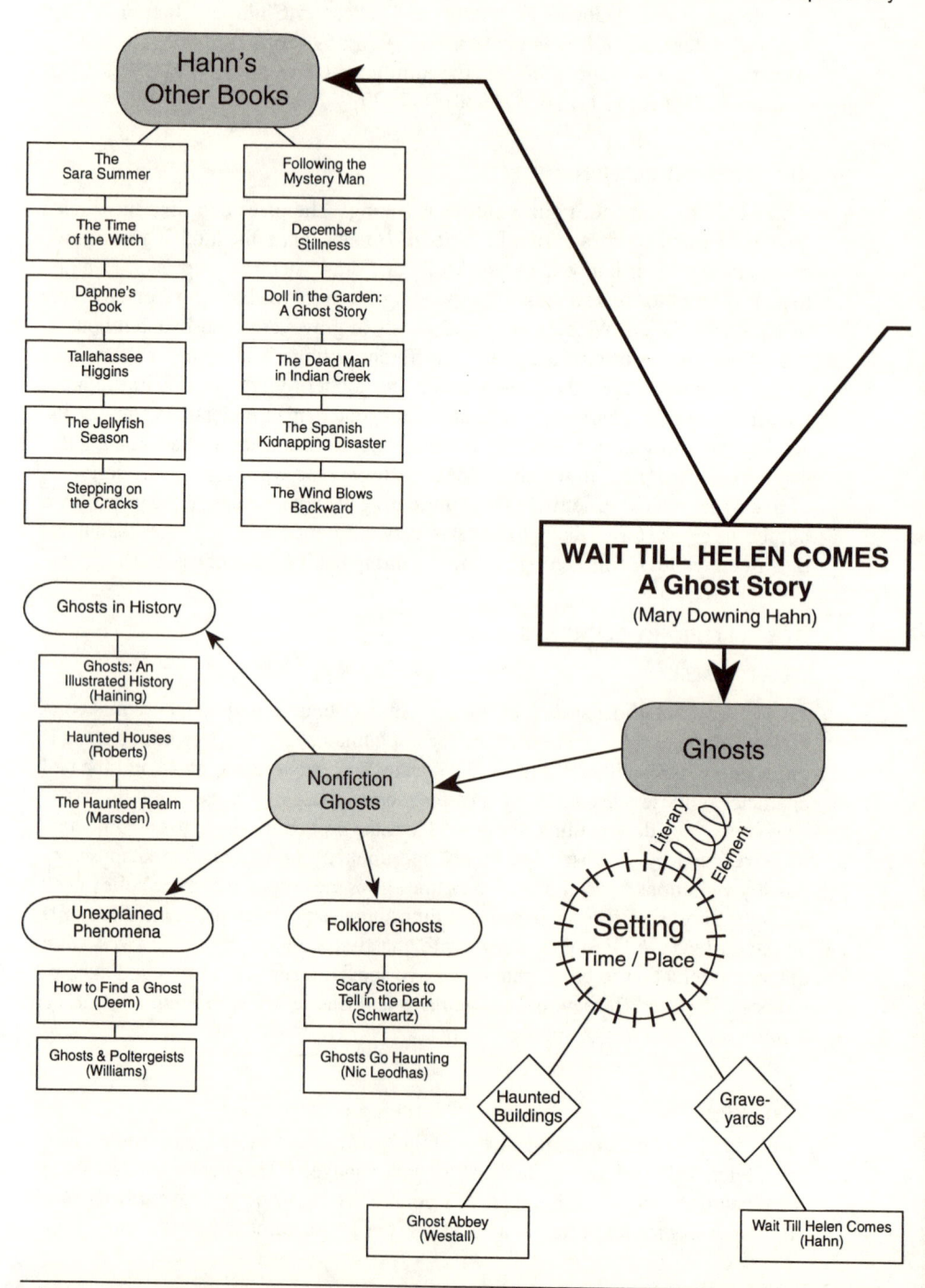

Figure 11. Web of *Wait Till Helen Comes*

Webbing 95

person appearing after death. All argument is against it, but all belief is for it."—Dr. Samuel Johnson

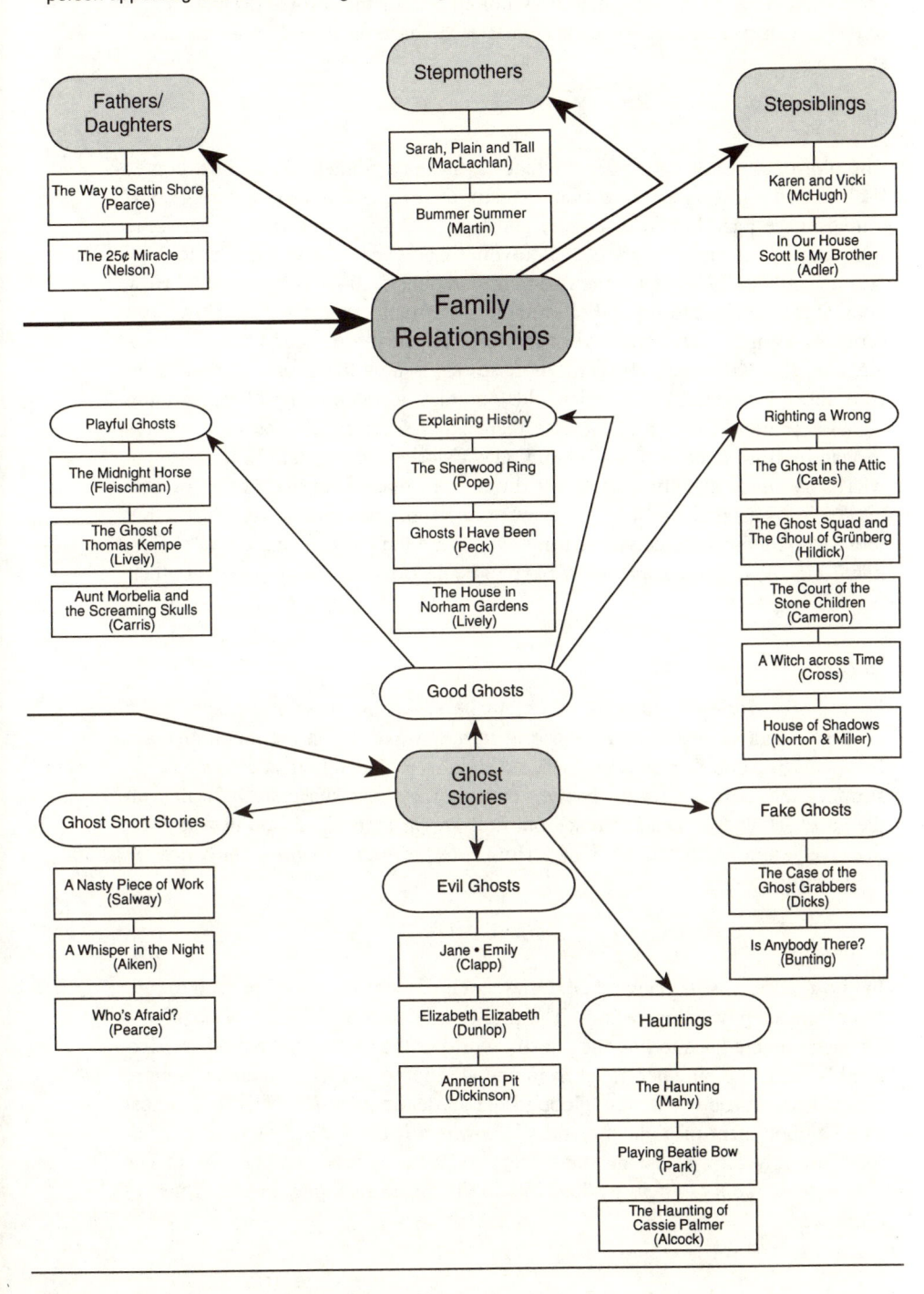

Family Relationships

- **Fathers/Daughters**
  - The Way to Sattin Shore (Pearce)
  - The 25¢ Miracle (Nelson)

- **Stepmothers**
  - Sarah, Plain and Tall (MacLachlan)
  - Bummer Summer (Martin)

- **Stepsiblings**
  - Karen and Vicki (McHugh)
  - In Our House Scott Is My Brother (Adler)

Ghost Stories

- **Playful Ghosts**
  - The Midnight Horse (Fleischman)
  - The Ghost of Thomas Kempe (Lively)
  - Aunt Morbelia and the Screaming Skulls (Carris)

- **Good Ghosts**
  - **Explaining History**
    - The Sherwood Ring (Pope)
    - Ghosts I Have Been (Peck)
    - The House in Norham Gardens (Lively)
  - **Righting a Wrong**
    - The Ghost in the Attic (Cates)
    - The Ghost Squad and The Ghoul of Grünberg (Hildick)
    - The Court of the Stone Children (Cameron)
    - A Witch across Time (Cross)
    - House of Shadows (Norton & Miller)

- **Ghost Short Stories**
  - A Nasty Piece of Work (Salway)
  - A Whisper in the Night (Aiken)
  - Who's Afraid? (Pearce)

- **Evil Ghosts**
  - Jane • Emily (Clapp)
  - Elizabeth Elizabeth (Dunlop)
  - Annerton Pit (Dickinson)

- **Fake Ghosts**
  - The Case of the Ghost Grabbers (Dicks)
  - Is Anybody There? (Bunting)

- **Hauntings**
  - The Haunting (Mahy)
  - Playing Beatie Bow (Park)
  - The Haunting of Cassie Palmer (Alcock)

mother or the father would have experienced it. Or collaborate with five of your classmates, with each of you assuming one of these roles. Remember to reread the story carefully to be sure what each character would know about the situation.

PLOT

The plot of a ghost story often includes a mystery. Sometimes a ghost comes back to find a lost object, to explain a historical event, or to right a wrong committed in the past. For instance, the ghosts in *The Sherwood Ring* reveal some little-known information about the Revolutionary War. Could the lies told by Heather in *Wait Till Helen Comes* be considered distractions from the plot? How does Dickinson create a parallel structure of evil in *Annerton Pit*? How do a series of events create terror without use of physical violence? One of the interesting things to think about in ghost stories is how the ghosts come and go from the spirit world to the real world. At times, a sudden drop of temperature signals the presence of a ghost. Are there other such signals that alert readers to visitors from another world? Many ghost stories also contain time travel. In what ways does ghostly time travel differ from that of science fiction or fantasy? Most ghosts depart our world when their missions are accomplished, but those who might be perceived as truly evil, as are the ghosts in *Jane-Emily, Elizabeth Elizabeth* and *Annerton Pit* have to be destroyed to free others from their powers.

MOOD

Some ghost stories frighten us; others make us laugh; while still others make us think about ourselves and our world in new ways. Often the mood changes from one of fright to a sense of peace and calm in which human characters are stronger and more sure of themselves because they have successfully dealt with the ghost. How does Hannah reach out in *A Witch across Time* and in what way does the setting influence the mood? How does the author of *Jane-Emily* portray the horrific?

SYMBOL

In ghost stories, as in many other stories, everyday objects are often used to represent special powers or feelings. The ring and the mirror in *Elizabeth Elizabeth*, for instance, are used to link the ghostly world of the past with the modern Elizabeth's world, helping her travel from one world to the other. Sometimes a more unusual object such as a glass globe in the garden in *Jane-Emily* is used almost as an embodiment of a ghost or the place where it resides and its power is felt most strongly. How is the ancient shield, the Tamarin, used symbolically in *The House in Norham Gardens*? What role do the paper dolls play in *The House of Shadows*?

EXPLORATIONS BASED ON THE WEB

It might be fun to develop a chart, based on reading books from this web, that describes ghosts using any of the patterns listed below. If you see another pattern, add it to the chart.

1. Ghosts who serve as a companion to a human character in the real world
2. Ghosts who try to entice a person into the spirit world
3. Ghosts who help someone through a bad time and then disappear
4. Ghosts who do the same thing over and over again
5. Ghosts who have a mission and, once that mission is completed, they disappear
6. Ghosts that still reside in the place of their death
7. Ghosts or poltergeists who are playful
8. Ghosts who seek to continue an evil pattern
9. Ghosts of the living, such as Scrooge's ghosts in *The Christmas Carol*
10. Ghosts that make human characters realize something about themselves

Once you have read a number of novels in this web (List 16 gives the names of all novels in the web), establish a set of rules for ghostliness that might be considered genre characteristics. You may wish to develop a diagram or a map of these characteristics with specific references to stories, characters, events, etc.

If you could look back in history and select a period of time or a series of events that interest you, decide what type of ghost might exist in that time and why that ghost might come back in our time.

Assume you are writing in the twenty-third century and elect a ghost story as the means of saying something about life today. Describe the ghost from today that might appear in your story. Why would that ghost want to appear so long after its own lifetime?

Look around your own home, school, or neighborhood to find a likely habitat for a ghost. Imagine what kind of a ghost might live in that place and what that ghost would do if it could visit you in your world. Write, draw, or act out the story you have created for your special ghost.

Most stories are about the relationship of the main characters to those close to them. In *Wait Till Helen Comes*, Heather's closeness to her father is threatened by his marriage and by the move to a new home large enough for the new stepmother and her children. Other books in this web focus on less-than-satisfactory family relationships. How do such relationships open the possibility of a ghost entering into a character's life?

Talk to your parents, grandparents, or other older people you know and ask them if they remember ever hearing about ghosts or other strange happenings that people really believed. Be sure to get as many details as possible and report the story as if it were happening now and you were a newspaper reporter or a TV newscaster.

Many scientists believe that what we call ghosts are actually instances of ESP or parapsychology, which they study in their laboratories. Find out as much as you can about ESP and parapsychology. You may even be able to do some experiments to test whether you or any of your friends may have ESP. Scientists disagree about the existence of these phenomena and so may the members of your group. If so, you might want to divide into two teams and have a debate. Be sure that you have collected evidence to support your position.

List 16. List of Books Placed in the Web for *Wait Till Helen Comes*

Adler, Carole S. *In Our House Scott Is My Brother.* New York: Macmillan, 1980.
Aiken, Joan. *A Whisper in the Night: Tales of Terror and Suspense.* New York: Delacorte, 1984.
Alcock, Vivien. *The Haunting of Cassie Palmer.* New York: Delacorte, 1980.
Bunting, Eve. *Is Anybody There?* New York: Harper & Row, 1988.
Cameron, Eleanor. *The Court of the Stone Children.* New York: Dutton, 1973.
Carris, Joan. *Aunt Morbelia and the Screaming Skulls.* Boston: Little, Brown, 1990.
Cates, Emily. *The Ghost in the Attic.* New York: Bantam, 1990.
Clapp, Patricia. *Jane-Emily.* New York: Lothrop, Lee & Shepard, 1969.
Cross, Gilbert B. *A Witch across Time.* New York: Atheneum, 1990.
Deem, James M. *How to Find a Ghost.* Boston: Houghton Mifflin, 1988.
Dickinson, Peter. *Annerton Pit.* Boston: Little, Brown, 1977.
Dicks, Terrance. *The Baker Street Irregulars in The Case of the Ghost Grabbers.* New York: Elsevier/Nelson, 1980.
Dunlop, Eileen. *Elizabeth Elizabeth.* New York: Holt, Rinehart and Winston, 1975.
Fleischman, Sid. *The Midnight Horse.* New York: Greenwillow, 1990.
Hahn, Mary Downing. *Daphne's Book.* Boston: Clarion, 1983.
Hahn, Mary Downing. *The Dead Man in Indian Creek.* Boston: Clarion, 1990.
Hahn, Mary Downing. *December Stillness.* Boston: Clarion, 1988.
Hahn, Mary Downing. *Doll in the Garden: A Ghost Story.* Boston: Clarion, 1989.
Hahn, Mary Downing. *Following the Mystery Man.* Boston: Clarion, 1988.
Hahn, Mary Downing. *The Jellyfish Season.* Boston: Clarion, 1985.
Hahn, Mary Downing. *The Sara Summer.* New York: Bantam, 1979.
Hahn, Mary Downing. *The Spanish Kidnapping Disaster.* New York: Clarion, 1991.
Hahn, Mary Downing. *Stepping on the Cracks.* New York: Clarion, 1991.
Hahn, Mary Downing. *Tallahassee Higgins.* Boston: Clarion, 1987.
Hahn, Mary Downing. *The Time of the Witch.* Boston: Clarion, 1982.
Hahn, Mary Downing. *Wait Till Helen Comes: A Ghost Story.* Boston: Clarion, 1986.
Hahn, Mary Downing. *The Wind Blows Backward.* New York: Clarion, 1993.
Haining, Peter. *Ghosts: The Illustrated History.* New York: Book Sales, 1988.

Hildick, E. W. *The Ghost Squad and the Ghoul of Grünberg*. New York: Dutton, 1986.
Lively, Penelope. *The Ghost of Thomas Kempe*. New York: Dutton, 1973.
Lively, Penelope. *The House in Norham Gardens*. New York: Dutton, 1974.
McHugh, Elisabet. *Karen and Vicki*. New York: Greenwillow, 1984.
McKissack, Patricia C. *The Dark-Thirty: Southern Tales of the Supernatural*. New York: Alfred Knopf, 1992.
MacLachlan, Patricia. *Sarah, Plain and Tall*. New York: Harper & Row, 1985.
Mahy, Margaret. *The Haunting*. New York: Atheneum, 1983.
Marsden, Simon. *The Haunted Realm: Ghosts, Spirits and Their Uncanny Abodes*. New York: Dutton, 1986.
Martin, Ann. *Bummer Summer*. New York: Holiday, 1983.
Matthews, Rupert. *The Supernatural*. Illus. by Peter Dennis. New York: Bookwright, 1989.
Nelson, Theresa. *The 25¢ Miracle*. New York: Bradbury, 1986.
Nic Leodhas, Sorche. *Ghosts Go Haunting*. Illus. by Nonny Hogrogian. New York: Holt, Rinehart & Winston, 1965.
Norton, Andre, and Phyllis Miller. *House of Shadows*. New York: Atheneum, 1984.
Park, Ruth. *Playing Beatie Bow*. New York: Atheneum, 1982.
Pearce, Philippa. *The Way to Sattin Shore*. New York: Penguin, 1985.
Pearce, Philippa. *Who's Afraid? And Other Strange Stories*. New York: Greenwillow, 1986.
Peck, Richard. *Ghosts I Have Been*. New York: Viking, 1977.
Pope, Elizabeth Marie. *The Sherwood Ring*. Boston: Houghton Mifflin, 1958.
Roberts, Nancy. *Haunted Houses: Tales from 30 American Homes*. Chester, Conn.: The Globe Pequot, 1988.
Salway, Lance. *A Nasty Piece of Work: And Other Ghost Stories*. New York: Clarion, 1983.
Schwartz, Alvin, comp. *Scary Stories to Tell in the Dark*. Philadelphia: Lippincott, 1981.
Westall, Robert. *Ghost Abbey*. New York: Scholastic, 1988.
Williams, Gurney. *Ghosts & Poltergeists*. New York: Franklin Watts, 1979.

Conclusion

Webbing is neither the only nor the best means of organizing information and ideas. It is, however, a versatile and very enjoyable means for young people to see relationships among ideas and materials. The organization of a visual representation of one's thought processes encourages a close look at the content of particular works as well as of the context for those works. Thus, webbing encourages a careful reading of sources in order to understand content and draw relationships in research. The pleasure young people take from seeing their ideas take shape in this visual form and the fact that there is no "right" way to represent ideas or show relationships also encourages dialogue and true cooperative learning. Probably the most important learning to result from creating and discussing webs is the confirmation that each person makes his or her own meanings in the world and that multiple acceptable and appropriate meanings can be made from the same set of source materials. Classroom teachers and library media specialists sharing webs with students should encourage them to include materials in their webs that are gender-fair and culturally diverse so that the voices of all peoples are available to young learners. The visual representation of information and ideas also may help to remind young people that there may be different points of view surrounding most issues and that real inquiry requires an examination and consideration of those alternative views. In this way, then, webbing is not only a useful tool for organizing information; it can be a means of expanding an understanding and an appreciation of others.

6

Staff Development and Workshop Initiatives

Staff Development

Information Power: Guidelines for School Library Media Programs states that "library media specialists are teachers and have a broad knowledge base that includes an understanding of media, the application of media to the learning process, the needs of students for information sources, and instructional strategies."[1] Surely such a person plays a significant role in both informal staff development and in more formal in-service education. In fact, school library media specialists have traditionally been key figures in that kind of staff development resulting from personal encounters with classroom teachers to discuss curriculum development or instructional planning. We have always built professional collections for faculty and administrators, routed appropriate journal articles and other items to teachers, and involved our colleagues in decisions about the purchase of materials and the coordination of those materials with teaching and learning. As members of curriculum committees and in our planning of instructional units with individual teachers, we have brought our special expertise about information and materials and our own perceptions of the process of teaching to bear on the work of other faculty members in the school. In addition, from our vantage point in the library media center, we have a unique perspective on the work of classroom teachers and can identify common concerns among members of the faculty and encourage and facilitate their getting together to discuss these concerns, benefiting from each other's ideas and experiences.

For instance, the library media specialist may notice that two teachers, perhaps at different age or grade levels, are dealing with the same content in very different ways or that they are having similar difficulties in selecting materials or designing teaching strategies. This is an ideal opportunity for the library media specialist to get these two teachers involved in a three-way discussion that will lead to the kind of professional sharing that is both the most natural and most rewarding form of staff development. Some library media specialists are so insightful in identifying such common concerns and so supportive in encouraging teachers to share their strengths that faculty are drawn to the library media center during free moments and after class hours just to keep up with what's going on professionally in the school.

These are some of the most common and consistent roles a library media specialist assumes in staff development or in our schools.[2] However, such activities are not enough. If we really are to play a teaching role in the school, it is no longer sufficient to think of our instructional consultant responsibilities in terms of these basic continuing practices plus an occasional workshop to introduce new ideas, new materials, or new technologies. We have already discussed the library media specialist's role as teacher of students in both the preactive and interactive stages. Now let us look at examples of ways library media specialists can extend their educational expertise to provide more formal in-service programs for other faculty members either at the building or district level. It should be pointed out that when library media specialists are teaching teachers, their interactive teaching may be a part of the teachers' preactive teaching.

In order to be effective leaders of staff development activities for other teachers as well as providers of educational opportunities for parents and caregivers, school library media specialists must be knowledgeable about basic principles of adult education.[3] Probably the greatest distinction between educational activities designed for school-age children and those for adults is that schooling is presumed to be the primary responsibility of children, while such activities are almost always secondary in the lives of adults. Discussions of adult education normally divide learning activities into three types: basic education, career education, and leisure or enrichment education. Obviously, the emphasis in our work with teachers is on career education or possibilities for improving their work with young people.

Adult learners ordinarily come to an educational activity with very different expectations from those of elementary or secondary school students. In most instances, adults are choosing to participate and their motivation is very specifically tied to the value they place on the educational experience. Often this is a very pragmatic value; they expect to see the usefulness in their lives and their work. Especially with teachers, whose work is also education, we must be certain that our respect for their prior knowledge is very obviously acknowledged and used in the planning and execution of current learning activities. We must assume self-directed learners who will share both the authority and responsibility for learning in cooperative, peer-group ventures. Teachers as learners demand realistic goals and require challenges and a variety of resources and learning experiences to meet their expectations and various learning styles. In addition, they expect a reasonable learning pace that neither rushes them through content without time for thought or hands-on experiences nor wastes their time. Adults often come to educational experiences with predetermined personal goals, with a need for a sense of control over the process, and with a desire for socially satisfying interactive learning; therefore, the teacher must respond with respect, with flexibility, and with shared responsibility and authority. This is especially true when a school library media specialist is teaching other teachers in the school.

Curricular changes, either the introduction of new options in an expanded multicultural program or the development of greater depth in traditional disciplines, provide excellent opportunities for library media specialists to demonstrate their competencies as teachers. A school that offers many options to students increases the number of subjects being taught and often expands into areas not previously included in the school curriculum. As control for some aspects of the curriculum shifts from teachers to students, there may be a shorter time span for faculty preparation, greater difficulty in acquiring course materials, and fewer guides available to suggest possible approaches and teaching strategies.

The responses of library media specialists to these increased demands and assistance to other teachers in planning instructional units are a valuable means of staff development. One type of response that library media specialists ought to consider in today's electronic environment is an array of in-service options that participants might access in their own time from their home computers or VCRs. Technology has eased the process of telecommunication to such a degree that more and more educational institutions are including it as a part of the organizational plan for schooling and a means for staff development.[4] Distance education not only offers opportunities for students in our schools but also opens avenues for advancement in competencies to the faculty of a school.

Although formal in-service activities, either in person or electronic, are important, perhaps the most significant impact the library media specialist has as a teacher of teachers is through informal one-to-one encounters. In helping another teacher prepare an instructional unit, the school library media specialist as instructional consultant becomes involved in the total teaching plan, not just the selection of materials. The discussion that ensues between these two faculty members is valuable in itself, but the library media specialist can, with thoughtful preplanning, make such discussion even more valuable and perhaps extend it to other members of the faculty. One way this might be done is by sharing some kind of schema or set of guidelines for a systematic instructional development process. One useful outline of this process, and exploration of the library media specialist's role, is found in Philip Turner's *Helping Teachers Teach*.[5] A document listing the steps of this process (needs assessment, performance objectives, learner analysis, test design, materials selection, activities development, implementation, and evaluation) would, at the very least, serve as a useful checklist for the library media specialist to use in conferences with other teachers. This can insure both a mutual understanding of what the teacher has in mind and an agreement that all necessary elements are being considered.

The T.I.E. Model of Cooperative Instructional Development, devised by Betty Cleaver and William Taylor, is another useful means for the library media specialist to prepare for or to examine the process of interaction with other teachers as an instructional consultant.[6] T.I.E. is an acronym for Talking, Involving, and Evaluating, the three stages of the process in which classroom teachers and library media specialists work together for improving instruction. Michael Eisenberg's and Robert Berkowitz's work on the "Big Six Skills" approach to information problem solving is yet another exciting way to think about working with teachers.[7] These approaches are most often used more informally with individual teachers or with small groups of cooperating teachers, but the ideas behind them and instruction in their use might be a very valuable in-service education unit in a formal presentation to an entire faculty.

Most classroom teachers would appreciate the organizational assistance provided in this way and would be encouraged to use these instructional development documents in subsequent preparations, thus making both their work and the work of the library media specialist somewhat easier. The library media specialist might distribute various outlines or schema to all teachers as a routine professional resource to facilitate the introduction of new curricular content. Since such systems for instructional design are abundant in educational literature, library media specialists need not appear to be setting themselves up as experts telling others how to do their work, but rather as persons whose special responsibility in the school is to sort through, select, and provide others with appropriate professional materials. Of course, the particular schema mentioned here come from the library media field, and classroom teachers should be encouraged to share similar models or schema that derive from general education or from specific disciplines.

In-Service Workshops

An in-service workshop in which the library media specialist goes through the stages and actually demonstrates to other teachers the instructional development process, as well as the use of media center resources available for the support of teaching and learning activities, might be a most efficient and effective means of teaching teachers. The library media specialist might also prepare his or her own plan or schema for a workshop for teachers and make that schema available to the rest of the faculty so they will see the advantages of the systematic approach for themselves as learners as well as teachers.

Figure 12 is a Management Control Schema the author has used for the preparation of in-service workshops, programs for parents, short-term courses, and other educational activities. It assumes a knowledge of standard elements of the instructional design process and focuses on practical considerations of time, money, and facilities required, which, as we all know, can have a major impact on success.

Many of the advanced media competencies discussed in previous chapters may quite profitably be made accessible to other faculty members through a workshop planned by focusing on appropriate teaching and learning knowledge and then checking practical details against this schema. If faculty members are not comfortable with videotaping, hypermedia, or distance learning, it is unlikely that even the most skillful students will be encouraged to make appropriate uses of these techniques in their schooling. Thus, library media specialists might offer specific courses in the use of such technologies. One also might, either at the building or district level, use the Management Control Schema for the preparation of an efficient plan for the training of paraprofessionals or volunteers.

Although the items outlined on this Management Control Schema are things most teachers regularly consider when planning educational activities, sometimes

I. Brief description of course or program
II. Needs Assessment
III. Target Audience
    Primary: Adults: Teachers, Parents, Administrators
              Students: age, grade or skill level
    Alternative, if feasible
IV. Time Frame
    Planning time
    Teaching time
V. Goals and Objectives (Relate to Needs Assessment)
VI. Teaching Strategies/Learning Activities
    How objectives will be achieved for each segment
VII. Personnel Requirement
    Primary: teacher, guest speakers, etc.
    Secondary: materials preparation, technical assistance, etc.
VIII. Materials and Equipment (list specific items)
    Materials selection
    Additions to collection
    Consumable items
    Rentals
    District loan/Public Library loans
    Interlibrary loans
    Electronic networks
IX. Item to Be Produced (if any)
    Print: instructional modules, handouts, worksheets, etc.
    Nonprint: videos, slides, tapes, transparencies, computer files, etc.
X. Facilities
    Spaces
    Furnishings
XI. Information Program (How others will be informed)
XII. Budget
XIII. Evaluation Procedures
XIV. Resources Used in Preparation (Bibliographies, etc.)

Figure 12. Management Control Schema

the use of such a list will encourage one to consider alternatives. For instance, a school library media specialist planning a staff development program on a particular topic might initially think only of a single school staff as the audience. Further consideration might lead one to plan with other library media specialists for a district-wide program. That decision could lead to many other changes in the planning process. For instance: What physical facilities are needed for the expanded audience? Will the equipment and other resources be adequate for the expanded space and number of participants? Will shared resources from several schools or district funds enable you to increase the breath or depth of coverage of the topic? Would an outside consultant or special materials be more attractive to the audience and encourage their active participation? Could an outside consultant bring new perspectives to your district's thinking on the topic? Is this an appropriate topic for cooperative planning with local public libraries or other agencies? The consideration of these and other questions may well enhance our own thinking and improve the quality of staff development and in-service education.

The series of in-service workshops that follow focus on teaching content that might be initiated by school library media specialists. In the preactive planning for both efferent and aesthetic aspects of these workshops, one might refer to the Model of the Teaching Process in chapter 2. For more practical aspects of designing programs for a particular time, place, and audience, the Management Control Schema above should be helpful. The workshops as presented here are, of necessity, incomplete. The teaching suggestions included will have to be adapted to a particular situation and group of participants as will the more practical aspects of their enactment.

Whatever their specific content, all of these workshops emphasize the evaluation, selection, and use of library media center resources. This is an accepted area of expertise of library media specialists and one that has an immediate, and often profound, influence on both teachers and students, limiting or expanding possibilities for personal or group inquiry. Thus, the selection of materials is an important phase of preactive teaching, influencing not only the content taught but also how that content is taught. As one of the most important aspects of planning for teaching, the evaluation and selection of educational resources should be a cooperative and collegial activity of teaching professionals. A primary goal of these workshops is to initiate a dialogue in which teachers, through the examination of a variety of resources, will explore different aspects of teaching content and, in the process, reflect upon and share their ideas, beliefs, and values concerning what is important within particular curricular content and in schooling in general.

In addition to the emphasis on educational resources, these workshops represent a valuing of many aspects of education and teaching discussed in the first two chapters of this work. They all encourage learners, teachers, and students to think both critically and creatively, to raise questions, and to use the results of their inquiry to make their own meanings. In order to stimulate such inquiry and meaning-making, controversial topics and innovative approaches to those topics, using literature across all areas of the school curriculum, are discussed. There is also an attempt to include materials that are gender-fair and multicultural so that different peoples, as well as different approaches to content, are represented whenever possible.

The first two workshops are direct, and very general, activities to encourage teachers to become more conscious of and involved in the process of evaluating and selecting materials in the preactive phase of teaching. Subsequent workshops focus on more specific content, topics or types of materials, but all of the sample workshops reflect the values and the concerns about teaching expressed throughout this book.

Workshop on Selection and Societal Issues

The first workshop is intended to take a broad view of the variety of materials available for young people today and some of the ways these resources might be used to stimulate student discussion of contemporary society. Many of the particular titles are controversial; all are discussible. The role of the school library media specialist is to get teachers or parents to experience these materials and to consider both their aesthetic and their efferent values to students. In the process of discussing such works, all participants will probably expand their own perceptions not only of specific works but of possibilities for sharing them with students and for relating them to the school curriculum.

The video productions of *Ralph S. Mouse*, *The House of Dies Drear*, and *The Wind in the Willows* are fairly standard visual interpretations of favorite young people's books that are intended to stimulate a discussion of similarities and differences between print and video. *When the Wind Blows* is a video version of a cartoon picture book about an elderly couple waiting for the wind to bring life-threatening radiation to them after a nuclear disaster. Obviously, the topic itself is controversial, but this work is especially so because the format is one usually thought of as for young children. *Jabberwocky* and *The Shooting Gallery* are striking animated films with sometimes violent images. The author's previous research on critical thinking and student meaning-making in the viewing of *The Shooting Gallery* might prove a useful aspect of examining this work.[8] Those selecting *Jabberwocky* based on their appreciation of the nonsense poem may well be startled by this film. *Beauty and the Beast*, like other Fairie Tale Theatre videos, presents an adult, somewhat tongue-in-cheek, version of this classic tale. Thus, one of the key ideas to be discussed in this workshop is the matching of materials to an appropriate audience.

Book titles in this workshop list range from playful picture books for young children to Thomas Baird's challenging and provocative novel for young adults. Both fiction and informational books are included. The list reinforces that even many books required in school curricula or considered "classics" are controversial. The more than one hundred years of censorship of *The Adventures of Huckleberry Finn*, often considered one of the most powerful antislavery works ever produced because of its realistic portrayal of the attitudes, beliefs, and language of the prejudiced white Americans of the time, is a case in point. It is the strength of these negative portrayals that convinces readers of the horrors of slavery. On the other hand, one can understand the concerns of African-Americans who fear that young adults reading this novel will just accept the use of the term "nigger" and the reversal of child-adult roles.[9] Some have also objected to *A Day No Pigs Would*

Die because of the natural violence and animal sexuality of harsh rural life in America.[10] Lesser-known, probably much more serious, charges against this book have been brought by Shaker scholars who claim Peck misrepresented himself in the author's notes and misrepresented the Shaker faith in his novel.

Our current, and very necessary, concern with racism, sexism, ageism, and other "isms" seems sometimes to have clouded our vision in the search for the best possible materials for student use. Everyone selecting materials for young people and helping students develop critical skills to evaluate such materials ought to be fully aware of the many subtle, and not so subtle, ways whole groups of people have been perceived in our society. The media brought into the school and that which is produced there should reflect these concerns, but the absence of such consciousness-raising images and ideas does not necessarily negate the value of the work. It is still possible to have a perfectly good story about a mother who stays home and bakes cookies, even if we agree that the image of women has been too limited or one-sided in the past. On the other hand, a book or film that presents a woman as a firefighter or state senator is not necessarily of high artistic value, and a poorly executed composition is likely to cause negative, rather than positive, responses to its subject matter. The materials included here, or those other library media specialists might substitute for this type of workshop, should encourage a discussion of these concerns.

Society's confrontations with new concerns and new values cannot change the fact that works of art have always dealt with unique individuals and situations, frequently unpleasant ones. Zeal for "political correctness" in today's world cannot erase a history in which slavery and the subservient role of women played very real parts, and it would be absurd to try to eliminate works discussing or showing these events. It is equally absurd to assume that any work of art including a racist character or remark is advocating racism or that one in which a character is confronted with an unresponsive social system is advocating nihilism. Such responses to aesthetic forms, attributing specific motives to their creators based on inappropriate evidence, can lead to a modern brand of witch-hunting that is as irrational and inhumane as the injustices we are attempting to stamp out. Adults must help students become more sensitive to the ways in which different peoples are portrayed in the various media, but ultimately the only place to eliminate prejudice effectively is not in literature but in life. If we censor materials we find objectionable we will no doubt make them more attractive to young people. What we must do is to stop confusing the contents of the composition with the intentions of the composer and then to hold these works up as mirrors to help all of us look more sensitively at what is happening or has happened in society. Then we may attack these injustices more aggressively in the real world.

We can, however, use various methods and media to stimulate student thought and feelings about injustice. The first step may be to encourage students to think about the various forms or instances of injustice they have seen or experienced in their own lives or through the mass media. Again, the intellectual process of organizing and categorizing individual items may lead to fruitful discussions and potential areas for further research. Alternatively, we might begin with a specific book such as Avi's *Nothing But the Truth*, which skillfully weaves together the perspectives of several characters in relation to the events of this story.[11] Older students might be exposed to film or video presentations such as *Date Rape: It Happened to Me*, which has as its purpose the sensitizing of teenagers to the psychological, emotional, and the legal ramifications of an act of sexual violence.[12] As a natural relationship to this film students might view two others that explore the position of women. *The Chrysanthemums*, drawn from John Steinbeck's story, reveals the inner struggle of a woman seeking to be valued in a male-dominated society of the 1930s.[13] *Half the Kingdom* demonstrates, through the voices of seven Jewish women around the world, the conflict of religion, cultural tradition, and contemporary feminist principles. This work goes beyond Judaism and reaches out to all women.[14] In this workshop adults will share their perceptions of a variety of materials and consider whether, and if so how, these materials might be used with young people.

As they engage in the kinds of inquiry suggested above, workshop participants will evaluate and discuss the issues raised using questions such as the following:

Do these materials reflect problems, aspirations, attitudes, and ideals of society?
Are they relevant to today's world and to today's young people?
Are they appropriate to the age, ability, and interest levels of the users? Do they represent differing viewpoints on controversial subjects? Are they free of stereotyping according to age, sex, race, and other factors?
Are they appropriate for inclusion in the school curriculum?

Participants will screen any of the following listed in List 17. (Since some of these videos are lengthy, it might be best to select a portion to screen or make them available before the workshop. Alternative videos might be chosen with attention to a particular school's characteristics and needs.)

List 17. Selected Videocassettes to Stimulate Thought on Societal Issues

Beauty and the Beast. Color, 50 minutes. Faerie Tale Theatre series. Playhouse Video, CBS/Fox Video, 1983.
The Chrysanthemums. Color, 22 minutes. Directed by Steve Rosen and Terri De Bonas. Distributed by Pyramid Films, 1990.
Date Rape: It Happened to Me. Color, 29:30 minutes. Directed by Ken Carpenter. Distributed by Pyramid Films, 1990.
Half the Kingdom. Color, 58 minutes. Directed by Francis Zuckerman/Roushell Goldstein. Distributed by Direct Cinema Limited, 1989.
The House of Dies Drear. Color, 116 minutes. WonderWorks Public Television's Children's and Family Consortium, 1984.
Jabberwocky. Color, 14 minutes. Sim Films. Weston Woods, 1973.

Ralph S. Mouse. Color, 40 minutes. Churchill Films, 1990.
The Shooting Gallery. Color, 16 minutes. Sim Films. Weston Woods, 1970.
When the Wind Blows. Color, 80 minutes. International Video Entertainment, 1986.
The Wind in the Willows. Color, 78 minutes. HBO Video, Thames Video Collection, 1984.

Participants will examine the following books in List 18. (Substitute comparable books to match grade range and curricular needs.)

List 18. Selected Books to Stimulate Thought on Societal Issues

Avi. *Nothing But the Truth.* Boston: Clarion, 1991.
Baird, Thomas. *Smart Rats.* New York: Harper & Row, 1990.
Beisner, Monika. *Catch That Cat! A Picture Book of Rhymes and Puzzles.* New York: Farrar, Straus and Giroux, 1990.
Briggs, Raymond. *Fungus the Bogeyman.* New York: Random House, 1979.
Browne, Anthony. *The Tunnel.* New York: Alfred Knopf, 1989.
Collington, Peter. *On Christmas Eve.* New York: Alfred Knopf, 1990.
Dickinson, Peter. *Eva.* New York: Delacorte, 1989.
Emberly, Michael. *Ruby.* Boston: Little, Brown, 1990.
Gordon, Sheila. *The Middle of Somewhere: A Story of South Africa.* New York: Orchard, 1990.
Henry David Thoreau: Walden. Text selections by Steve Lowe. Illus. by Robert Sabuda. New York: Philomel, 1990.
Klause, Annette C. *Silver Kiss.* New York: Delacorte, 1990.
Martin, Rafe. *The Rough-Face Girl.* Illus. by David Shannon. New York: G. P. Putnam's, 1992.
Myers, Walter Dean. *Malcolm X: By Any Means Necessary.* New York: Scholastic, 1993.
Peck, Robert Newton. *A Day No Pigs Would Die.* New York: Alfred Knopf, 1972.
Provensen, Alice. *The Buck Stops Here: Presidents of the United States.* New York: Harper & Row, 1990.
Ringgold, Faith. *Tar Beach.* New York: Crown, 1991.
Scieszka, Jon, and Lane Smith. *Stinky Cheese Man and Other Fairly Stupid Tales.* New York: Viking, 1992.
Shulevitz, Uri. *Toddlecreek Post Office.* New York: Farrar, Straus and Giroux, 1990.
Stanley, Diane, and Peter Vennema. *Bard of Avon: The Story of William Shakespeare.* Illus. by Diane Stanley. New York: Morrow, 1992.
Twain, Mark. *The Adventures of Huckleberry Finn.* Boston: Houghton Mifflin, 1958.

As workshop participants engage in the kinds of inquiry suggested above, the following probe questions may help to focus their discussion:

> What specific ideas, attitudes, or information do the videos and books you have just examined communicate?
> Do the contents of these materials represent the highest informational and aesthetic standards?
> Do the materials contribute to heightening affective responses? Intellectual responses? Aesthetic responses?
> What aspects of imagination are addressed in these works?
> Do these materials confirm, illuminate, or extend life experiences?
> Is there sufficient cultural diversity shown in the range of items?
> Do materials respond to various levels of students' interests, from the merely curious to the deeply committed?
> Will the materials help children and youth become more critical of their own perceptions of the world and of aesthetic forms and meanings?
> Would you use these materials with children and young people? If not, why not? For what age group are they most appropriate?
> Do these materials cause you to reconsider your beliefs about the rights of children and youth to sophisticated levels of information and aesthetic content?

Workshop on Selection and Bibliographic Access

Participants will review existing selection policies in their schools—or draft a preliminary selection policy if none exists–and then examine these policies in light of specific instructional and personal needs of users. Copies of *The ALAN Review* issue on censorship (vol. 20, no. 2, Winter 1993) should also be available. Special attention should be drawn to Gloria Treadwell Pipkin's "Challenging the Conventional Wisdom on Censorship," which questions the value of selection policies in dealing with challenges to materials.[15] The following goals might be adopted for the workshop:

> Participants will evaluate various selection criteria through a series of workshop activities.
> Participants will identify and use a range of bibliographic sources for the selection of materials.
> Participants will explore the relationships between teaching and learning strategies and the availability and use of resources.

As they complete the various exercises in this workshop, participants will:

> Identify and use a variety of tools for selection
> Identify alternative sources for selection.
>
> Participants will examine and compare the items provided in List 19.

List 19. Selected List of Bibliographic Resources

Sampling of school library media center collection development policies.

Sampling of general and specialized selection tools, such as Lyn Miller-Lachmann, *Our Family Our Friends Our World: An Annotated Guide to Significant Multicultural Books for Children and Teenagers* (New Providence, N.J.: R.R. Bowker, 1992); *From Page to Screen: Children's and Young Adult Books on Film and Video*, ed. by Joyce Moss and George Wilson (Detroit, Mich.: Gale Research, 1992); Stephanie Zvirin, *The Best Years of Their Lives: A Resource Guide for Teenagers in Crisis* (Chicago, Ill.: American Library Association, 1992); and Anthony L. Manna and Cynthia Wolford Symons, *Children's Literature for Health Awareness* (Metuchen, N.J.: Scarecrow Press, 1992).

Sampling of review periodicals, such as *School Library Journal, Kirkus, Horn Book, Booklist, The New Advocate, VOYA* and *Book Links*.

Sampling of journals specific to subject fields that review materials for children and young people, such as *English Journal, Reading Teacher, Social Studies Education, Science* and *Children*.

Sampling of catalogs of publishers, distributors, producers, etc.

Sampling of alternative sources for materials, such as museum catalogs, environmental association catalogs, and small press catalogs.

Participants will select a topic and use various tools to develop a preview or purchase list that matches their grade, subject content, and student profiles. The probes for discussion that follow might help in the understanding of bibliographic access:

- Do the standard bibliographic tools represent the broad spectrum of interests of the students we seek to serve?
- Do standard bibliographic tools represent aspects of the topic chosen in significant range and depth?
- What is the level of information needed to determine whether or not a particular item reviewed is pertinent to your topic and to the collection as a whole?
- Do the classification numbers and subject headings suggested in various tools and selection aids increase or decrease access to specific aspects of your topic?
- Does the structure and organization of a tool such as *Book Links* help in the enlargement of your view on both topic and materials?
- To what extent does the existence of district centers, county cooperatives, and networks alter the selection and acquisitions policies at the building level?
- Having participated in all stages of this unit, what conclusions do you reach concerning bibliographic access and the selection of both topics and materials for learning?

Workshop on Selection and Mathematics

As they complete the various exercises in this workshop, participants will examine math materials according to the following criteria:

Do these materials contribute to the specific objectives of the instructional program in mathematics?
Do these materials represent sound mathematical concepts?
Are they appropriate to the interests and the learning levels of students?
Are they authoritative, realistic, factual, open-ended?
Do they stimulate inquiry?

Participants will examine a range of computer software and children's books in mathematics listed in Lists 20 and 21. This workshop offers suggestions for such materials, but alternative titles might be substituted from a particular school library media center collection or from alternative selection sources. In this workshop, the examples given represent a range of materials appropriate for young children.

List 20. Selected Computer Software on Mathematics for Younger Children

Blockers and Finders II. Apple II and IBM. Sunburst, 1989.
Hop to It. Apple II. Sunburst, 1990.
Math Bingo. Apple II. DLM, 1991.
Math Blaster: In Search of Spot. IBM. Davidson, 1993.
Math Blaster Mystery. Apple II, Apple IIGS, IBM. Davidson, 1989.
Math Blaster Plus! Apple II, Apple IIGS, IBM. Davidson, 1987.
Math Magic; A Mystical Mission. IBM. Mind Play, 1991.
Math Rabbit. Apple II and IBM. Learning Company, 1986.
Number Maze. Apple Mac. Great Wave Software, 1988.
Number Munchers. Apple II. MECC, 1986.
Super Solvers: Treasure Mountain! IBM. Learning Company, 1990.
Taking Chances. Apple II. Sunburst, 1991.
Treasure Math Storm. IBM. Learning Company, 1992.
Winker's World of Numbers. Apple II. Sunburst, 1989.

List 21. Selected Books on Mathematics for Younger Children

Anno, Mitsumasa. *Anno's Counting Book*. New York: Harper & Row, 1986.
Anno, Mitsumasa. *Anno's Math Games III*. New York: Philomel, 1991.
Anno, Mitsumasa. *Anno's Mysterious Multiplying Jar*. New York: Putnam, 1983.
Bang, Molly. *Ten, Nine, Eight*. New York: Greenwillow, 1983.
Christelow, Eileen. *Five Little Monkeys Jumping on the Bed*. New York: Clarion, 1989.
Dennis, J. Richard. *Fractions Are Parts of Things*. Illus. by Donald Crews. New York: Harper & Row, 1971.
Feelings, Muriel. *Moja Means One: A Swahili Counting Book*. Illus. by Tom Feelings. New York: Dial, 1971.
Geisert, Arthur. *Oink*. Boston: Houghton Mifflin, 1991.

Geisert, Arthur. *Pigs from 1 to 10*. Boston: Houghton Mifflin, 1992.
Hoban, Tana. *Circles, Triangles and Squares*. New York: Macmillan, 1974.
Hutchens, Pat. *The Doorbell Rang*. New York: Greenwillow, 1986.
Kaplan, Majorie. *Henry and the Boy Who Thought Numbers Were Fleas*. Illus. by Heidi Chang. New York: Four Winds, 1991.
Pomerantz, Charlotte. *The Half-Birthday Party*. New York: Clarion, 1986.
Schwartz, David M. *How Much Is a Million?* Illus. by Steven Kellogg. New York: Lothrop, 1985.
Schwartz, David M. *If You Made a Million*. Illus. by Steven Kellogg. New York: Lothrop, 1989.
Seuss, Dr. *One Fish, Two Fish, Red Fish, Blue Fish*. New York: Random House, 1960.
Spier, Peter. *Noah's Ark*. New York: Doubleday, 1977.
Tafuri, Nancy. *Who's Counting*. New York: Greenwillow, 1986.
Tompest, Ann. *Grandfather Tang's Story*. Illus. by Robert A. Parker. New York: Crown, 1990.
Viorst, Judith. *Alexander Who Used to Be Rich Last Sunday*. New York: Atheneum, 1978.
Wildsmith, Brian. *Professor Noah's Spaceship*. New York: Oxford University, 1980.

Participants will also examine a sampling of curriculum guides, units of study in elementary school mathematics, and the *MathFinder Sourcebook*.[16]

> Given a specific section of a mathematics curriculum or a unit guide, what materials does the library media center have to support these topics (particularly considering specific rather than generic materials)?
> Examining the same curriculum materials, what do the stated objectives imply about learners and the supportive materials required?
> How do we allow for alternative approaches to curricular content?
> Having participated in all stages of this workshop, what conclusions do you reach concerning selection and the mathematics curriculum?
> Do these materials encourage the integration of the computer and other technologies into teaching strategies?

Workshop on Challenges to Intellectual Freedom

Materials have frequently been the target of censors in school library media centers in this country. In most instances, a specific item has been challenged; in others, it is the generic topic (AIDS, Abortion, Feminism, Secular Humanism, New Age Ideas, Homosexuality, Satanism) that some individuals or organized groups believe should not be represented in our schools. Participants, in reading or viewing a work, should consider its intrinsic value as an aesthetic work and its relation to the school curriculum, discuss the pros and cons of the challenges to that work, and prepare evidence to support a position in relation to the challenges. It is much

Staff Development and Workshop Initiatives   115

easier for many in the library profession to see things from a liberal perspective, but one might want to include items that those from a liberal perspective would seek to ban.

The workshop that follows is a means for discussion and exploration of intellectual freedom and access to information. The organization of this workshop differs somewhat from the others, with a primary focus on professional materials related to the topic (see Lists 22 and 23) before dealing with questions of intellectual freedom in regard to specific materials for young people (see figure 13). Participants are first asked to select and read a number of articles and to examine several books on intellectual freedom.

List 22. Key Background Readings and Resources on Intellectual Freedom

ALA Office for Intellectual Freedom and Intellectual Freedom Committee. *Intellectual Freedom Manual*. 4th ed. Chicago: American Library Association, 1992.

Banned Books Week: Celebrating the Freedom to Read Resource Book. Robert Doyle, ed. Chicago: American Library Association, 1991.

Burress, Lee. *Battle of the Books: Literary Censorship in the Public Schools, 1950–1985*. Metuchen, N.J.: Scarecrow, 1989.

Celebrating Censored Books. Lee Burress and N. Karolides, eds. Racine, Wisc.: Wisconsin Council of Teachers, 1985.

Censored Books: Critical Viewpoints. Niholas J. Karolides, Lee Burress and John M. Kean, eds. Metuchen, N.J.: Scarecrow, 1993.

Delfattore, Joan. *What Johnny Shouldn't Read*. New Haven, Conn.: Yale University, 1992.

The Intellectual Freedom Committee Young Adult Services Division. *Hit List: Frequently Challenged Young Adult Titles; References to Defend Them*. Chicago: American Library Association, 1989.

Jenkinson, Edward. *Censors in the Classroom: The Mind Benders*. Carbondale, Ill.: University of Southern Illinois, 1979.

Reichman, Henry. *Censorship and Selection: Issues and Answers for Schools*. Chicago: American Library Association, 1988.

List 23. Supplementary Resources on Intellectual Freedom

Berman, Jerry, and Janlori Goldman. *A Federal Right of Information Privacy: The Need for Reform*. Washington, D.C.: Benton Foundation, 1989.

"The Constitution and the American Way of Life." *Journal of American History* 74, no. 3 (December 1987).

Cox, Archibald. *The Court and the Constitution*. Boston: Houghton Mifflin, 1989.

Curry, Richard O. *Freedom at Risk: Secrecy, Censorship, and Repression in the 1980s*. Philadelphia, Penn.: Temple University, 1988.

Gerhardt, Lillian N. "Ethical Back Talk: III." *School Library Journal* 36, no. 6 (June 1990): 4.

Jenkinson, Edward B. "Classroom Questions: Respect for Student Privacy Isn't Asking Too Much." *American School Board Journal* 176, no. 11 (November 1989): 27–30.

Jenkinson, Edward B. *The Schoolbook Protest Movement: 40 Questions and Answers*. Bloomington, Ind.: Phi Delta Kappa Educational Foundation, 1986.

Mnookin, Robert H. *In the Interest of Children: Advocacy, Law Reform, and Public Policy*. New York: W. H. Freeman, 1985.

Parker, Barbara, and Stefanie Weiss. *Protecting the Freedom to Learn: A Citizen's Guide*. Washington, D.C.: People for the American Way, 1983.

Price, Janet R., Alan H. Levine, and Eve Cary. *The Rights of Students*. 3d ed. Carbondale, Ill.: Southern Illinois University, 1988. (An American Civil Liberties Union Handbook)

Schimmel, David, and Louis Fischer. *Parents, Schools, and the Law*. Columbia, Md.: The National Committee for Citizens in Education, 1988.

After exploring the content of the above materials, participants will be divided into groups, each of which will work with one title from the list in figure 13. The group will discuss the issues represented in that item and then explore the policies and procedures for dealing with challenges to intellectual freedom and the responses to be prepared in light of the particular work.

POLICIES AND PROCEDURES

Re-examine the policies and procedures for dealing with challenges to materials currently in effect in your school. Are these adequate and appropriate? Do they need to be revised to account for changes in education or new types of materials in the library media center?

RESPONSE

Prepare a response to the specific objection to the content. Is there such a thing as a universal response, either to all challenges to intellectual freedom or to all challenges of a particular item? If not, why not? What factors might cause us to vary either the nature or the extent of the response? Consider the following:

1. Who has challenged the material?
    —Parent, student, teacher, principal, school board member, concerned citizen, parish priest, police chief, local psychologist, mayor
    —Individual or group
    —Local concern or representative of a regional or national effort by an official organization

Staff Development and Workshop Initiatives 117

2. Type of school?
   —Public, private, parochial
   —General or special magnet
3. Age or grade level of students?
   —K–12 school
   —Elementary
   —Middle school
   —High school
4. Location of the school?
   —Urban, suburban, rural
   —Region or area of the country
   —Proximity to public library, book stores, etc.
5. Acknowledged worth of material?
   —Reviews, awards, etc.
6. Use of material in school?
   —Required or optional

HS   Mark Twain. *The Adventures of Huckleberry Finn.* Racist language, offensive to blacks, derogatory remarks. The book "creates an emotional block for black students that inhibits learning."

HS   Eric Remarque. *All Quiet on the Western Front.* War is depicted as brutal and dehumanizing, too violent for the child.

HS   George Bernard Shaw. *Androcles and the Lion.* Shaw was an atheist.

HS   Michael Crichton. *The Andromeda Strain.* Too much attention to sex.

HS   Richard Peck. *Are You in the House Alone?* Description of rape.

MS   Judy Blume. *Are You There God? It's Me, Margaret.* "I wouldn't let anyone read that, it's smut." Vulgar and obscene language, sexually explicit, anti-religious sentiment.

HS   Aldous Huxley. *Brave New World.* Too frequent sex passages, objected to test-tube babies. Immorality of baby factory. Profanity, sex reference, immoral, not suitable for high school students, students not mature enough to understand it.

MS   Katherine Paterson. *Bridge to Terabithia.* Language.

HS   Geoffrey Chaucer. *Canterbury Tales.* Risque language in some tales. Unhealthy characters and nasty words. "We don't read things like this in my house and I don't expect my daughter to be subjected to that at school."

HS   J. D. Salinger. *Catcher in the Rye.* Not proper for teenagers, dirty words, writing and talk, profanity and sex. Book is shocking. Too sophisticated, gross, shocking vulgarity in profusion, bad language, lack of plot. Language.

MS   Bernard Evslin. *Cerberus.* (Monsters of Mythology series) "Call Hades Lord." "Titles of Chapters 7, 39, 43, 63, 71, and 77." Illustrations.

HS   Robert Cormier. *The Chocolate War.* Pervasive vulgarity. "Humanistic and destructive of religious and moral beliefs and of national spirit." "Ultimately failed

---

Figure 13. List of Challenged Materials and Typical Objections[17, 18]

118   Staff Development and Workshop Initiatives

because of the pessimistic ending." The novel fostered negative impressions of authority, of school systems and of religious schools.

HS   Alice Walker. *The Color Purple.* Inappropriate portrayal of religion, sexually explicit and excessive violence. "Sexual and social explicitness" and its "troubling ideas about race relations, man's relationship to God, African history and human sexuality." The school principal felt "it might incite rape."

HS   Arthur Miller. *The Crucible.* Language throughout book, no historical benefit. Objected that *The Crucible* taught witchcraft. Morally corrupting child, Satan figures in the plot.

ES   Michael Willhoite. *Daddy's Roommate.* Depiction of homosexuality as a positive lifestyle.

MS   Robert Newton Peck. *A Day No Pigs Would Die.* Language. "It is bigoted against Baptists and women and depicts violence, hatred, animal cruelty, and murder." "Derogatory references to Baptists."

MS   Natalie Babbitt. *The Devil's Storybook.* "Children should not read stories about the Devil other than in the Bible."

MS   Ann Frank. *Diary of a Young Girl.* E. Roosevelt's prejudiced introduction. Objected to the discussion of the mistreatment of the Jewish people. Sex.

MS   Julia Cunningham. *Drop Dead.* Would frighten children.

HS   Bernard Malamud. *The Fixer.* Vivid grossness of scenes of immature juniors and seniors, the end of chapter 8, "she stood naked." Language.

HS   Daniel Keyes. *Flowers for Algernon.* Subject matter related to sex. Included profanity and explict sex acts.

ES   Leslea Newman. *Gloria Goes to Gay Pride.* Depiction of homosexuality as a positive lifestyle.

HS   *Go Ask Alice.* A filthy book, makes drugs sound exciting. "A true story and very shocking—language not fit for anyone, let alone children—should be banned and destroyed."

HS   John Steinbeck. *Grapes of Wrath.* Vulgarity. Objectionable language and sexual activity, against church beliefs. Profanity. Demeaning to Southerners.

HS   Charles Dickens. *Great Expectations.* Theme of the book was objectionable.

MS   Katherine Paterson. *The Great Gilly Hopkins.* "I do not see the need for fifth graders to read materials with words such as 'hell' and 'damn' scattered through it." "Over forty instances of profanity."

HS   Robert Graves. *Greeks, Gods, and Heroes.* Language too graphic.

HS   Rumer Godden. *Greengage Summer.* People in picture not decently dressed.

HS   John Gardner. *Grendel.* Language.

ES   Eve Merriam. *Halloween ABC.* Illus. by Lane Smith. "The consensus of opinion was that the book's general content as well as the illustrations reflect an offensive, evil, satanic theme which is inappropriate for younger age children."

HS   William Shakespeare. *Hamlet.* Language and immorality.

ES   Leslea Newman. *Heather Has Two Mommies.* Depiction of lesbian household as a positive lifestyle.

Figure 13—*Continued*

MS John Bellairs. *The House with a Clock in Its Walls.* It could encourage a student's interest in the occult.

ES Thomas Rockwell. *How to Eat Fried Worms.* Cruelty to animals.

HS Langston Hughes. *Works of Langston Hughes.* Hughes had communist front connections; was a "willing tool of this intellectual conspiracy to destroy us."

HS Maya Angelou. *I Know Why the Caged Bird Sings.* A form of pornography, disturbing mind implants. Sex—unfit for high school use, graphic description of young girl raped by her stepfather and of one other sexual encounter.

ES Maurice Sendak. *In the Night Kitchen.* Nudity.

ES Margot Zemach. *Jake and Honeybunch Go to Heaven.* Stereotypes African-Americans. Makes fun of God and Heaven.

HS Lois Duncan. *Killing Mr. Griffin.* Advocates killing a teacher. Language.

HS Ursula Le Guin. *Lathe of Heaven.* "Advocacy of Non-Christian religions," profanity, poor sentence structure.

HS Shirley Jackson. *The Lottery.* Violence. Objected on religious grounds, it was paganistic in their viewpoint. "Includes obscene language, and promoted the occult, devil worship and secular humanism."

HS Eli Wiesel. *Night.* One passage had a man's hand on a woman's breast.

HS John Steinbeck. *Of Mice and Men.* Rough language, too depressing, sexual activity, against church beliefs. Took the name of the Lord in vain. Profanity. Language.

HS T. H. White. *The Once and Future King.* Objected to the relationship between Lancelot and Guinevere.

HS William Shakespeare. *Othello.* Sex.

HS Judith Guest. *Ordinary People.* The book is morally bad, it contains profanity, sexual innuendos and takes the name of the Lord in vain.

MS S. E. Hinton. *The Outsiders.* "Too much violence."

HS Stephen Crane. *The Red Badge of Courage.* Profane language.

HS Howard Pyle. *Robin Hood.* Robin and his "merry men" were following the "straight communist line" while dashing through Sherwood Forest.

HS Nathaniel Hawthorne. *The Scarlet Letter.* Involvement of clergy in fornication—"degrades Christian ministry as a whole." Adultery. Too frank and revealing.

ES *The Three Billy Goats Gruff.* It was "too violent for children."

HS Harper Lee. *To Kill a Mockingbird.* Immoral, obscene trash, unsuitable, rape scene, indecent, vulgar.

ES AnnaLena McAfee and Anthony Browne. *The Visitors Who Came to Stay.* Shows unmarried couple living together. Many sexual images in illustrations.

ES Sharmot. *Who's Afraid of Ernestine?* "I find this content [page on vampires] inappropriate. I think the innocence should be preserved in our youth."

MS Roald Dahl. *The Witches.* Satanic, occult and new age content.

MS Madeleine L'Engle. *Wrinkle in Time.* No clear distinction between good and evil. Linking the name of Jesus Christ with artists and leaders.

MS Marjorie Rawlings. *The Yearling.* Unsuitable language.

Workshop on Versions and Variants of Traditional Literature

Both literary and cultural studies might be enhanced by an examination of multiple versions and variants of a particular folk or fairy tale. Such a study is also fascinating to most young people who may be familiar with only one interpretation and set of illustrations for a story such as *The Crane Wife*, which comes from a very different cultural tradition (see List 24). An alternative tale, one that students are likely to be much more familiar with, is *Beauty and the Beast* (see List 25). This is an especially good example because there are so many versions appealing to a range of age or grade levels and so many different interpretations over time. Some of the titles included in the *Beauty and the Beast* list are adult versions, and teachers will need to examine these to determine their appropriateness for the particular audience and teaching or learning activity. An essential reading for teachers is Betsy Hearne's study of *Beauty and the Beast* in which she offers example after example of how this tale has been interpreted in different times and places. Students might begin such a study by comparing and contrasting one of the earliest versions of this traditional tale with the well-known Disney version and then with Nancy Willard's story with Barry Moser's illustrations set in New York's Hudson Valley. Of course, the various videos of *Beauty and the Beast* add another fascinating dimension to the study of this tale.

An alternative approach, especially for older children, might be to explore how an individual interpreter of folktales deals with the differences among tales and legends of various peoples. Does a compiler or interpreter inevitably inject some of his or her own personality into the tales and thus render them less authentic? For this investigation, use the books by Lattimore in List 26.

Participants may also find it helpful to see the video about Paul Yee (Videocassette. Color, 15 minutes. School Services of Canada) and examine his *Tales from Gold Mountain: Stories of the Chinese in the New World* (Illus. by Simon Ng. New York: Macmillan, 1989) and *The Curses of Third Uncle* (Toronto: James Lorimer, 1986) as a way to focus on the use of historic documents as a portion of the folklore and ethnicity of a people.

Traditional literature presents an excellent opportunity to introduce ideas of similarities and differences among peoples in multicultural studies or global education. Participants will be encouraged:

> To use a particular genre as a means of increasing aesthetic response and of fostering thinking skills;
> To increase the multicultural literacy of children;
> To foster an appreciation of the diversity of folklore as it moves through time and across cultural lines.

Using "Thinking About Folklore: Lessons for Grades K–4," by Carole Slattery *(Journal of Youth Services in Libraries* 4, no. 3 [Spring 1991]: 249–58); "Introduction," by Kay E. Vandergrift in *The Unreluctant Years: A Critical Approach to*

Children's Literature by Lillian Smith (Chicago: American Library Association, 1991, vii-xxix); and Betsy Hearne's two-part article "Respect the Source" (*School Library Journal* 39, nos. 7–8 [July–August, 1993]: 22–27, 33–37) as the basic readings, consider the following questions:

> In what ways might the study of versions and variants of a folktale help students to develop critical thinking skills?
> How do differing versions of the same tale lend themselves to increasing students' abilities to see nuances contained in alternative interpretations?
> How are the cultural context, the place of origin, and characteristics of particular peoples revealed in the telling of the tale?
> Does the clarity of language in folktales increase students' sensitivity to language and their ability to use it effectively and affectively?

List 24. Selected Versions of *The Crane Wife* and Related Tales

Bang, Molly. *Dawn*. New York: Morrow, 1983.
Bang, Molly. *The Paper Crane*. New York: Greenwillow, 1985.
Bartoli, Jennifer. *The Story of the Grateful Crane*. Illus. by Kozo Shimizu. Chicago: Albert Whitman, 1977.
Coerr, Eleanor. *Sadako and the Thousand Paper Cranes*. Illus. by Ronald Himler. New York: G. P. Putnam's Sons, 1977.
Ginsburg, Mirra. "The Crane's Feather." In *The Master of the Winds and Other Tales from Siberia*. New York: Crown, 1970.
Laurin, Anne. *Perfect Crane*. Illus. by Charles Mikolaycak. New York: Harper & Row, 1981.
Morimoto, Junko. *The White Crane*. Sydney, Australia: Collins, 1983.
Pratt, Davis, and Elsa Kula. "The Crane Wife." In *Magic Animals of Japan*. Berkeley, Calif.: Parnassus, 1967.
Uchida, Yoshiko. "The Princess and the Fisherman." In *The Dancing Kettle and Other Japanese Folk Tales*. New York: Harcourt, Brace & World, 1949.
Wolkstein, Diane. *White Wave: A Chinese Tale*. Illus. by Ed Young. New York: Thomas Y. Crowell, 1979.
Yagawa, Sumiko. *The Crane Wife*. Trans. by Katherine Paterson. Illus. by Suekichi Akaba. New York: Morrow, 1981.
Yamaguchi, Tohr. *The Golden Crane: A Japanese Folktale*. Illus. by Marianne Yamaguchi. New York: Henry Holt, 1963.

Given the ideas suggested by Slattery, Hearne and Vandergrift, how might this exercise be used in the curriculum and who would teach which portions? What elements of the story remain constant in all versions? What elements change? What do illustrations, if any, convey about the culture of the story's origin? To what extent is memory an important element in the exploration of folktales? Which versions would be most appropriate for younger children? For older readers?

List 25. Selected Versions of *Beauty and the Beast*

BOOKS

Brett, Jan. *Beauty and the Beast*. New York: Clarion, 1989.

Brown, Kay. *Beauty and the Beast*. Illus. by Gerry Embleton. New York: Derrydale, 1978.

Collection, Madame D'Aulnoy. *Beauty and the Beast*. Illus. by Etienne Delessert. Mankato, Minn.: Creative Education, 1984.

Crane, Walter. *Beauty and the Beast and Other Tales*. London: Thames and Hudson and the Metropolitan Museum of Art, 1982. (Reproduction)

Crump, Fred Jr. *Beauty and the Beast*. Nashville, Tenn.: Winston-Derek, 1992.

deBeaumont, Marie Leprince. *Beauty and the Beast*. Trans. by Richard Howard. Illus. by Hilary Knight. Afterword by Jean Cocteau. New York: Simon & Schuster, 1990.

Disney's Beauty and the Beast. Illus. by Ron Dias. Adapted from the film by A. L. Singer. New York: Disney, 1991.

Edens, Cooper. *Beauty and the Beast*. San Diego, Calif.: Green Tiger, 1989. (Illustrations selected and arranged by Cooper Edens from the Green Tiger's collection of old children's books.)

Fast, Jonathan. *The Beast*. New York: Random House, 1981.

Fleischman, Paul. *Shadow Play*. Illus. by Eric Beddows. New York: Harper & Row, 1990.

Gerstein, Mordicai. *Beauty and the Beast*. New York: Dutton, 1989.

Hambly, Barbara. *Beauty and the Beast*. Based on the series created by Ron Koslow. New York: Avon, 1989.

Harris, Rosemary. *Beauty and the Beast*. Illus. by Errol Le Cain. London: Faber & Faber, 1979.

Hayes, Sarah. *Beauty and the Beast*. Illus. by David Scott. New York: Derrydale, 1985.

Hearne, Betsy. *Beauty and the Beast: Visions and Revisions of an Old Tale*. Chicago: University of Chicago, 1989.

McKinley, Robin. *Beauty: A Retelling of the Story of Beauty and the Beast*. New York: Harper & Row, 1978.

Mayer, Marianna. *Beauty and the Beast*. Illus. by Mercer Mayer. New York: Four Winds, 1978.

Pearce, Philippa. *Beauty and the Beast*. Illus. by Alan Barrett. New York: Thomas Y. Crowell, 1972.

Perrault, Charles. *Beauty and the Beast*. Illus. by Charles Moore. New York: Rizzoli, 1991.

Pini, Wendy. *Beauty and the Beast: Night of Beauty*. Based on the series created by Ron Koslow. Chicago: First Pub IL, 1990.

Southgate, Vera. *Beauty and the Beast*. Illus. by Robert Ayton. Moughborough, England: Ladybird, 1980.

Tepper, Sheri S. *Beauty*. New York: Doubleday, 1991.

Willard, Nancy. *Beauty and the Beast.* Illus. by Barry Moser. San Diego, Calif.: Harcourt Brace Jovanovich, 1992.

VIDEOS

Beauty and the Beast. Color, 100 minutes. Republic Pictures Home Video, 1988. (Made up of "Once Upon a Time in the City of New York" and "A Happy Life")
Beauty and the Beast. Color, 100 minutes. Republic Pictures Home Video, 1989. (Made up of "To Reign in Hell" and "Orphans")
Faerie Tale Theatre Beauty and the Beast. Color, 50 minutes. Playhouse Video, 1987.
Jean Cocteau's Beauty and the Beast. B/W, 90 minutes. Embassy Home Entertainment, 1985.
Walt Disney Classic Beauty and the Beast. Color, 84 minutes. Walt Disney Home Video, 1992.

List 26. Selected Titles by Deborah Nourse Lattimore

The Dragon's Robe. New York: Harper & Row, 1990.
The Flame of Peace: A Tale of the Aztecs. New York: Harper & Row, 1987.
The Prince and the Golden Ax: A Minoan Tale. New York: Harper & Row, 1988.
Punga: The Goddess of Ugly. San Diego, Calif.: Harcourt Brace, 1993.
The Sailor Who Captured the Sea: A Story of the Book of Kells. New York: HarperCollins, 1991.
Why There Is No Arguing in Heaven: A Mayan Myth. New York: Harper & Row, 1989.
The Winged Cat: A Tale of Ancient Egypt. New York: HarperCollins, 1992.

Workshop on Authentic Female Voices

It is essential to provide young people, both male and female, with authentic female voices writing about their lives and their cultures, especially in light of the research on gender bias reported by the AAUW and referred to in chapter 1. The responsibility to seek out information about feminist scholarship and feminist literary criticism (see List 27) is critical to those in schooling who care about presenting young scholars with the full range of human experiences. The books in List 28 are selected because they represent distinct female voices. The titles in the first list are primarily professional readings, although some of these works are accessible to and of interest to secondary school students. Some of the books in the second list are adult titles popular with young adults, which, because of their mature themes, may be considered inappropriate in some schools and, therefore, need to be examined from that perspective. Others are picture books enjoyed by young children but that could also be included in a more formal study of female voices with older readers. Although these materials were selected to sample the narratives of various cultures and literary genres as well as age or grade levels, one might focus on one specific aspect of female narratives such as voices of Native American women or African-American slave narratives to extend student understandings of a "particular period in American history."

List 27. Feminist Theory

Altmann, Anna E. "Welding Brass Tits on the Armor: An Examination of the Quest of Metaphor in Robin McKinley's *The Hero and the Crown.*" *Children's Literature in Education* 23, no. 3 (September 1992): 143–56.

Between Women: Biographers, Novelists, Critics, Teachers and Artists Write about Their Work on Women. Ed. by Carol Ascher, Louise DeSalvo and Sara Ruddick. Boston: Beacon, 1984.

Brown, Lyn Mikel, and Carol Gilligan. *Meeting at the Crossroads.* Cambridge: Harvard University, 1992.

Christian, Barbara. *Black Feminist Criticism: Perspectives on Black Women Writers.* New York: Pergamon, 1985.

Double Stitch: *Black Women Write about Mothers and Daughters.* Ed. by Patricia Bell-Scott. Boston: Beacon, 1991.

Gender in the Classroom: Power and Pedagogy. Ed. by Susan L. Gabriel and Isaiah Smithson. Urbana, Ill.: University of Illinois, 1990.

Gilligan, Carol. *In a Different Voice: Psychological Theory and Women's Development.* Cambridge: Harvard University, 1982.

Hancock, Emily. *The Girl Within.* New York: Dutton, 1989.

Heilbrun, Carolyn G. *Reinventing Womanhood.* New York: Norton, 1979.

Heilbrun, Carolyn G. *Writing a Woman's Life.* New York: Norton, 1988.

McRobbie, Angela. *Feminism and Youth Culture: From Jackie to Just Seventeen.* Boston: Unwin Hyman, 1991.

Making Connections. Ed. by Carol Gilligan, Nona P. Lyons and Trudy J. Hanmer. Cambridge: Harvard University, 1990.

Many Women's Voices. Comp. by Susan Altan. Boston: NAIS Council for Women in Independent Schools, 1992.

Showalter, Elaine. *A Literature of Their Own: British Women Novelists from Bronte to Lessing.* Princeton, N.J.: Princeton University, 1976.

White, Barbara A. *Growing Up Female: Adolescent Girlhood in American Fiction.* Westport, Conn.: Greenwood, 1985.

List 28. Female Voices in Fiction, Biography, and Poetry

Angelou, Maya. *I Know Why the Caged Bird Sings.* New York: Bantam, 1970.

Atwood, Margaret. *The Handmaid's Tale.* Boston: Houghton Mifflin, 1986.

Avi. *The True Confessions of Charlotte Doyle.* New York: Orchard, 1990.

Brent, Linda. *Incidents in the Life of a Slave Girl: An Authentic Historical Narrative Describing the Horrors of Slavery as Experienced by Black Women.* New York: Harcourt Brace Jovanovich, 1973.

Caines, Jeannette. *Just Us Women.* Illus. by Pat Cummings. New York: Harper & Row, 1982.
Carter, Dorothy Sharp. *His Majesty, Queen Hatshepsut.* Illus. by Michelle Chessare. New York: Harper & Row, 1987.
Dickinson, Emily. *The Complete Poems of Emily Dickinson.* Boston: Little, Brown, 1955.
Erdrich, Louise. *The Beet Queen.* New York: Henry Holt, 1986.
Erdrich, Louise. *Love Medicine.* New York: Henry Holt, 1984.
Erdrich, Louise. *Tracks.* New York: Henry Holt, 1988.
Giovanni, Nikki. *Gemini: An Extended Autobiography on My First 25 Years of Being a Black Poet.* Indianapolis: Bobbs-Merrill, 1976.
Greenfield, Eloise. *Mary McLeod Bethune.* Illus. by Jerry Pinkney. New York: Harper & Row, 1977.
Greenfield, Eloise. *Rosa Parks.* Illus. by Eric Marlow. New York: Harper & Row, 1973.
Greenfield, Eloise. *Sister.* Illus. by Moneta Barnett. New York: Harper & Row, 1974.
Hautzig, Esther. *The Endless Steppe: Growing Up in Siberia.* New York: Harper & Row, 1968.
Hendry, Frances Mary. *Quest for a Maid.* New York: Farrar, Straus & Giroux, 1990.
Hurston, Zora Neal. *Their Eyes Were Watching God.* Illus. by Jerry Pinkney. Foreword by Ruby Dee. Urbana, Ill.: University of Illinois, 1991.
I Dream a World: Portraits of Black Women Who Changed America. Ed. by Brian Lanker. New York: Stewart Tabori and Chang, 1989.
Johnston, Norma. *Louisa May: The World and Works of Louisa May Alcott.* New York: Four Winds, 1991.
Lee, Tanith. *Black Unicorn.* New York: Atheneum, 1991.
LeGuin, Ursula. *Tehanu: The Last Book of Earthsea.* New York: Atheneum, 1990.
LeGuin, Ursula. *The Tombs of Atuan.* New York: Atheneum, 1971.
Lyons, Mary E. *Letters from a Slave Girl: The Story of Harriet Jacobs.* New York: Scribners, 1992.
McKinley, Robin. *The Hero and the Crown.* New York: Greenwillow, 1985.
Mori, Kyoko. *Shizuko's Daughter.* New-York: Henry Holt, 1993.
Morrison, Toni. *Tar Baby.* New York: Alfred Knopf, 1981.
Paterson, Katherine. *Lyddie.* New York: Lodestar, 1991.
Rodowsky, Colby. *Julie's Daughter.* New York: Farrar, Straus & Giroux, 1985.
Sills, Leslie. *Inspirations: Stories about Women Artists.* New York: Albert Whitman, 1989.
Staples, Suzanne Fisher. *Shabanu: Daughter of the Wind.* New York: Alfred Knopf, 1989.
Voigt, Cynthia. *Dicey's Song.* New York: Atheneum, 1982.
Walker, Alice. *The Color Purple.* New York: Harcourt Brace Jovanovich, 1982.
Walsh, Jill Paton. *Grace.* New York: Farrar Straus & Giroux, 1991.

Williams-Garcia, Rita. *Blue Tights*. New York: Dutton/Loadstar, 1988.
Woolf, Virginia. *A Room of One's Own*. New York: Harcourt Brace, 1929.
Yolen, Jane. *Briar Rose*. New York: T. Doherty Associates, 1992.

Working with Parents and Caregivers

In addition to more formal in-service workshops such as the above (which might be adapted for another audience) and the many opportunities for informal staff development with teachers, library media specialists also work with parents and caregivers when appropriate. Homework is one area in which many parents, and our colleagues in the public library, would appreciate some help. Most parents care about their children's education and want them to do well in school. Too often this concern turns into a battle over homework, and parents either give up or give in and do some of the homework for their children. Watching parents do their children's homework is a major cause of distress among youth professionals in the public library, but they often feel that they have no right to question users in respect to school activities. If we assume that parents have students' best interests in mind when they do the research or even write a report for a busy student, what they may need most is some help in knowing what is really in the young person's best interest.

Workshops or publications suggesting appropriate ways to assist with homework might encourage parents to raise questions with students, helping their children to clarify assignments and determine both what they already know and what they need to find out. A parent might begin with those basic journalistic questions, "Who, What, Where, When, Why, and How?" Adults can also help students see relationships and recognize comparison and contrast, cause and effect, and the like as means of organizing and presenting information. Any reliable source on critical thinking, information skills, or the research process can help, but the best support parents can give children is shared time to think together about problems, tasks, responses, and responsibilities. Specific suggestions to parents on how to use the "homework problem" to get in touch with and encourage their children academically might be the focus of a workshop. A pamphlet on this topic could be distributed at these workshops, Parent Teachers Association meetings, school visits, the public library, or sent home with students' report cards. Pamphlets take a great deal of time and effort if they are to be informative and effective, but an investment for topics such as this are likely to save time and frustration over the course of a school year.[19] In addition to such a pamphlet, school library media specialists, perhaps in cooperation with public librarians, could offer an evening workshop for parents or parents and students on this topic.

Another area in which school library media specialists might initiate teaching activities with parents and caregivers is that of family or intergenerational literacy.[20] Such programs are particularly appropriate for cooperative ventures with other school personnel, with our colleagues in the public library, and with other community agencies concerned with literacy. Our expertise in selecting materials and sharing them with young people is precisely what is needed to help parents develop their skills as models of reading behaviors for their children. Our knowledge of child development and the school curriculum enables us to suggest language development and pre-reading activities that will lead to reading-writing activities in the home. Too often school library media specialists do not initiate contacts with the parents and care givers of their students and thus miss opportunities to reach those who ultimately have the greatest influence on the learning behaviors of young people.

Conclusion

Changes in educational thought or priorities naturally lead to new opportunities for in-service education. Teachers need help in keeping up with the massive influx of materials about these changes, and certainly they need help in interpreting them in ways that will inform and improve their own practice of teaching. The library media specialist can not only collect, sort, and provide abstracts of these materials but can organize workshops or informal discussion sessions to help transform theory to practice. For instance, workshops on topics such as "Organizing Classrooms for Independent Learning," "Discipline in the Whole Language Environment," or "Evaluating Student and Teacher Portfolios as an Assessment Technique" might be appropriate in a school attempting to move from a textbook-and-teacher-centered program to more open student-centered learning. These cooperative learning ventures can be a part of an attitude of "reflection-in-action" in which all members of the teaching team use a kind of improvisation, sharing ideas and coaching each other in an attempt to solve real-life teaching and learning problems.[21]

Too often, however, we have looked at staff development and in-service education as if they were only special means of helping teachers add new competencies to their teaching repertoires. It is equally important, perhaps more so, for teachers to examine their existing skills and reconsider old ideas, practices, and materials in order to improve their work with and for children. The library media specialist who is perceived as a strong, insightful, and yet nonthreatening leader of teachers in a school can help to bring the whole faculty together in a cooperative learning team that will enhance the capabilities, the competence, and the concerns of all. The library media center can be the focal point for the development of that kind of shared vision of what education and teaching might be—a vision that makes a school a pleasant and a profitable place for both students and teachers to learn and grow in their understanding and appreciation of the world.

7

Evaluation and the School Library Media Specialist

Evaluation is, in a very real sense, the beginning as well as the end of most human endeavor. Schooling originates with the question What do we value? It is in the answers to this question that the work of library media specialists and other teachers takes root. In fact, the very act of teaching is one of evaluation, that is, the process of attributing value to our subject matter and to our students. As teachers we seek and point out to students the best in that subject matter and in themselves so that they might perceive the whole process of education as an ongoing search for excellence.

In the history of education, however, evaluation has more often been used as a means of selection or exclusion than as an aid to personal or curricular development. Tests of student achievements have frequently been interpreted as measures of student worth and have been used to grant or deny access to further schooling. Even when they have not controlled access to formal education, tests have been used to sort students into various programs or tracks that may become inescapable paths to a particular kind or level of schooling. Unfortunately, such sorting also carries with it a labeling of personal potential, often based on inaccurate or inadequate evidence.

There are at least two major barriers to sound evaluation of school library media programs and services. First is the confusion between evaluation and assessment.[1] Assessment, the process of gathering data (usually quantitative data based on testing, to be used for evaluative purposes), is too often substituted for evaluation itself. When this occurs, the locus of value may be lost because assessment tests may not target those aspects of the program most valued by either teachers or students, and because all data must be interpreted within a particular context to be useful as evaluation. Second, the most important and most valued results of our work in school library media centers do not necessarily reveal themselves fully in the time and space we share with students. If one of our major goals is to encourage lifelong learning and lifelong reading, we must acknowledge that standard evaluative techniques administered at the end of a particular time period or sequence of activities will not necessarily indicate progress toward that goal.

Types of Evaluation

There are many types of evaluation and techniques for its accomplishment. Major distinctions are made between quantitative and qualitative measures, that is, between "hard" numerical data and "soft" narrative, anecdotal, or observational means of evaluation. Quantitative data are often studied and manipulated in the abstract and at some distance from actual learners. Qualitative data depend upon perspective and context and are ordinarily done in proximity to, or even in collaboration with, the person being evaluated. Good teachers have always relied heavily on "soft" evidence and personal judgment in making decisions about individual students and classroom activities. Those at the school, state, or national level do not normally possess the same kind of personal or observational information about students, nor would they be able to deal with the volume of such evidence or be familiar enough with the persons or the contexts to evaluate it. Thus, they rely on more distanced numerical data in their decision making. Although standardized numerical data have a place in evaluation, it is teachers who can make the best decisions about their students and classroom or library media center programs, and they must be empowered to do so. This is especially true considering the evidence that standardized tests are filled with biases of race, gender, social class, culture, ethnicity, and even of geography and specific school curriculum.

Educators also make distinctions among diagnostic, formative, and summative evaluations. Diagnostic evaluations are used prior to instruction to determine skill levels, prior knowledge, learning characteristics, or learning difficulties in order to place students in appropriate educational situations. Formative evaluation takes place during instruction to provide feedback to both teacher and students and to adjust learning environments to improve performance. Summative evaluation occurs at the end of a unit of work or a particular time period and most often results in some type of certification or grading of student achievement. At each of these stages of evaluation, both quantitative and qualitative measures may be used.

It may also be useful to think of evaluation as being programmatic, instructional, or personal; that is, focusing on overall programs, on specific instructional units, or on persons. In practice, these forms of evaluation usually correspond to a focus on states, districts, or schools (programmatic), on classroom or library media center activities (instructional), or on students or teachers (personal). Each of these is important, but it is in the balancing of the three that the best evaluation takes place. The important thing is to match the type of evaluation and the specific techniques used with the intent of education providers and of those being evaluated, thereby focusing the evaluative instruments on the appropriate element or elements of schooling.[2]

Standards for school library media centers have probably been the most influential forces in attempting to determine the overall value of all components of a library media center's contributions to the education of students. They have been especially useful in relation to input measures or measures of the resources allocated to library media center facilities and programs. Standards are also useful for diagnostic planning, encouraging professionals to consider possibilities and to set priorities. Questions that emerge in reading *Information Power: Guidelines for School Library Media Programs* are helpful to library media specialists in weighing their own values, considering various alternatives, setting priorities, establishing goals and objectives, and evaluating their work.[3] AASL has also published a checklist to evaluate school library media programs in relation to current guidelines.[4] Some states have used the guidelines from *Information Power* to develop their own assessment instruments to evaluate school library media programs.[5] Ultimately it is the output of our programs and services that must be evaluated; such instruments, in correlation with the judgments of practicing professionals, may be the basis for that evaluation.

Project TAP

Project TAP (Time Allocation and Priorities) is a survey instrument based, to a large extent, on the content and language of *Information Power* (see the Appendix). In this instance, two library educators developed the instrument in an attempt to capture an overall picture of the activities and attitudes of school library media specialists in New Jersey. It originated with concerns about the direction school library media services are moving in this state—in fact, in the whole nation. Discussions with colleagues, observations of school library media centers, and readings of professional literature all seemed consistent in the placement of managerial aspects of our profession and a rather narrow view of instruction in information skills in priority positions. Responses to the publication of *Information Power* seemed to confirm these driving forces for school library media specialists.

As with any investigation, this study was rooted in the values of the investigators. Although we certainly value good management, information skills, the research process, and the integration of all media, we focused, in this study, on our concern that the sharing and teaching of literature, long a strength of the profession, was being gradually eroded in an emphasis on research skills and library media center management. We had noted with increasing alarm that less and less attention is paid to the aesthetic appreciation of books and reading in school library media centers. In a time when literacy is in a critical state in this country, school library media specialists, the very people who should be assuming a major role, seem to be abdicating their responsibilities in this area. In addition, educators, including library media specialists, seem to have lost sight of the fact that, although decoding skills are a necessary component of schooling, it too frequently happens that, in the process of learning those decoding skills, young people lose sight of the joys of reading. Emphasis throughout schooling is placed on skills and on information comprehension, not on the wonders of language, the joys of experiencing fine literature, and the challenge of an intellectually and aesthetically stimulating idea. The transaction between literary text and reader opens new worlds for children, enabling them to confirm, extend, and illuminate their own life experiences while appreciating those of others. The whole language movement has become increasingly important in schools and should naturally lead to a greater emphasis on reading on the part of students. Unfortunately this does not automatically follow.

In spite of this renewed emphasis on literature in whole language programs, it appears that many school library media specialists do not see a role for themselves in sharing and discussing books and other media. Increasingly they are willing to sacrifice their work with literature in favor of managerial duties and instruction in information skills or the research process. Even those who emphasize the critical thinking process over specific information skills do not seem to acknowledge that aesthetic content is as rich a stimulus to thought as is scientific or informational content. In fact, ideas fired with aesthetic feeling lead to the most critical and involved thought. Thus, we set out to identify the practices and the specific priorities and time allocations of professional school library media specialists through this investigation.

With these concerns in mind, we devised a number of research questions:

Is teaching and sharing literature a higher priority with elementary school library media specialists than with those in secondary schools?

Are library media specialists driven by what might be labeled a management model?

Does the library media specialist concentrate on those aspects of management that are identified by *Information Power* ?

What specific priority does the library media specialist give to the sharing and the discussion of literature?

Although we did have additional research hypotheses, these questions dominated our investigation. Much of the language in the instrument was based on *Information Power* and was used with permission of the American Library Association. We added those questions that addressed reading and literary activities as well as questions that examined in some detail the teaching role of the library media specialist. Since the specific use of technology was of interest to the investigators, we used one of the questions from the study designed by Marilyn Miller.[6] We also raised questions about the extent of networking and cooperative ventures among school library media specialists. The instrument of the study was piloted and corrections were made to address problems in design. The response rate was low, perhaps due to the length and complexity of the instrument and the time of distribution (shortly before the holidays), but the majority of those who did respond confirmed that many library media specialists in New Jersey do not believe that literary activities are a part of their responsibility, even in the lower grades, and that many schools lack basic technological and media resources for student use.

The instrument itself is included in the Appendix as an example that might be used or modified either by an individual library media specialist for programmatic evaluation or by a district or cluster of districts to assess the state of the program and the priorities (often subconscious values) that influence what we do as school library media specialists.

Much simpler evaluative tools are useful to focus on particular aspects of the school library media program. The paired self-evaluation inventories in figure 14 were developed by this author for use in the examination of school and public library cooperation. Used in a workshop, they challenge youth specialists in both institutions to examine their own practices, begin a dialogue, and go beyond the suggestions contained in these documents to explore alternatives for cooperative ventures to better serve our shared clientele.

These examples are very different types of evaluation, but both are instruments to help professionals think about and evaluate their work outside of the immediacy of that work. Like all such instruments they are subject to the dangers of one's perceptions and misperceptions of one's own work. Sometimes respondents record what they intend to do or wish to do in a situation rather than what actually happens, or they may attempt to answer in a way that will provide the responses they assume the investigators wish to receive.

The majority of the established means of evaluation in schools, however, focus on the modes of and the results of specific teaching and learning activities in classrooms. In an age of accountability many tools have been designed to measure the specific results of the work of students and teachers.[7] Most commonly this type of assessment consists of teacher-effectiveness studies, teacher-made tests, standardized tests, and the reporting of student scores as indicative of teacher, school, or district success in specific learning activities. Unfortunately, our concentration on these types of evaluation too often conveys the impression that it is only those things that are measurable that we value. It is also true that much instructional evaluation comes too late to be of any real assistance to students or teachers.

Workshops such as those discussed in chapter 6 are important in helping faculty prepare for teaching, but school library media specialists also use them as a natural means to assist in staff development at the postactive stage, of the educational design process. During these workshops the library media specialist can suggest a number of opportunities for teachers to evaluate their work with students. While helping another teacher in program planning or the selection of materials, specific teaching concerns or classroom problems will be discussed. In such instances library media specialists can often do more than just offer a friendly ear and supportive response; they can provide the means for teachers to investigate their own teaching in a nonthreatening way. The specific means to this investigation will depend primarily on the interests and concerns of the teacher and, secondarily, on the resources available in the school. Such encounters also depend, of course, on the presence of trust and mutual respect for each other as teachers.

Evaluation of Teaching

There are many ways to examine one's own work as a teacher and many people who might be involved. It is nearly impossible for teachers not to evaluate their work, in some way, as it is happening. Our own feelings about what we do and the

SCHOOL LIBRARY MEDIA SPECIALIST

1. Do you know the names and phone numbers of the director and the youth services personnel in your local public library?
2. Have you made every effort to inform the public library about the school curriculum and assignments and to inform students and teachers about programs and activities of the public library?
    - Requested information from the public library?
    - Requested information from classroom teachers to be shared with the public librarian?
    - Devised simple but informative questionnaires to keep yourself and public library personnel abreast of topics and assignments?
    - Arranged specific times and procedures for sharing such information with public librarians?
    - Requested time to meet with youth services specialists in the public library?
    - Asked to be included on the distribution list of newsletters and other public library publications?
    - Attended Friends of the Library meetings to inform yourself about the public library and offer your support?
    - Requested reference copies of textbooks to be placed in the public library for assistance with homework assignments?
    - Sent lists of new materials prepared for teachers or students to the public library?
3. Have you made every effort to work with public library personnel to assist students?
    - Worked together in goal setting and data collection, recognizing similarities and differences in mission?
    - Offered to help set up curriculum-related collections in the public library?
    - Participated in a joint evaluation of the use of such collections?
    - Informed classroom teachers about student informational needs that can or cannot be met at the public library?
    - Explored the possibility of resource sharing to meet student needs, including the possibility of school library media center loans to the public library, especially during school vacations?
    - Invited public library personnel to the school library media center to observe and discuss resources and services?
    - Worked with the public library to establish a "Homework Helper" program?
    - Established an efficient document delivery system between schools and the public library?
4. Have you informed the public library about potential changes in the school curriculum and about current topics of discussion such as the Whole Language movement or cultural literacy and the core curriculum?
5. Have you contacted special area teachers (art, music, physical education, etc.) to

Figure 14. Self-Evaluation Inventory: School–Public Library Cooperation

inform them of school and public library resources that might assist them in their work with students?
6. Have you invited youth specialists from the public library to participate in planning sessions in the school?
7. Have you requested an opportunity to join public library youth services specialists in speaking to their library administrators or the library board about the library and information needs of young people?
8. Have you offered to advertise public library programs and services to parents, teachers, and students?
9. Have you offered to share new materials with public library personnel—either in the public library or the school library media center?
10. Have you asked public library youth specialists to participate in cooperative reviewing of materials—and then made every effort to schedule meetings at their convenience?
11. Do you invite public librarians to do booktalks in the school on topics of special interest to teachers and students?
12. Do you keep public library personnel informed about changes in media center policies and procedures, especially about technological changes such as an OPAC?
13. Have you asked public librarians about your students' abilities to use the library and cooperatively planned bibliographic instruction to meet student needs?
14. Do you work with the public library to register students for library cards?
15. Do you work with the public library to enroll students in summer reading programs?
16. Have you planned and participated in cooperative programming with your public library youth services specialists?
17. Do you share professional development opportunities—or at least share transportation to professional meetings?
18. Are you purchasing hardware, particularly computers, that are compatible with those in the public library?
19. Are you at least working toward establishing an electronic network among the schools and the public library (especially e-mail and a union catalog)?

PUBLIC LIBRARY YOUTH SERVICES LIBRARIANS

1. Do you know the names and phone numbers of all the school library media specialists and school principals in your community?
2. Have you made every effort to inform yourself and your colleagues about the school curriculum and student assignments?
   - Requested information from the school library media specialist?
   - Requested information from classroom teachers?
   - Devised simple but informative questionnaires to keep abreast of topics and assignments?

Figure 14—*Continued*

- Arranged specific times and procedures for the collection of the above instruments?
- Requested time to meet with the school library media specialists and teachers in the school building?
- Asked to be included on the distribution list of curriculum bulletins, newsletters, etc.?
- Attended school board and open informational meetings for parents and community about curriculum changes, etc.?
- Requested reference copies of textbooks for the public library?
- Sent lists of new materials to school library media specialists?

3. Have you made every effort to inform school personnel about how the public library can assist them and their students?
   - Worked together in goal setting and data collection, recognizing similarities and differences in mission?
   - Offered to set up curriculum-related collections in the public library?
   - Provided feedback to school personnel on the use of such collections?
   - Informed school personnel about student informational needs that can and cannot be met at the public library?
   - Offered loans of materials to the school library media center or to classrooms?
   - Invited school personnel to the public library to observe and discuss resources and services?
   - Worked with the schools to establish a "Homework Helper" program?
   - Established an efficient document delivery system between schools and the public library?

4. Have you helped to inform parents about the school curriculum, especially about educational change and current topics of discussion such as the Whole Language movement or cultural literacy and the core curriculum?

5. Have you contacted special area teachers (art, music, physical education, etc.) to inform them of library resources that might assist them in their work with students?

6. Have you invited school library media specialists to participate in planning sessions of youth services personnel in the public library?

7. Have you requested invitations to speak at teachers meetings and back-to-school nights or at least prepared materials to be distributed at such meetings?

8. Have you offered to display school-related materials and student work in the public library and then given appropriate publicity to such displays?

9. Have you offered to share new materials with school personnel—either in the public library or the school library media center?

10. Have you asked library media specialists and classroom teachers to participate in cooperative reviewing of materials—and then made every effort to schedule meetings at their convenience?

11. Do you offer to do booktalks in the school on topics of special interest to teachers and students?

12. Do you keep school personnel informed about changes in library policies and procedures, especially about technological changes such as an OPAC?
13. Do you offer bibliographic instruction for students in the public library?
14. Do you work with the schools to register students for public library cards?
15. Do you work with the schools to enroll students in summer reading programs?
16. Have you planned and participated in cooperative programming with school library media specialists?
17. Do you share professional development opportunities—or at least share transportation to professional meetings?
18. Are you purchasing hardware, particularly computers, that are compatible with those in the schools?
19. Are you at least working toward establishing an electronic network between the schools and the public library (especially e-mail and a union catalog)?

Figure 14—*Continued*

responses of students are the most obvious sources of information; it is often this informal feedback that leads us to look more systematically at our work. Probably the easiest and most useful means to getting additional information about our teaching is to gain another perspective by asking another teacher to observe and discuss perceptions of our teaching with us. The more the observer already knows about the teacher's concerns and ways of working with students, the more helpful the observation should be. The library media specialist is often an ideal person to do this because he or she may already know a great deal about what is going on in that classroom, is familiar with the students, and is in a role different enough from that of the classroom teacher not to be viewed as competitive or as a threat. Student observations can also be very valuable, but it is difficult for most teachers to devise a means to enable students to observe accurately and to respond openly and honestly.[8]

Probably the best kind of evaluation is self-evaluation, but the interactive nature of teaching makes it extremely difficult for a teacher to do such evaluation without outside help. Even if a teacher is too timid or threatened to allow another professional to observe, the library media specialist can assist in compiling data for teacher self-analysis through technological means. A wireless microphone worn around a teacher's neck or attached to a shirt or blouse pocket will enable that teacher to record interactions with students and will also pick up many audio clues to what is going on in the classroom. The tape recorder may be placed so it does not become obtrusive in the situation and also to make it obvious that no one else is listening in on the taping. The teacher may then listen to the tape, perhaps using one of the coding systems for the analysis of verbal interactions in the classroom to gain added insights.[9] This kind of activity, at least on a second or third try, should encourage the teacher to involve a trusted colleague, perhaps the library media specialist, in the analysis. Of course, there is always the option of erasing the tape.

Analysis of Verbal Interactions

The analysis of verbal interactions in the classroom was one of the most common forms of evaluation of teaching in the 1960s and 1970s, as educators studied what were considered the most "effective" verbal behaviors of teachers.[10] This type of research has largely been replaced by studies that focus more narrowly on the teaching of specific content or on those that attempt to identify the nature of learning communities.[11] Verbal interaction analysis, however, still reveals a great deal about group relationships and may be an appropriate way to introduce other means of analysis to teachers. Its advantage is that it can be done fairly simply and privately and the results often give teachers a sense that there are specific actions they might take that will improve their performances and perhaps the work of students.

Photo-Analysis of Teaching

Teachers who analyze verbal interactions in the classroom soon realize that some equally important aspects of classroom interaction must be seen rather than heard. A very simple, yet impressive and informative, means to look at teaching is that of photo-analysis. Even shots from a camera worn around the teacher's neck can provide useful information about certain aspects of classroom interaction, organization, and use of facilities. Students may also be encouraged to photograph what they consider to be the most important, the most exciting, or the most disturbing things they see in the classroom at various times. If photo-analysis is to be a really useful tool, an outside photographer, perhaps the library media specialist or a talented student, as well as a systematic plan for taking pictures, will be required. The library media specialist can assist the teacher in formulating such a plan and in deciding what most needs to be observed. A sample plan and the format for preserving and analyzing the photographs are represented by the accompanying diagram in figure 15.

Using this diagram, the photographer and teacher first identify the specific students whose activities are to be followed. Perhaps a teacher might select a so-called model student, one who is sometimes difficult or disruptive, and one somewhere in the middle range. It is also necessary to determine a position or two from which almost all the classroom can be observed in a long-range shot and to decide upon the specific time interval to be used. In a very busy and active open classroom with a great deal of movement, the time interval might be five minutes, while in a more traditionally structured situation, it might be every fifteen or twenty minutes. A time interval as short as five minutes would probably be unwieldy and unproductive to observe for more than an hour at a time; a forty-five minute period seems about right for an initial attempt. If the interval is larger, one might photograph a greater proportion of a teacher's daily work; but the larger the interval, the more that is lost between. Depending upon what one plans to record in the photographs, intervals of no less than five or no more than fifteen minutes

Time Intervals	Teacher	Student A	Student B	Student C	Classroom

Figure 15. Photo-Analysis Diagram

seem to work best. The photographer would normally take a shot of the classroom clock as an additional check on fitting the photographs accurately into the diagram after developing.

Black-and-white snapshots are not only inexpensive, especially in a school that buys bulk film and does its own developing; they are also a very dramatic means of presentation of the data. A sketch of the preceding diagram serves as the shot control for the photographer, and then an enlarged version on a roll of brown paper can be the means of display. Once the photos are mounted appropriately, the teacher can look down a particular column to follow his or her own activity, or that of any of the several students photographed. To see what all four were doing at a particular time, one looks across the chart. The overall classroom shot places the activities and positions of individuals into the larger context. The end product of this photographic activity is not only a revealing tool for the analysis of teaching but also a dramatic display, almost a work of art. An alternative means of presenting this type of material is on slides, which can be projected simultaneously. This may appear to be a much more flashy way of showing others what goes on in the teaching environment, but it is not nearly as satisfactory as an analytical tool for teachers.

The particular framework to be used depends, of course, upon the focus of the analysis. If the teacher is primarily concerned with classroom organization, traffic patterns, and use of facilities, the focus will probably be on certain areas of the room rather than on particular individuals. Many other variations might be devised according to the needs and interests of the participants, and this could prove to be not only an important but a popular analytical tool that, in itself, might encourage teachers to think about alternative ways of viewing their classrooms. Those wishing to determine whether gender bias exists in their classrooms might follow the activities of matched male-female pairs of students or, alternatively, monitor which students select classroom content considered to appeal more to one gender than another.[12]

Video Analysis of Teaching

The use of videotape allows a teacher to analyze teaching activities from a recording containing both sight and sound. The introduction of motion also allows one to follow individuals or teams of learners or to track events as they occur in the teaching environment. Here too, however, the teacher needs to draw up a plan with the camera operator to be sure that the videotape will yield the kind of data needed for analysis. Although it would appear that a videotape is closer to the reality of a situation than either the audio recording or the photo-analysis, this is not necessarily so. The camera operator may pick up only a very atypical aspect of the environment, ignoring that which would be most fruitful to study. It is possible, in a technologically wealthy school, to use several video cameras to capture much the same range of views of the environment as suggested for still photography. It is even possible to view the shots from several cameras simultaneously by splitting the images on the screen. One of the problems of videotaping most teaching and learning environments is sound control and the synchronization of sound with image in a very busy situation. If it is impossible to tape with natural light, or if videotaping would require cords running all over the room for lights and microphones, it is probably best to consider alternative techniques. Of course, if the focus is on teaching behaviors, the teacher can be miked and the camera will follow his or her activities. The analysis, then, allows that teacher to see not only teaching strategies but also patterns of response to student behaviors and the number of contacts with various students. Quite often the intent is to observe and evaluate one's teaching of particular content within an instructional unit.

Discussing the Results of Analysis

If such evaluations are to serve as more than a private mirror on the one hand or an ego trip or public relations stunt on the other, someone must take the lead and set the tone for in-depth analysis. As a knowledgeable participant in all kinds of schooling endeavors and yet one who has no direct supervisory or administrative power over other teachers, the library media specialist is frequently the best candidate for such a task. He or she may enable other teachers to look at their own teaching in these ways, first by modeling the process, then by mentoring, providing support and technical assistance. The very process of determining the technical requirements before taping or filming a teacher in action must begin with some discussion of teaching concerns. As a first step, the library media specialist may stimulate the interest by displaying a large photo-analysis chart of library media center activities in the hall or on a bulletin board. Such displays are usually striking as well as fascinating and will almost always encourage other teachers to ask for help in using the same approach in their classrooms or the gymnasium and sometimes even the principal's office.

This is an opportune time for the library media specialist to get all interested people together, perhaps informally, to discuss the possibilities of such a technique. Having already done a thorough analysis of the library media center photos, the library media specialist can point out some of the things already learned from the display and ask others to comment on what is revealed to them. If the talk is open and free about both positive and negative activities and the library media center environment, using the photo-analysis chart as a referent, others may feel less threatened and see the value of having colleagues discuss their work with them. Library media specialists who are unwilling to open their own work to such discussion have no right asking others to do so. A very important result of this kind of evaluation is the alleviation of teachers' all-too-common feelings of isolation to engage in cooperative research with colleagues.

In discussing any of these technological recordings of teaching, the library media specialist might make available samples of some of the many means that have been devised for instructional evaluation and be prepared to compare and contrast the kinds of information that can be obtained from each. Obviously, if one is interested in an analysis of verbal interactions, probably the most developed area of such study, an audiotape recording is the simplest and most economical means to collect the necessary data. For those who have difficulty analyzing from a tape, a typed transcript is often produced. However, this increases the costs in terms of both time and money, and tonal quality, which may be important for interpretation, is lost. Analysis of a series of photographs may reveal a great deal about classroom organization, the overall social system, patterns of student behavior, the use of facilities, and perhaps even something on management and control. Videotape, of course, provides continuous language and tone along with gesture, facial expression, and other visual clues to meaning.

In addition to the specific type of information needed for analysis and the cost of different kinds of records, another factor determines what means of observation will be most useful. Students and teachers who are not used to being taped may find the microphone or the camera a distraction in the situation. The degree of intrusion is certainly a factor to be considered since any observer, especially one with a camera or a microphone, has impact on the social and emotional climate in the room. We all know that the first time someone with a camera joins a group of people, the camera itself causes them to change their behavior in some ways. Once the camera has been there a while, however, most people tend to forget its presence and go about their normal activities. Students who work with nonprint media themselves and are used to its existence in the environment are not likely to be disturbed or distressed by it.

Alternative Forms of Evaluation

Traditional forms of evaluation may be important for many educational purposes, but they are not sufficient for all aspects of teaching and are frequently not carefully enough matched to the most critical elements of the teaching encounter. This is especially true for the work of school library media specialists, whose teaching often has as its aim affective or long-range goals rather than immediate behavioral objectives. How might one evaluate, for instance, literature-sharing activities with young people, the cumulative development of critical skills in evaluating media, or the real value of the research process and information skills? In each instance, there are specific skills or aspects of content that can be tested, but such testing itself may distract from the overall purposes of the learning activities or discourage or turn students away from those activities. Accurate responses to specific questions about literary works, media productions, or research tools do not necessarily correspond with the development of attitudes and appreciations that will ultimately result in lifelong reading, learning, and critical thought.

Most library media specialists and other teachers are familiar with Bloom's and Krathwohl's analysis of cognitive and affective behavioral goals and the various levels of each, but too few of us seriously consider them when planning and evaluating our work with students.[13] We tend to focus on cognitive goals, often at the level of simple knowledge or comprehension and assume that the more complex intellectual skills and affective goals will take care of themselves. That which serves only one low-level goal is an inefficient use of teaching time and a disservice to students. Of what value is it for students to learn about the resources of a library media center if, at the same time, they do not learn to value those resources and the possibilities for their use? True, it is very difficult to design evaluative instruments that allow teachers to assess behavior at the higher cognitive levels (application, analysis, synthesis, evaluation), or at various affective levels. Given the large numbers of students to deal with, our examinations often measure comparatively simple factual knowledge or recall. Too often, exams are prepared primarily for ease in correcting them without a thorough examination of the instruments themselves to determine whether they are adequately assessing the key elements or the real intent of the teaching composition. Of course, many such exams are devised by, scored by, and the results analyzed by those at great distance from the actual learning situation.

Many of the types of evaluative tools that focus on the work of individuals take into account only the aspects of that individual that can be objectified, quantified, and measured, and the results are often reported as the composite of many individual scores in order to evaluate the instruction in a particular classroom, school, or region. That which is truly unique and personal is ignored. Many lists of competencies or behavioral objectives are probably far more valuable as planning guides than as assessment tools for the examination of individual performance.[14]

Aesthetic Analysis

If the primary intent of those involved in a teaching encounter is to move toward more long-range educational outcomes or toward affective goals rather than to specific behavioral objectives, other tools and techniques must be used for evaluation. In a previous chapter, teaching is described as a compositional act and, as such, one that requires evaluative procedures closer to those employed by the arts. In *The Scientific Basis of the Art of Teaching*, N. L. Gage acknowledges the long history of the concern for the artistry of teaching and puts our scientific knowledge about the field in perspective as the base upon which that artistry flourishes.[15] As a compositional or artistic product, schooling may be examined for some elements similar to those considered in aesthetic criticism.[16] For instance:

Is the composition thinkable? Are students able to comprehend, reflect upon, and use it productively?

Is it believable? Is it convincing as an authentic place to be, to work, and to grow?

Does it evoke response? Does it encourage participants to become involved in real inquiry rather than just activities?

Is it significantly formed? Is the schooling composition one that gives pleasure and intellectual challenge to students?

Is there a balance of tension and equilibrium? Are there times for humor as well as seriousness, relaxation as well as hard work, aloneness as well as community activities, the aesthetic as well as the scientific?

Does it allow for aesthetic distancing? Are students encouraged to step back and take time to reflect upon their work and themselves?

Is there theme and order? Is there an overall sense of purpose within which each person can find a place for his or her uniqueness?

Does the composition have impact and import? Is the educational community worth being a part of and are the human endeavors carried on there of real significance?

Although evaluation must be personally designed for each student, there are some general concerns that should be addressed in every instance. The following questions may be helpful in evaluating a schooling composition for each of the persons who participate in it.

Does the schooling composition:
Increase appreciation, enjoyment, enthusiasm, and delight?
Allow for differing levels of interest from curiosity to concern to real commitment?

Help the student to become both more self-sufficient and more cooperative?
Provide for intellectual, social, and personal growth?
Enlarge awareness and refine discrimination?
Lead to wider and deeper perceptions that turn events into ideas?

The answers to such questions are inevitably subjective, but asking them does help to put the results of our more scientific measures in perspective and allows us to consider the totality of the person and the situation as well as those fragments that are quantifiable. Obviously, such questions can only be answered by individual human beings exercising personal judgment in the discriminating search after excellence. That is what criticism is all about. It is not as precise as measurement, but it is a far better tool for evaluating many aspects of our work as teachers.

Strategies for Personal Evaluation

Even when the teaching composition is sound, both scientifically and aesthetically, one must still evaluate its effectiveness for particular persons within that composition. An evaluator needs to be concerned with the overall personal, social, and affective goals that the teacher has determined for the schooling composition and those that each student has set for himself or herself. As teachers of students and of other teachers, library media specialists must be especially conscious of each person's own decision making, self-determination, and self-evaluation. Ultimately the best evaluator of any person's achievement is that person himself or herself. The whole process of education might be described as that of becoming increasingly critical, in the best sense of the word, of one's own understanding of oneself and of the world. However, such self-evaluation on the part of those we teach does not negate the teacher's responsibility to evaluate his or her own work as well as that of students. School library media specialists have developed some useful tools for the evaluation of their work.[17]

Our own professionalism and demands for accountability require more than just a "feels right," intuitive evaluation of our work, and there is now a great deal of information about means of assessment other than tests.[18] In fact, much of what we know about learning naturally leads us to consider a variety of evaluative strategies that match what is really important in the teaching-learning encounter. The figure "Linking Instruction and Assessment: Implications from Cognitive Learning Theory" in Joan Herman's *A Practical Guide to Alternative Assessment* provides an excellent overview of such strategies.[19] Unfortunately, however, the inclusion of library and information skills on standardized tests has caused us, like too many of our classroom colleagues, to concentrate on those aspects of our work that can be or may be tested. If we are truly to empower students as well as teachers (including school library media specialists), we must begin to use alternative assessment techniques that give both groups increased control over their work. Classroom teachers and library media specialists must work together to allow students to pursue self-directed projects that grow out of their own interests and learning styles. Students should also be encouraged to work cooperatively with others who have differing abilities but share an interest in the particular topic or project. Further, they should be allowed to choose how they will demonstrate mastery. Such practices not only shift the burden of responsibility for learning to students, where it ultimately must rest, but help to convince them that goal-directed personal inquiry, disciplined thought, and hard work to achieve a goal can be rewarding and enjoyable. What more can we ask of an educational activity?

In the pursuit of such self-determined learning goals, students discover that ideas, information, and knowledge have a variety of real-life values far more important than a score on an achievement test. If students have enough personal investment in what they consider real work, they will want to share that work with others and try to present it in ways that will demonstrate its importance and, perhaps, influence others. Exhibits, models, experiments, artistic performances, letters, and multimedia productions are just a few of the many personal means an individual or group might use to evaluate their work. Such activities would probably be used as diagnostic or as formative assessments to give students and teachers a sense of work-in-progress as well as for summative assessments, which should be both final evaluation and celebrations of the successful completion of a project.

Portfolio Evaluation

Much discussion in recent years has focused on portfolios of student work as evaluative tools, especially for the reading-writing process in whole language classrooms.[20] A similar cumulative collection of student work, whether it be a logbook of experiments or evidence of using quantitative analysis in problem solving, might help students to evaluate and reflect upon their own growth in the understanding of science or mathematics. A fascinating and informative description of one such alternative form of assessment is that of the video portfolios at the Key School in Indianapolis, Indiana.[21]

Sometimes called "process-folios," these selections of work, showing the development of students' learning over time, shift the responsibility for and ownership of the learning activities to the students themselves. Teachers are also forced to be reflective practitioners in a student-centered, resource-rich learning environment. Teachers become guides, facilitators, or coaches to students as they help to orchestrate the resources and activities of multifaceted learning environments. They are constantly aware and involved and yet step back to reflect on what is happening and on the progress being made. Ultimately, both students and teachers are freed from the imposition of someone else's demands to do work that matters to them; external assessment becomes far less important than the developing personal recognition of the value of one's own endeavors. Of course, this will require a real restructuring of schools as places that truly value authentic, personal, and cooperative ventures and recognize that simple standardized assessments are not adequate to evaluate learning. In such schools, the results of students' work might even be items they really care about rather than impersonal numbers or letters on a report card.

It is sad to realize that, after the first few years of school when writing and drawings are displayed on the family refrigerator, it is rare for students to produce anything in school that they are proud of and wish to keep and share with others. How exciting it would be for youngsters to have a portfolio and project collection reflecting their years of schooling that, in later years, could be shared with their own children. Video portfolios especially lend themselves to this intergenerational sharing because children could see both the trepidation and excitement their parents experienced in school, and parents would be reminded of themselves as students. Such sharing would be an invaluable record of the importance of learning in the family and the glimpse of parent as child could help open the doors to important family dialogue.

Teachers, too, might benefit from having their work evaluated using some of these alternative assessment techniques. Lee Shulman has been a leader in encouraging educators to consider various approaches to both self-assessment and more formal outside evaluations.[22] The Teachers Assessment Project (TAP) of Stanford University concentrated on two approaches: simulations and portfolios.[23] Advocates of the use of teacher portfolios admit that they "are messy to construct, cumbersome to store, difficult to score and vulnerable to misrepresentation."[24] They do, however, provide a record of what teachers really care about, what works with students, and the growth of both the art and craft of teaching. Wolf suggests that portfolios may play an even more important role in the restructuring of American education. "In fact, while they have an indispensable role to play in the evaluation of teachers' pedagogical competence, their larger contribution may lie in the ways that they can reshape the profession of teaching. Portfolios can give teachers a purpose and framework for preserving and sharing their work, provide occasions for mentoring and collegial interactions, and stimulate teachers to reflect on their own work and on the act of teaching."[25]

Given all these approaches to the evaluation of schooling, how are library media specialists to incorporate them in their work? If cooperative learning adventures are really the norm in schools, we are unlikely to be teaching isolated library skills, but instead will be members of a number of teaching teams. As such, library media specialists will work with students to help them evaluate those aspects of their work that have to do with the critical use of information and media. Projects initiated by the library media specialist can also be evaluated using a variety of innovative means. Research capabilities, for instance, could be demonstrated by the development of hypermedia stackware, which could then be shared with others, perhaps added to the library media center collection. Displays, videos, and portfolio collections of various media and materials not only assess student competence in literary, media, or information curricula but also provide them with a product of which they can be proud.

As library media specialists, we must be responsible not only for making use of a variety of materials and means of evaluation in looking at our own work but also for informing other teachers of alternative evaluative tools and techniques.[26] Thus, each of us participates in that ongoing search for value that is evaluation.

Conclusion

The particular view of teaching envisioned in this monograph is one that is student-centered and materials-centered. Library media specialists who truly believe in young people as critical and creative thinkers who make their own meanings in the world assist in that process by creating learning environments rich in resources. The library media specialist as teacher possesses both an understanding of teaching and learning strategies and a real knowledge of the contents of the library media center collection. It is that knowledge of resources that enables one to recognize why and how to use particular items with students and teachers to supplement, amplify, enrich, and provide alternatives to school curricula and personal interests and needs. The ability to select precisely the right materials to empower young people as competent learners or to satisfy aesthetic needs is a measure of our respect for students and for ourselves as professionals.

Historically, school library media specialists have been recognized and rewarded for building collections of fine literature for youth. With more recent emphases on management and the information search process, a strong focus on materials and collections is often seen as an evasion of our primary responsibilities. What we must remember, however, is that teaching and learning take place when the best possible materials are matched to particular content, to student learning styles and to teaching strategies. It is the ideas, information, and aesthetic content of a variety of resources in all media that expand one's personal repertoire and increase appreciation and understanding of others.

The school library media specialist is a teacher. I began with this statement and I end with it. Throughout this monograph I have attempted to share some of my understandings and my concerns about the act of teaching and the practical implications for very specific teaching activities of school library media specialists. This is not to deny that library media specialists function as administrators, as managers, and in many other capacities in schools. However, if we do not recognize and fully accept our teaching responsibilities, we are depriving ourselves of one of the most rewarding and most joyful aspects of our work as well as depriving students and teachers of the best that we have to offer. Our work as information specialists and educational consultants in the school can only be fully realized through our competence as teachers. Through teaching we reach out and make connections with students and help them in turn to reach out to connect with others in the world. In this way, we play a vital part in providing the best possible education for those who will shape the world of the twenty-first century.

Notes

Chapter 1

1. Among the many books on restructuring American education, the following proved most helpful. *Contemporary Issues in U.S. Education*, Kathryn M. Borman and others, eds. (Norwood, N.J.: Ablex, 1991); Robert V. Bullough, Jr., *The Forgotten Dream of American Public Education* (Ames, Iowa: Iowa State University, 1988); Philip C. Schlechty, *Schools for the Twenty-First Century: Leadership Imperatives for Educational Reform* (San Francisco, Calif: Jossey-Bass, 1990); *Education Reform: Making Sense of It All*, Samuel B. Bacharach, ed. (Boston: Allyn and Bacon, 1990); Joseph Murphy. *Restructuring Schools: Capturing and Assessing the Phenomena* (New York: Teachers College, 1991); Edward B. Fiske, *Smart Schools, Smart Kids: Why Do Some Schools Work?* (New York: Simon & Schuster, 1991); and *Redefining Student Learning: Roots of Educational Change*, ed. by Hermine H. Marshall (Norwood, N.J.: Ablex, 1992). The May 1991 issue of *Educational Leadership* 48, no. 8 is devoted to the topic: "Restructuring Schools: What's Really Happening?"

2. Barbara Stripling, *Libraries for the National Goals* (Syracuse, N.Y.: ERIC Clearinghouse on Information Resources, 1992).

3. *America 2000: An Education Strategy: Sourcebook* (Washington, D.C.: U.S. Government Printing Office, 1991).

4. Ibid., 4.

5. Daniel D. Barron, "School-Based Management and School Library Media Specialists," *School Library Media Activities Monthly* 7, no. 6 (February 1992): 47–50.

6. Andrew Gitlin and Karen Price, "Teacher Empowerment and the Development of Voice," in *Supervision in Transition*, ed. by Carl D. Glickman (Alexandria, Va.: Association for Supervision and Curriculum Development, 1992), 62.

7. *World Class Standards for American Education* (Washington, D.C.: U.S. Department of Education, October 1992), pamphlet.

8. To order *Curriculum and Evaluation Standards for School Mathematics*, write to the National Council of Teachers of Mathematics, Order Processing, 1906 Association Drive, Reston, VA 22091. Item number 398E1, ISBN 0-87353-273-2, $25.00

9. For an overview of some of the differing views on *America 2000* and on the question of national standards, read the following: Dennis P. Doyle, "America 2000," *Phi Delta Kappan* 73, no. 3 (November 1991): 185–91; Harold Howe II, "America 2000: A Bumpy Ride on Four Trains," *Phi Delta Kappan* 73, no. 3 (November 1991): 192–203; *Voices from the Field: 30 Expert Opinions on America 2000, The Bush Administration Strategy to "Reinvent" America's Schools* (Washington, D.C.: William T. Grant Foundation Commission on Work, Family and Citizenship and the Institute for Educational Leadership, 1991); "The Quest

for Higher Standards," *Educational Leadership* 48, no. 5 (February 1991): 4–69; and "The Challenge of Higher Standards," *Educational Leadership* 50, no. 5 (February 1993): 4–81.

10. Marian Wright Edelman, *The Measure of Our Success* (Boston: Beacon, 1992).

11. *What Your First Grader Needs to Know: Fundamentals of a Good First-Grade Education*, ed. by E. D. Hirsch, Jr., The Core Knowledge Series: Resource Books for Grades One Through Six (New York: Doubleday, 1991). See also these other books edited by E. D. Hirsch, Jr., *What Your Second Grader Needs to Know: Fundamentals of a Good Second-Grade Education* (New York: Doubleday, 1991), *What Your Third Grader Needs to Know: Fundamentals of a Good Third-Grade Education* (New York: Doubleday, 1992), *What Every Fourth Grader Needs to Know: Fundamentals of a Good Fourth-Grade Education* (New York: Doubleday, 1992), and *A First Dictionary of Cultural Literacy: What Our Children Need to Know* (Boston: Houghton Mifflin, 1989).

12. Harlow G. Unger, *What Did You Learn in School Today?: A Parent's Guide for Evaluating Your Child's School* (New York: Facts on File, 1991).

13. Ibid., 113.

14. *The Graywolf Annual Five: Multi-Cultural Literacy*, Rick Simonson and Scott Walker, eds. (Saint Paul, Minn.: Graywolf, 1988), 191–200.

15. Thomas Kellaghan and George F. Madaus, "National Testing: Lessons for America from Europe," *Educational Leadership* 49, no. 3 (November 1991): 87–93.

16. Catharine R. Stimpson, "Meno's Boy: Hearing His Story—& His Sister's," *Academe* 77, no. 6 (November-December 1991): 25–31.

17. C. Beth Schaffner and Barbara E. Buswell, *Opening Doors: Strategies for Including All Students in Regular Education* (Colorado Springs, Colo.: PEAK Parent Center, 1991) and Barbara E. Buswell and Judy Veneris, *Building Integration with I.E.P.* (Colorado Springs, Colo.: PEAK Parent Center, 1989).

18. Among the books that should prove helpful are: *Toward the Thinking Curriculum: Current Cognitive Research*, Lauren B. Resnick and Leopold E. Klopfer, eds. 1989 Yearbook of ASCD (Alexandria, Va.: Association for Supervision and Curriculum Development, 1989); Louis E. Raths and others, *Teaching for Thinking: Theory, Strategies, and Activities for the Classroom* (New York: Teachers College, 1986); Robert J. Marzano and others, *Dimensions of Thinking: A Framework for Curriculum and Instruction* (Alexandria, Va.: Association for Supervision and Curriculum Development, 1988); and Richard J. Stiggins and others, *Measuring Thinking Skills in the Classroom* (Washington, D.C.: National Education Association, 1986). An interesting alternative is found in Frank Smith, *To Think* (New York: Teachers College, 1990).

19. Karen Sheingold synthesizes her views on this in "Restructuring for Learning with Technology: The Potential for Synergy," *Phi Delta Kappan* 73, no. 1 (September 1991): 17–27, and *Restructuring for Learning with Technology*, ed. by Karen Sheingold and Marc S. Tucker (New York: Bank Street Center for Technology and Education and the National Center on Education and the Economy, 1990).

20. Sheingold, *Phi Delta Kappan*, 19.

21. David Cohen, "Teaching Practice," in *Contributing to Educational Change: Perspectives on Research and Practice*, ed. by Philip Jackson (Berkeley, Calif.: McCutchan, 1988), 27–84.

22. Kay E. Vandergrift, "Privacy, Schooling, and Minors," *School Library Journal* 37, no. 1 (January 1991): 26–30.

23. Sheingold, *Phi Delta Kappan*, 19.

24. Ibid.

25. Paul McCarty, "Bringing the World into the Classroom," *Principal* 71, no. 2 (November 1991): 8–10; for additional information on World Classroom, contact Dr. Varnell Bench at Utah State University, Logan, UT 84322, or call 801-750-1474.

26. Karen Gould, "Indiana's High-Tech Elementary School," *Principal* 71, no. 2 (November 1991): 11–13; additional information on LinkWay may be obtained by calling 404-238-1070.

27. Alvin Poussaint, "In a Minority District in Maryland, a Magnet School That Really Draws," *New York Times*, 3 March 1993, sec. B 13.

28. *Public Schools of Choice. ASCD Issues Analysis* (Alexandria, Va.: Association for Supervision and Curriculum Development, 1990).

29. D. R. Moore and S. Davenport, "School Choice: The New Improved Sewing Machine" (Chicago: Design for Change, 1989) and "Schools of Choice?" *Educational Leadership* 48, no. 4 (December 1990/January 1991): 4–72.

30. Bonnie Blodgett, "The Private Hell of Public Education," *Lear's* 5, no. 2 (April 1992): 54.

31. *The AAUW Report: How Schools Shortchange Girls*, prepared by the Wellesley College Center for Research on Women (Washington, D.C.: American Association of University Women, 1992).

32. "Creating a Gender-Fair Federal Education Policy," *American Association of University Women Outlook* 87, no. 1 (Spring 1993): 3.

33. *School-University Partnerships in Action: Concepts, Cases, and Concerns*, ed. by Kenneth A. Sirotnik and John Goodlad (New York: Teachers College, 1988); Franklin P. Wilbur and Leo M. Lambert, *Linking America's Schools and Colleges: Guide to Partnerships and National Directory* (Washington, D.C.: American Association for Higher Education, 1991). For questions about the possibilities of partnerships in library education, see Linda Catelli, "School-University Partnerships: The Transference of a Model," in *Library Education and Leadership: Essays in Honor of Jane Anne Hannigan*, ed. by Sheila S. Intner and Kay E. Vandergrift (Metuchen, N.J.: Scarecrow, 1990) 127–40.

34. Renate Nummela Caine and Geoffrey Caine, *Making Connections: Teaching and the Human Brain* (Alexandria, Va.: Association for Supervision and Curriculum Development, 1991).

35. Susan Hill and Tim Hill, *The Collaborative Classroom: A Guide to Co-Operative Learning* (Portsmith, N.H.: Heinemann, 1990); Robert E. Slavin, "Synthesis of Research on Cooperative Learning," *Educational Leadership* 48 (February 1991): 72–82.

36. A number of books and articles have been written on whole language but among them the following are most useful: Eleanor R. Kulleseid, ed., "Conversations in Print," in *School Library Media Annual* 6 (Englewood, Colo.: Libraries Unlimited, 1988), 3–59; Constance Weaver and others, *Understanding Whole Language: From Principles to Practice* (Portsmith, N.H.: Heinemann, 1990); Ralph Peterson and Maryann Peterson, eds., *Grand Conversations: Literature Groups in Action* (New York: Scholastic, 1990); Ralph Peterson, *Life in a Crowded Place: Making a Learning Community* (Portsmith, N.H.: Heinemann, 1992); Kenneth S. Goodman, *What's Whole in Whole Language?* (Portsmith, N.H.: Heinemann, 1986); Linda Leonard Lamme and Linda Ledbetter, "Libraries: The Heart of Whole Language," *Language Arts* 67, no. 7 (November 1990): 735–41, and "Whole Language," *Teacher Magazine* 2, no. 9 (August 1991): 20–47.

37. Brian Cambourne, "Language, Learning and Literacy," in *Towards a Reading-Writing Classroom*, ed. by Andrea Butler and Jan Turbill (Portsmouth, N.H.: Heinemann, 1989), 5–9.

38. See the research of the author on meaning-making and children: Kay E. Vandergrift, "The Child's Meaning-Making in Response to a Literary Text," *English Quarterly* 22, no. 3-4 (Winter 1990): 125–40, and "Meaning-Making and the Dragons of Pern," *Children's Literature Association Quarterly* 15 (Spring 1990): 27–34.

39. The model developed by the author draws from a number of disciplines and from more than twenty-five years of practical experience working with young people and literature for its theoretical base. The brief mention of some of these sources is not intended to demonstrate specific relationships between previous work and current study, but merely to identify and pay tribute to those whose work has influenced my own. The perception of the reader as one who both brings meaning to and takes meaning from a literary text is grounded in the transactional theory of Louise Rosenblatt. Other reader-response theorists and critics whose work informs my own are Stanley Fish for his work in interpretive strategies and interpretive communities and Wolfgang Iser for his discussions of gaps or "areas of indeterminacy" in a text. Feminist literary criticism has offered alternative patterns in the work of Showalter and Heilbrun. Alan Purves and Robert Protherough are among those who have documented the recreative powers of school-age children in response to literary texts. From developmental psychology and education have come work on critical thinking, whole language, and metacognition. John Dewey's classic work on the development of thinking skills has been reexamined and expanded in recent years as educators study the development of higher-order thinking skills across all areas of the school curriculum, and in relation to specific subjects such as reading. The whole language approach of Kenneth S. Goodman and others to language arts instruction, the speech act theory of literary discourse of Pratt, and the importance of informal writing as a way of ordering and shaping thought about literature. Also important to the understanding of the process through which community meanings are created are studies of communication and paralinguistics, such as Colin Cherry, and of the sociology of knowledge defined by Berger and Luckmann.

40. Lawrence A. Cremin, *The Genius of American Education* (New York: Random House, 1965), 23.

41. Kay E. Vandergrift, *Children's Literature: Theory, Research, and Teaching* (Englewood, Colo.: Libraries Unlimited, 1990).

42. Kay E. Vandergrift, "Exploring the Concept of Contextual Void: A Preliminary Analysis," in *Library Education and Leadership: Essays in Honor of Jane Anne Hannigan*, ed. by Sheila S. Intner and Kay E. Vandergrift (Metuchen, N.J.: Scarecrow, 1990), 349–63.

43. Kay E. Vandergrift, "Hypermedia: Breaking the Tyranny of the Text," *School Library Journal* 35, no. 3 (November 1988): 30–35. See also George P. Landow, *Hypertext: The Convergence of Contemporary Critical Theory and Technology* (Baltimore, Md.: The Johns Hopkins University, 1992).

44. Vandergrift, "Contextual Void," 353.

45. Stephen T. Kerr, "Lever and Fulcrum: Educational Technology in Teachers' Thought and Practice," *Teachers College Record* 93, no. 1 (Fall 1991): 132.

46. Ibid., 122.

47. Karen Sheingold and Martha Hadley, *Accomplished Teachers: Integrating Computers into Classroom Practice* (New York: Bank Street College of Education, Center for Technology in Education, 1990).

48. Howard Rheingold, *Virtual Reality* (New York: Summit, 1991), and Stewart Brand, *The Media Lab: Inventing the Future at MIT* (New York: Viking, 1987).

49. Gillian Rubinstein, *Space Demons* (New York: Pocket, 1989), and Gillian Rubin-

stein, *Skymaze* (New York: Orchard, 1991). *Space Demons* won the Australian National Children's Book Award in 1988.

50. Cremin, *Genius*, 11.

51. Jonathan Kozol, *Savage Inequalities* (New York: Crown, 1991), 152.

52. American Association of School Librarians and Association for Educational Communications and Technology, *Information Power: Guidelines for School Library Media Programs* (Chicago: American Library Association, 1988), 1.

Chapter 2

1. See the regular updates by Patsy H. Perritt. "School Library Media Certification Requirements: 1992 Update," *School Library Journal* 38, no. 6 (June 1992): 30–49.

2. A number of works could be cited for this discussion of the teaching role of the school library media specialist. See Lillian Biermann Wehmeyer, *The School Librarian as Educator*, 2d ed. (Littleton, Colo.: Libraries Unlimited, 1984); Kay E. Vandergrift, *The Teaching Role of the School Media Specialist* (Chicago: American Library Association, 1979); Philip M. Turner, *Helping Teachers Teach: A School Library Media Specialist's Role* (Littleton, Colo.: Libraries Unlimited, 1985); David V. Loertscher, *Taxonomies of the School Library Media Program* (Englewood, Colo.: Libraries Unlimited, 1988); Patricia G. Winn, *Integration of the Secondary School Library Media Center into the Curriculum: Techniques and Strategies* (Englewood, Colo.: Libraries Unlimited, 1991).

3. Michael Bell and Herman Totten, "Cooperation in Instruction between Classroom Teachers and School Library Media Specialists: A Look at Teacher Characteristics in Texas Elementary Schools," *School Library Media Quarterly* 20, no. 2 (Winter 1992): 83.

4. See, for example, Patricia Glass Schuman, "Librarians: Images and Realities," in *Library Education and Leadership: Essays in Honor of Jane Anne Hannigan*, ed. by Sheila S. Intner and Kay E. Vandergrift (Metuchen, N.J.: Scarecrow, 1990), 27–34.

5. Teaching is explored in numerous books, but among the most helpful are Michael Dunkin and Bruce Biddle, *The Study of Teaching* (New York: Holt, Rinehart and Winston, 1974); Gary Fenstermacher and Jonas Soltis, *Approaches to Teaching* (New York: Teachers College, 1986); Philip W. Jackson, *The Practice of Teaching* (New York: Teachers College, 1986); Rachel Pinder, *Why Don't Teachers Teach Like They Used To?* (London: Hilary Shipman, 1987); and *Perspectives on Effective Teaching and the Cooperative Classroom*, ed. by Judy Reinhartz (Washington, D.C.: National Education Association, 1984).

6. The author has a detailed exploration of this thesis in her *Children's Literature: Theory, Research and Teaching* (Englewood, Colo.: Libraries Unlimited, 1990).

7. Louise M. Rosenblatt, *The Reader, The Text, The Poem* (Carbondale, Ill.: Southern Illinois University, 1978).

8. Vandergrift, *Children's Literature*, 64–72.

9. Classroom interaction research is the focus of attention in a number of books and journal articles. Among the most useful are *Controversies in Classroom Research: A Reader*, 2d ed. (Buckingham, England: Open University, 1993); *Classroom Talk: Speaking and Listening Activities from Classroom-Based Teacher Research* (Portsmith, N.H.: Heinemann, 1991); Doralyn R. Roberts and Judith A. Langer, *Supporting the Process of Literary Understanding: Analysis of a Classroom Discussion*, Report Series 2.15, Eric no. ED337780,

1991; *Interaction Analysis: Theory, Research and Application,* Edmund J. Amidon, comp. (Reading, Mass.: Addison-Wesley, 1967); and Donn Byrne, *Techniques for Classroom Interaction* (London: Longman, 1987).

10. Bruce Joyce and Marsha Weil, *Models of Teaching,* 3d ed. (Englewood Cliffs, N.J.: Prentice-Hall, 1986).

11. American Association of School Librarians and Association for Educational Communications and Technology, *Information Power: Guidelines for School Library Media Programs* (Chicago: American Library Association, 1988).

12. It might prove helpful to use Sandy Whiteley, "A World View—Children's Atlases," *Book Links* 2, no. 1 (September 1992): 44–47.

13. Mark Monmonier, *How to Lie with Maps* (Chicago: The University of Chicago, 1991), 1.

14. Ibid., 2.

15. Joyce and Weil, *Models,* 165–86.

16. William J. Gordon and Tony Poze, *The Metaphoric Way of Learning and Knowing* (Cambridge: Porpoise, 1971).

17. Joyce and Weil, *Models,* 48–60

18. *GTV: A Geographic Perspective on American History* (National Geographic Society in cooperation with Optical Data, 1991, CD-ROM).

19. Pat Brisson, *Kate Heads West,* Illus. by Rick Brown (New York: Bradbury, 1990); *Kate on the Coast* (New York: Bradbury, 1992); and *Your Best Friend, Kate* (New York: Macmillan, 1989).

20. Pat Brisson, *Magic Carpet,* Illus. by Amy Schwartz (New York: Bradbury, 1991).

21. See, for example, Kathryn Lasky, *Beyond the Divide* (New York: Macmillan, 1983); Amy Ehrlich, *Where It Stops Nobody Knows* (New York: Dial, 1988); Cynthia Voigt, *Homecoming* (New York: Atheneum, 1981); Bruce Brooks, *Midnight Hour Encore* (New York: Harper & Row, 1986); and Sheila Burnford, *The Incredible Journey* (Boston: Little, Brown, 1961).

Chapter 3

1. Jacqueline C. Mancall, Shirley Aaron, and Sue Walker, "Educating Students to Think: The Role of the School Library Media Program," *School Library Media Quarterly* 14 (Fall 1986): 18–47.

2. American Association of School Librarians and Association for Educational Communications and Technology, *Information Power: Guidelines for School Library Media Programs* (Chicago: American Library Association, 1988), 1.

3. Penelope A. Moore and Alison St. George, "Children as Information Seekers: The Cognitive Demands of Books and Library Systems," *School Library Media Quarterly* 19, no. 3 (Spring 1991): 161–68.

4. Ibid., 168.

5. Leslie Edmonds, Paula Moore and Kathleen M. Balcom, "The Effectiveness of an Online Catalog," *School Library Journal* 36, no. 10 (October 1990): 28–32. It should be noted that newer technologies may alter some findings as reported in this article.

6. Christine L. Borgman and Mark H. Chignell, "Designing an Information Retrieval Interface Based on Children's Categorization of Knowledge: A Pilot Study," Paper sub-

mitted to the 1989 International Conference on Research and Development in Information Retrieval sponsored by the Special Interest Group for Information Retrieval (SIGIR) Association for Computing Machinery, 22 pages; Christine Borgman and others, "From Hands-on Science to Hands-on Information Retrieval," *Proceedings of the 52nd American Society for Information Science Annual Meeting* 26 (1989): 96–103; Christine Borgman and others, "Children's Use of an Interactive Catalog of Science Materials," *Proceedings of the 53rd American Society for Information Science Annual Meeting* 27 (1990): 55–68; and Virginia Walter and Christine Borgman, "The Science Library Catalog: A Prototype Information Retrieval System for Children," *Journal of Youth Services in Libraries* 4, no. 2 (1991): 159–66.

7. Readers may find Philip Turner's book, particularly pages 99–119 and pages 227–34, helpful in this aspect. Philip Turner, *Helping Teachers Teach* (Littleton, Colo.: Libraries Unlimited, 1985).

8. Herman A. Witkin and others, *Psychological Differentiation: Studies of Development* (Potomac, Md.: Wiley, 1974). An application of their theories is in Paula Kay Montgomery's dissertation (1989); a brief report is found in "Cognitive Style and the Level of Cooperation between the Library Media Specialist and the Classroom Teacher," *School Library Media Quarterly* 19, no. 3 (Spring 1991): 185–91.

9. Carol Collier Kuhlthau, *School Librarian's Grade by Grade Activities Program: A Complete Sequential Skills Plan for Grades K–8* (West Nyack, N.Y.: The Center for Applied Research in Education, 1981); Carol Collier Kuhlthau, *Teaching the Library Research Process: A Step by Step Program for Secondary School Students* (West Nyack, N.Y.: The Center for Applied Research in Education, 1985); Michael Marland, ed., *Information Skills in the Secondary Curriculum*, Schools Council Curriculum Bulletin 9 (London: Methuen Educational, 1981); Nancy O'Hanlon, "Good Intentions Are Not Enough: Toward Cooperative Teaching of Basic Information Seeking Competencies," *Ohio Media Spectrum* 44, no. 1 (Spring 1992): 14–19; and *Library Research Skills Workbook. Grades 7-12*, comp. by the editors of *The Book Report* (Worthington, Ohio: The Book Report/Linworth, 1990).

10. It would be useful to examine Michael Eisenberg's work on curriculum mapping in conjunction with the process of determining competencies. See Michael B. Eisenberg, "Curriculum Mapping and Implementation of an Elementary School Library Media Skills Curriculum," *School Library Media Quarterly* 12 (Fall 1984): 411–18.

11. See *The Mind's Treasure Chest*, videocassette, color, 94:30 minutes (McHenry, Ill.: Follett Software Co., 1991). *The Mind's Treasure Chest*, an "educational film . . . on the subject of libraries and learning," is a recent effort to improve upon years of often poor quality commercial materials for library instruction. This video does make effective use of filmic techniques, combining a kind of superhero motif with a fast-paced look at informational technologies. The greatest strength of this film, endorsed by AASL and other educational organizations, is in the high school protagonist's growing recognition of and respect for information and ideas. Unfortunately, however, the length of the film will preclude its use with most junior and senior high school audiences for whom it was intended. Even as two 45-minute segments, this film is probably too long to be used in many school settings. Tighter scripting and editing would have improved this film and made it more accessible to a variety of audiences.

12. Carol C. Kuhlthau, "Information Search Process: A Summary of Research and Implications for School Library Media Programs," *School Library Media Quarterly* 18, no. 1 (Fall 1989): 19.

13. Others, such as Michael Eisenberg and Robert Berkowitz, Ann Irving, Barbara Stripling, and Judy Pitts have also developed models of the information process, but none of them are research-based as is that of Kuhlthau. What is noteworthy is the similarity among all the models when stripped to the essentials. See Michael B. Eisenberg and Michael K. Brown, "Current Themes Regarding Library and Information Skills Instruction: Research Supporting and Research Lacking," *School Library Media Quarterly* 20, no. 2 (Winter 1992): 103-10.

14. Kuhlthau "Information Search," 23.

15. Ibid., 21.

16. Eisenberg and Brown "Current Themes," 108.

17. *Writing from Sources* is an undergraduate text that might prove useful to school library media specialists in this aspect of instruction. Brenda Spatt, *Writing from Sources* (New York: St. Martin's, 1983).

18. *Activities to Promote Critical Thinking: Classroom Practices in Teaching English, 1986* (Urbana, Ill.: National Council of Teachers of English, 1986), 50.

19. Arthur N. Applebee, *Contexts for Learning to Write: Studies of Secondary School Instruction* (Norwood, N.J.: Ablex, 1984). See also Glynda Ann Hull, "Research on Writing: Building a Cognitive and Social Understanding of Composing," in *Toward the Thinking Curriculum: Current Cognitive Research*, ed. by Lauren B. Resnick and Leopold E. Klopfer (Alexandria, Va.: Association for Supervision and Curriculum Development, 1989), 104-28.

20. Using his own model, Eisenberg translates it to practical instruction. See Michael Eisenberg and Robert Berkowitz, *Information Problem-Solving: The Big Six Skills Approach to Library and Information Skills Instruction* (Norwood, N.J.: Ablex, 1990).

21. Much has been written on this topic, but the following may prove most helpful. G. Freedman and E. G. Reynolds, "Enriched Basic Reader Lessons with Semantic Webbing," *Reading Teacher* 33 (1980): 677-83. Another article of importance is Eleanor R. Kulleseid, "Extending the Research Base: Schema Theory, Cognitive Styles, and Types of Intelligence," *School Library Media Quarterly* 15 (Fall 1986): 41-48.

22. Eyewitness Books and Amazing Eyewitness Juniors are produced by Alfred Knopf and cover a wide range of topics including Bird, Butterfly & Moth, Invention, Weather, Mammal, Music, Pond & River, Shell, Skeleton, Sports, Tree, Money, Insect, Rocks & Minerals, Fish, Monkeys, Spiders, Snakes, Crocodiles & Reptiles, etc.

23. Michele Byam, *Arms and Armor* (New York: Alfred Knopf, 1988). This topic may be problematic for some, but the book is very useful in a library media center collection and may itself stimulate discussion about controversial issues such as gun control.

24. Piero Ventura, *There Once Was a Time* (New York: Putnam, 1986).

25. Russell Freedman, *The Wright Brothers: How They Invented the Airplane* (New York: Holiday House, 1991).

26. Judith St. George, *Mason and Dixon's Line of Fire* (New York: Putnam, 1991).

27. *David Macaulay in His Studio*, videocassette, color, 25 minutes (Boston: Houghton Mifflin, 1981); *Pyramid*, videocassette, color, 60 minutes (Unicorn; distributed by Dorset Video, 1988).

28. Patricia Lauber, *Great Whales: The Gentle Giants*, Illus. by Pieter Folkens (New York: Henry Holt, 1991).

29. Kay E. Vandergrift, "Hypermedia: Breaking the Tyranny of the Text," *School Library Journal* 35, no. 3 (November 1988): 30-36.

Chapter 4

1. A scholarly presentation on this is found in Gillian Thomas, *A Position to Command Respect: Women and the Eleventh Britannica* (Metuchen, N.J.: Scarecrow, 1992).

2. Beverly Klatt, "Abraham Lincoln: Deified Martyr, Flesh and Blood Hero, and a Man with Warts," *Children's Literature in Education* 23, no. 3 (September 1992): 119–29.

3. *The Columbian Quincentenary: An Educational Opportunity* (Washington, D.C.: National Council for the Social Studies, 1991), 4.

4. "When Worlds Collide: How Columbus's Voyages Transformed Both East and West," Columbus Special Issue: *Newsweek* (Fall/Winter 1991), 182 pages. (A Joint Project with the Smithsonian's Natural History Exhibit "Seeds of Change")

5. Among the most useful works for comparative study are the following: Madeleine B. Stern, *Louisa May Alcott* (Norman, Okla.: University of Oklahoma, 1950); *Louisa May Alcott: Selected Fiction*, ed. by Daniel Shealy, Madeleine Stern and Joel Myerson (Boston: Little, Brown, 1990); *The Selected Letters of Louisa May Alcott*, ed. by Joel Myerson, Daniel Shealy and Madeleine Stern (Boston: Little, Brown, 1987); and *The Journals of Louisa May Alcott*, ed. by Joel Meyerson, Daniel Shealy and Madeleine Stern (Boston: Little, Brown, 1989). For a younger audience an entire issue of *Cobblestone* was devoted to Alcott. See *Cobblestone: The History Magazine for Young People* 9, no. 12 (December 1988): 4–47.

6. Eleanor H. Ayer, *Boris Yeltsin: Man of the People* (New York: Dillon, 1992).

7. This work is available as a video, *Lincoln: A Photobiography*, videocassette, color, 65 minutes (American School Publishers, 1989).

8. *James Daugherty*, videocassette, color, approx. 20 minutes (Weston Woods Studios, n.d.).

9. Kay E. Vandergrift and Jane Anne Hannigan, "Makers of Magic: Children's Authors and Illustrators on Video," *School Library Journal* 38, no. 4 (April 1992): 26–31.

10. This concept of docudrama as historical manipulation formed a major portion of the plot in the following novel: Arthur Hailey, *The Evening News* (New York: Doubleday, 1990).

11. "The Perilous Path of the Docudrama: Presenting the Facts," *The Economist* 315 (April 7, 1990): 104.

12. Albert Auster, "The Missiles of October: A Case Study of Television Docudrama and Modern Memory," *Journal of Popular Film and Television* 17 (Winter 1990): 164–72.

13. *Amy Fisher, My Story*, Television program (NBC, December 28, 1992); *Casualties of Love: The Long Island Lolita Story*, Television program (CBS, January 3, 1993); and *The Amy Fisher Story*, Television program (ABC, January 3, 1993). Additionally, the *Donahue* show presented Mary Jo and Joey Buttafuoco on NBC Tuesday, January 5, 1993, to respond to the various portrayals.

14. *One Against the Wind*, Television program (CBS, December 1, 1991).

15. The following book should prove helpful in exploring this issue: Patricia Marks Greenfield, *Mind and Media: The Effects of Television, Video Games, and Computers* (Cambridge: Harvard University, 1984).

16. The form that Eisenberg and Berkowitz present might be usefully placed on the computer to act as a suggestion for students to select an appropriate presentation format. Michael Eisenberg and Robert Berkowitz, *Information Problem-Solving: The Big Six Skills*

Approach to Library and Information Skills Instruction (Norwood, N.J.: Ablex, 1990), 122–23.

17. Laserdisc collections are becoming more plentiful and are useful not only for completing assignments but they also allow young people to browse. *Insects* (Smithsonian Laserdisc Collection, Lumivision Corporation, narrated by James Earl Jones), done in cooperation with the Smithsonian, offers innumerable examples of visual beauty as well as solid informational content.

18. Kay E. Vandergrift and Jane Anne Hannigan, "Reading Visual Images: Videos in the Library and Classroom," *School Library Journal* 39, no. 1 (January 1993): 20–25.

19. An article in *School Library Journal* accuses the author of this book of bigotry but says that a library that censored another of her books "robbed some readers of insight into what bigotry is really like and why the changes in this century have been so momentous." Carolyn Caywood, "Bigotry by the Book," *School Library Journal* 38, no. 12 (December 1992): 41.

Chapter 5

1. Donna E. Norton, "Using a Webbing Process to Develop Children's Literature Units," *Language Arts* 59, no. 4 (April 1982): 348–56; *Children's Literature in the Classroom: Weaving Charlotte's Web*, ed. by Janet Hickman and Bernice Cullinan (Norwood, Mass.: Christopher-Gordon, 1989); and, John H. Clarke, "Using Visual Organizers to Focus on Thinking," *Journal of Reading* 34, no. 7 (April 1991): 526-34.

2. A version of this web from *The Taken Girl* by Vining was first published as a segment of the following: Kay E. Vandergrift and Jane Anne Hannigan, "Oldies But Goodies: Hidden Treasures from Your Shelves," *School Library Journal* 37, no. 9 (September 1991): 174–79.

3. Eloise McGraw, *The Striped Ships* (New York: Margaret McElderry Books, 1991).

Chapter 6

1. American Association of School Librarians and Association for Educational Communications and Technology, *Information Power: Guidelines for School Library Media Programs* (Chicago: American Library Association, 1988), 34.

2. For information about staff development activities and their influence on student achievement see Bruce Joyce and Beverly Showers, *Student Achievement through Staff Development* (New York: Longman, 1987).

3. Malcolm Knowles, *The Modern Practice of Adult Education: Pedagogy versus Andragogy*, 2d ed. (Chicago: Association Press/Follett, 1980).

4. A number of works on this topic are available but among the most useful are John R. Verduin, Jr., and Thomas A. Clark, *Distance Education: The Foundations of Effective Practice* (San Francisco, Calif.: Jossey-Bass, 1991); *Contemporary Issues in American Distance Education*, ed. by Michael G. Moore (Oxford: Pergamon, 1990); D. R. Garrison, *Understanding Distance Education* (London: Routledge, 1989); John Carey, "Plato at the Keyboard: Telecommunications Technology and Education Policy," *The Annals of the Academy of Political and Social Science* 514 (March 1991): 11–21; and Cornelia Brun-

ner, "Gender and Distance Learning," *The Annals of the Academy of Political and Social Science* 514 (March 1991): 133–45.

5. Philip M. Turner, *Helping Teachers Teach: A School Library Media Specialist's Role* (Littleton, Colo.: Libraries Unlimited, 1985). See also Jerrold E. Kemp, *The Instructional Design Process* (New York: Harper & Row, 1985); and Walter Dick and Lou Carey, *The Systematic Design of Instruction*, 2d ed. (Glenview, Ill.: Scott, Foresman, 1985).

6. Betty P. Cleaver and William D. Taylor, *The Instructional Consultant Role of the School Library Media Specialist* (Chicago: American Library Association, 1989).

7. Michael B. Eisenberg and Robert E. Berkowitz, *Information Problem-Solving: The Big Six Skills Approach to Library and Information Skills Instruction* (Norwood, N.J.: Ablex, 1990); and also *Curriculum Initiative* (Norwood, N.J.: Ablex, 1988); and *The Resource Companion* (Norwood, N.J.: Ablex, 1988).

8. Kay E. Vandergrift, "Critical Thinking Misfired: Implications of Student Responses to *The Shooting Gallery*," *School Library Media Quarterly* 15, no. 2 (Winter 1987): 86–91.

9. For various considerations of this work see: Toni Morrison, *Playing in the Dark: Whiteness and the Literary Imagination* (Cambridge: Harvard University, 1992), 54–57; Justin Kaplan, *Born to Trouble: One Hundred Years of Huckleberry Finn* (Washington, D.C.: Library of Congress, 1985); *Satire or Evasion? Black Perspectives on Huckleberry Finn*, ed. by James S. Leonard and others (Durham, N.C.: Duke University, 1992); *Huck Finn among the Critics: A Centennial Selection*, ed. by M. Thomas Inge (Frederick, Md.: University Publications of America, 1985); Victor A. Doyno, *Writing Huck Finn: Mark Twain's Creative Process* (Philadelphia, Penn.: University of Pennsylvania, 1991); and Shelley Fisher Fishkin, *Was Huck Black? Mark Twain and African American Voices* (New York: Oxford University, 1993).

10. Robert Newton Peck, *A Day No Pigs Would Die* (New York: Alfred Knopf, 1972).

11. Avi, *Nothing But the Truth* (Boston: Clarion, 1991).

12. *Date Rape: It Happened to Me*, videocassette, color, 29:30 minutes, directed by Ken Carpenter. Distributed by Pyramid Films, 1990.

13. *The Chrysanthemums*, videocassette, color, 22 minutes, directed by Steve Rosen and Terri De Bonas. Distributed by Pyramid Films, 1990.

14. *Half the Kingdom*, videocassette, color, 58 minutes, directed by Francine Zuckerman and Roushell Goldstein. Distributed by Direct Cinema Limited, 1989.

15. Gloria Treadwell Pipkin, "Challenging the Convential Wisdom on Censorship," *The ALAN Review* 20, no. 2 (Winter 1993): 35–37.

16. *MathFinder Sourcebook: A Collection of Resources for Mathematics Reform*, written and ed. by Laurie Kreindler and Barbara Zahm (Armonk, N.Y.: The Learning Team, 1992).

17. These titles and the quotations about them, for the most part, have been taken from the research reported by Lee Burress in *Battle of the Books: Literary Censorship in the Public Schools, 1950-1985* (Metuchen, N.J.: Scarecrow, 1989). In addition, banned titles have been located in *School Library Journal*, as well as in the *Newsletter on Intellectual Freedom* and *Hit List*, both published by the American Library Association.

18. It would be useful to obtain the latest lists of banned items from both the Office of Intellectual Freedom of ALA and the Office of the People for the American Way in Washington, D.C.

19. Lillian N. Gerhardt, editorial, "On Pamphlets Needed Now," *School Library Journal* 38, no. 1 (January 1992): 4.

20. There are many resources in this area, and the following have proved espe-

cially helpful. Debra W. Johnson and Leslie Edmonds, *Family Literacy Library Programs: Models of Service* (Des Moines, Iowa: Iowa State Library, 1990); Ellin Greene, *Books, Babies, and Libraries* (Chicago: American Library Association, 1991); and Margaret Monroe and Kathleen Heim, *Partners for Lifelong Learning: Public Libraries and Adult Education* (Washington, D.C.: Office of Educational Research and Improvement, 1991).

21. Donald A. Schon, *The Reflective Practitioner: How Professionals Think in Action* (New York: Basic, 1983) and *Educating the Reflective Practitioner* (San Diego, Calif.: Jossey-Bass, 1987); Carl A. Grant, *Preparing for Reflective Teaching* (Boston: Allyn and Bacon, 1984).

Chapter 7

1. George F. Madaus and Ann G. A. Tan, "The Growth of Assessment," in *Challenges and Achievements of American Education*, ed. by Gordon Caweli, 1993 Yearbook of the Association for Supervision and Curriculum Development (Alexandria, Va.: ASCD, 1993), 53–79.

2. For a selection of instruments to evaluate school library media programs, see David V. Loertscher, *Taxonomies of the School Library Media Program* (Englewood, Colo.: Libraries Unlimited, 1988). See also Marilyn Shontz, "Evaluation of Library Resource Center Programs," *Emergency Librarian* 19, no. 1 (September/October 1991): 8–24.

3. American Association of School Librarians and the Association for Educational Communications and Technology, *Information Power: Guidelines for School Library Media Programs* (Chicago: American Library Association, 1988).

4. *Information Power: Checklist for School Library Media Programs*, prepared by Judith K. Meyers for an AECT/AASL Implementation Workshop for *Information Power: Guidelines for School Library Media Programs*, August 20, 1988 (Chicago: American Library Association, 1988).

5. Kathy Howard Latrobe, "Evaluating Library Media Programs in Terms of *Information Power*: Implications for Theory and Practice," *School Library Media Quarterly* 21, no. 1 (Fall 1992): 37–45.

6. From "Expenditures for Resources in School Library Media Centers," *School Library Journal* 39, no. 10 (October 1993): 26–36. Permission to reprint from Reed Publishing, USA.

7. *Expanding Student Assessment*, ed. by Vito Perrone (Alexandria, Va.: Association for Supervision and Curriculum Development, 1991); and, *Advances in Research in Teaching*, vol. 1, ed. by Jere Brophy (Greenwich, Conn.: JAI, 1989).

8. There are a number of useful studies on the college level that deal with student evaluation. A careful analysis of the *American Educational Research Journal* and the *Third Handbook of Research on Teaching* might be most helpful in the design of materials.

9. Donn Byrne, *Techniques for Classroom Interaction* (New York: Longman, 1987); *Controversies in Classroom Research: A Reader*, 2d ed. (Buckingham, England: Open University, 1993); *Classroom Talk: Speaking and Listening Activities from Classroom-Based Teacher Research* (Portsmith, N.H.: Heinemann, 1991); Ned A. Flanders, *Interaction-Analysis in the Classroom: A Manual for Observers* (Ann Arbor, Mich.: University of

Michigan, 1960); and Arno Bellack and others, *The Language of the Classroom: Final Report*, USOE Cooperative Research Project No. 2023 (New York: Teachers College, 1966).

10. One of the best summaries of earlier studies may be found in Michael J. Dunkin and Bruce J. Biddle, *The Study of Teaching* (New York: Holt, Rinehart and Winston, 1974). The April 1992 issue of *Educational Leadership* (vol. 49, no. 7) entitled "Beyond Effective Teaching" is an excellent overview of contemporary approaches to evaluation.

11. Ethnographic research has increased in the 1980s and 1990s and is proving fruitful in the examination of interaction. See, for example, R. F. Ellen, *Ethnographic Research: A Guide to General Conduct* (London: Academic, 1984) and James P. Spradley, *The Ethnographic Interview* (New York: Holt, 1979).

12. American Association of University Women, *The AAUW Report: How Schools Shortchange Girls* (Washington, D.C.: AAUW Educational Foundation, 1992). The AAUW has a number of publications that would help in evaluating gender bias and in providing a means to change such bias such as: *The AAUW Report: How Schools Shortchange Girls, Executive Summary* (1992); *The AAUW Report Action Guide* (1992), which includes concrete strategies for combating gender bias; and *Video: Shortchanging Girls, Shortchanging America* (1991), an examination of inequities girls face in America's schools featuring education experts and public policy leaders.

13. *Taxonomy of Educational Objectives: The Classification of Educational Goals. Handbook 1. Cognitive Domain*, ed. by Benjamin S. Bloom (New York: McKay, 1956) and D. R. Krathwohl and others, *Taxonomy of Educational Objectives: The Classification of Educational Goals, Handbook 2. Affective Domain* (New York: McKay, 1964).

14. Although rather old, for library media specialists, the Behavioral Requirements Analysis Checklist (BRAC) is a good example of this. The key words *behavioral* and *competency-based* appearing in the title and subtitle might lead one to believe that this checklist could be used for rather precise measurement of a library media specialist's performance. The fact that it could not, in no way reduces the value of this tool, which by the very listing of seven hundred tasks to be performed causes library media specialists to reconsider and reevaluate their own professional priorities. See *Behavioral Requirements Analysis Checklist: A Compilation of Competency-Based Job Functions and Task Statements for School Library Media Personnel*, ed. by Robert N. Case and Anna Mary Lowrey (Chicago: American Library Association, 1973).

15. N. L. Gage, *The Scientific Basis of the Art of Teaching* (New York: Teachers College, 1978).

16. Edward F. Kelly, "Curriculum Evaluation and Literary Criticism: Comments on the Analogy," *Curriculum Theory Network* 5 (1975): 87–106; E. W. Eisner. "On the Uses of Educational Connoisseurship and Criticism for Evaluating Classroom Life," *Teachers College Record* 78 (1977): 345–58.

17. *Guidelines for Performance Appraisal of School Library Media Specialists*, Prepared by the Professional Development/Library Education Committee of the American Association of School Librarians (Chicago: American Library Association, 1988); and Ken Haycock, "Evaluation of the Teacher-Librarian: A Discussion Guide," *Emergency Librarian* 18, no. 4 (March/April 1991): R 1–8.

18. One of the best books on the subject is that by Joan L. Herman and others, *A Practical Guide to Alternative Assessment* (Alexandria, Va.: Association for Supervision and Curriculum Development, 1992).

19. Ibid., 19–20.

20. Robert J. Tierney and others, *Portfolio Assessment in the Reading-Writing Class-*

room (Norwood, Mass.: Christopher-Gordon, 1991) and Susan Mandel Glazer and Carol Smullen Brown, *Portfolios and Beyond: Collaborative Assessment in Reading and Writing* (Norwood, Mass.: Christopher-Gordon, 1993).

21. Edward B. Fiske and others, *Smart Schools, Smart Kids* (New York: Simon & Schuster, 1991), 115–44.

22. Lee Shulman, "Assessment for Teaching: Initiative for the Profession," *Phi Delta Kappan* (September 1987): 38–44; Lee Shulman, "The Paradox of Teacher Assessment," in *New Directions for Teacher Assessment* (Princeton, N.J.: Educational Testing Service, 1989), 13–27; and Lee Shulman, "A Union of Insufficiencies: Strategies for Teacher Assessment in a Period of Educational Reform," *Educational Leadership* (November 1988):36–41.

23. Lee Shulman and others, *Toward Alternative Assessments of Teaching: A Report of Work in Progress* (Stanford, Calif.: Teacher Assessment Project, Stanford University, 1989).

24. Kenneth Wolf, "The Schoolteacher's Portfolio: Issues in Design, Implementation, and Evaluation," *Phi Delta Kappan* 73, no. 2 (October 1991): 129.

25. Ibid., 136.

26. *Measures of Excellence for School Library Media Centers*, ed. by David V. Loertscher (Littleton, Colo.: Libraries Unlimited, 1988) provides a range of evaluative measures for school library media center services including involvement of teachers, student involvement in audiovisual production, and media use in the classroom.

APPENDIX

PROJECT

TAP

TIME ALLOCATION & PRIORITIES

INVESTIGATORS:

Kay E. Vandergrift
Daniel O. O'Connor

School of Communication, Information and Library Studies, Rutgers University, New Brunswick, New Jersey.

Funded by a SCILS Faculty Research Grant, Rutgers University, 1989.

DATA ON THE LIBRARY MEDIA CENTER

1. The grade range of the school is from grade _____ to grade _____.
2. The budget for total materials expenditures is _____.
3. The student population is _____.
4. Is a curriculum and/or a scope and sequence chart available for library media skills?
    Yes _____ No _____
5. What is the date of the last revision?
    _____
6. The library media center has the following:
    _____ Online Circ System
    _____ Online Catalog (OPAC)
    _____ Computer for management of the LMC
    _____ Computer with modem
    _____ Access to online data bases
    _____ CD-ROM
    _____ Computers for student use in the media center
    _____ Databases such as BookBrain and/or BookWhiz
    _____ Fax machine
    _____ Copying machine
7. When the microcomputers that are managed by the library media center staff are in the LMC, how are they being used? (Please check as many as apply)
    _____ Reading guidance/literary enrichment
    _____ Library media skills instruction
    _____ Library media center management (check all that apply)
        _____ circulation
        _____ acquisition
        _____ cataloging
        _____ inventory
        _____ overdues
        _____ budgeting/spreadsheets
        _____ ILL
        _____ Other (Please indicate)
            _____
8. Check those items that are included in your curriculum for library media skills:
    _____ The parts of a book
    _____ The Dewey Decimal System
    _____ Searching on Dialog
    _____ Distinguishing points of view in literary works
    _____ Media production
    _____ The use of setting in various forms of story
    _____ Periodical indexes
    _____ Use of INFO-TRAC II
    _____ Traditional motifs in literature
    _____ Persuasive techniques in media
    _____ Approaches to literary criticism
    _____ The steps of the research process
    _____ Recognition of various plot structures
    _____ Use of the card catalog (or online catalog)
    _____ Dictionary skills
    _____ Distinguishing between realistic and fanciful fiction
    _____ Use of atlases and geographical dictionaries
    _____ Use of cross references
    _____ Recognition of symbolic language in a story
    _____ Parts of a newspaper
    _____ Understanding "efferent" and "aesthetic" approaches to interpretation
    _____ Computer skills
    _____ Listening and viewing skills
    _____ Understanding of literary genre
    _____ Biographical tools
    _____ Note-taking techniques
    _____ Operation of AV equipment
    _____ Use of almanacs
    _____ Interpretation of illustrative materials (Pictures, Maps, Charts, Graphs)
    _____ Preparation of footnotes and bibliographies
    _____ Techniques of character development in story
    _____ Identification of point of view in fiction

DATA ON THE LIBRARY MEDIA SPECIALIST

1. The size of the library media center staff is:
   _____ Professionals
   _____ Clericals
   Volunteers:
   _____ Adult
   _____ Student

2. What national and local professional associations do you belong to?
   _____
   _____
   _____

3. What professional development activities did you participate in during the past year?
   _____ National Conference
   _____ Local/Regional Conference
   _____ Institute
   _____ Workshop
   _____ Seminar
   _____ Course
   _____ Lecture

4. How would you assess yourself as a reader?
   _____ An infrequent reader
   _____ An occasional reader
   _____ A moderate reader
   _____ A frequent reader
   _____ A very frequent reader

5. Do you participate in Regional Book Selection activities?
   _____ Never
   _____ Monthly
   _____ Once a semester
   _____ Once a year
   _____ Other (Please indicate _____)

6. What is the primary book reviewing journal you use in collection development?
   _____

7. Do you engage in any cooperative activities with your local public library? If so, what?
   _____

164　Appendix

INSTRUCTIONS: All responses are approximations. We are not concerned with absolute accuracy but with *your perceptions* of priorities. In the Time column, indicate with a plus ⊞ if this item occupies an important portion of your time or with a minus ⊟ if it does not.

LIBRARY MEDIA SPECIALIST **MANAGEMENT** RESPONSIBILITIES	PRIORITIES OF SCHOOL ADMINISTRATOR AS YOU PERCEIVE THEM RATE 1 - 7 Lowest Moderate Highest 1 2 3 4 5 6 7	YOUR PRIORITIES RATE 1 - 7 Lowest Moderate Highest 1 2 3 4 5 6 7	TIME + OR −
Defines the library media center program, mission, goals and objectives.			
Articulates the purposes for planning, the outcomes expected and the evaluation procedures to be used.			
Involves students, teachers and administrators in the planning process.			
Designs, formulates, justifies, administrates and evaluates the library media budget.			
Defines personnel needs, selects qualified personnel, develops staff competencies, establishes standards of performance and evaluates personnel performance.			
Implements circulation systems and policies that promote ready and free access to collection materials.			
Assesses changing needs of the curriculum and of individual users.			
Reads professional journals/book reviews			
Evaluates and selects resources for the collection			
Arranges facilities to create an environment that encourages the use of various media, facilitates inquiry, helps motivate students to use the materials and services necessary for learning, and provides the design flexibility needed to accommodate new technologies.			
Demonstrates effective leadership by articulating the vision of the library media program with enthusiasm and confidence.			
Promotes and markets the program of the library media center.			
Practices interpersonal skills in working interactively with various constituencies—teachers, students, administrators, parents, and the community.			
Provides periodic maintenance through inventory, and the removal of outdated or inaccurate collection materials.			
Provides the logical organization of collection materials, preferably with standardized procedures, and with an aim toward automation.			
Participates in network activities.			
Establishes flexible policies and procedures for the use of resources, emphasizing maximum access to all users.			
Provides retrieval systems for accurate and efficient access to information resources.			

Appendix   165

LIBRARY MEDIA SPECIALIST **INSTRUCTION** RESPONSIBILITIES	PRIORITIES OF SCHOOL ADMINISTRATOR AS YOU PERCEIVE THEM RATE 1 - 7 Lowest Moderate Highest 1 2 3 4 5 6 7	YOUR PRIORITIES RATE 1 - 7 Lowest Moderate Highest 1 2 3 4 5 6 7	TIME + OR −
Provides assistance in identifying, locating, and interpreting information housed in and outside the library media center.			
Uses a variety of instructional methods with different user groups.			
Teaches the structures of various media and the distinctive uses of compositional elements in media such as film, video, computer graphics, etc.			
Demonstrates the effective use of newer media and technologies.			
Teaches the information curriculum as an integral part of the content and objectives of the school's curriculum.			
Teaches compositional elements of story.			
Includes instruction in accessing, evaluating, and communicating information.			
Teaches production in a variety of media.			
Integrates systematic learning activities with library media resources to emphasize higher-order cognitive strategies (critical thinking skills) for selecting, retrieving, analyzing, synthesizing, and evaluating information.			
Explores archetypal patterns in literature and popular media.			
Relates television advertising to the folk tradition.			
Teaches the steps of the research process.			
Discusses literary works from the viewpoint of feminist criticism.			
Teaches metacognitive skills to students.			
Teaches students to articulate alternative responses to a particular work of art.			
Participates in school, district, departmental and grade-level curriculum design and assessment projects.			
Helps teachers develop instructional activities.			
Provides continuing education to teachers in the selection, evaluation and use of materials and emerging technologies for the delivery of information and instruction.			
Develops unit objectives that build viewing, listening, reading and critical thinking skills.			
Analyzes learner characteristics that will influence design and use of media.			

Appendix

LIBRARY MEDIA SPECIALIST **PROGRAM** RESPONSIBILITIES	PRIORITIES OF SCHOOL ADMINISTRATOR AS YOU PERCEIVE THEM RATE 1 - 7 Lowest Moderate Highest 1 2 3 4 5 6 7	YOUR PRIORITIES RATE 1 - 7 Lowest Moderate Highest 1 2 3 4 5 6 7	TIME + OR −
Designs, promotes, executes and evaluates programs for students based on their developmental needs and the goals of the library media program.			
Offers programs on materials selection for parents and caregivers.			
Provides a variety of programs including storytelling, book talking, media discussion, and other appropriate activities.			
Designs programs to introduce teachers to new materials.			
Spends time talking with individual students about their film and television viewing.			
Develops book lists related to current student interests or topical concerns.			
Spends time talking with individuals about favorite books.			
Organizes poetry sharing sessions for students and teachers.			
Helps older students prepare for storytelling activities with younger children.			
Discusses literary ideas with students.			
Provides readers' advisory service, helping students to develop personal reading, viewing, listening plans.			
Encourages reading for pleasure as well as for information and instruction.			

LIBRARY MEDIA SPECIALIST **CLERICAL & CUSTODIAL** RESPONSIBILITIES	PRIORITIES OF SCHOOL ADMINISTRATOR AS YOU PERCEIVE THEM RATE 1 - 7 Lowest Moderate Highest 1 2 3 4 5 6 7	YOUR PRIORITIES RATE 1 - 7 Lowest Moderate Highest 1 2 3 4 5 6 7	TIME + OR −
Shelving materials.			
Preparing catalog copy.			
Ordering supplies.			
Filing.			
Photocopying materials.			
Student discipline.			
Circulation statistics.			
Arranging chairs, tables, etc.			
Checking publishers/distributors lists.			
Typing (word processing) booklists, etc.			
Preparing displays.			
Materials/Equipment Repair.			
Preparing new materials for circulation.			
Inventories.			
General housekeeping duties.			

Please indicate your overall evaluation of priorities and time allocations for the four major categories.

LIBRARY MEDIA SPECIALIST RESPONSIBILITIES	PRIORITIES OF SCHOOL ADMINISTRATOR AS YOU PERCEIVE THEM RATE 1 – 7 Lowest Moderate Highest 1 2 3 4 5 6 7	YOUR PRIORITIES RATE 1 – 7 Lowest Moderate Highest 1 2 3 4 5 6 7	HOURS YOU SPENT ON THIS RESPONSIBILITY DURING THE PREVIOUS WEEK	DAYS YOU SPEND ON THIS RESPONSIBILITY DURING AN AVG. MONTH
MANAGEMENT				
INSTRUCTION				
PROGRAM (Individual & Group Activities)				
CLERICAL & CUSTODIAL				

Please provide an assessment, in your own words, of your role and responsibilities. Be honest and specific in completing the following three statements.

I. In my view the primary role of the library media specialist is . . .

II. In my view the library media specialist has the following responsibilities in the development of library media skills . . .

_____

III. In my view the library media specialist has the following responsibilities in the development of literary abilities . . .

_____

THANK YOU FOR YOUR COOPERATION.

Index

AAUW. *See* American Association of University Women
Adult education, 102, 126–27
Aesthetic analysis, 142–43
Aesthetic dimension, and learning, 49
America 2000, 1, 2, 4, 18
American Association of University Women (AAUW), 9
Assessment
  of school library media center, 128
  of students, 4, 45, 143
  See also Evaluation
Authors, biographical resources for, 67–71

Bennet, William J., 4
Berkowitz, Robert, 103
Bibliographic access, for selection, 111–14
"Big Six Skills" approach, 103
Biographical resources, for authors, illustrators, 67–71

Caregivers, consultations with, 126–27
CD-ROM databases, 56–57
Checklist, for competencies, 45
Choice, of schools, 7–9
Cleaver, Betty, 103
Costs, and education, 18
Cultural Literacy, 4
Curriculum
  approach to, 6–7
  changes in, 102–3
  content of, 4–6
  and media specialists, 29–30

Disabilities, and public law, 6
Docudrama, use of, 71–72

Education
  aspects of learning, 11–15
  change in, 17–20
  choice issues in, 7–9
  costs of, 18–19
  gender equity in, 9–11
  national goals for, 1, 18, 19
  time factor for change in, 19
  traditional information skills for, 42–50
Educational materials, 18
Eisenberg, Michael, 103
Eisenhower Math and Science Education Act, 10
Elementary and Secondary Education Act (ESEA), 10
ESEA. *See* Elementary and Secondary Education Act
Evaluation
  alternative forms of, 141–46
  biographical resources for authors, illustrators, 67–71
  of docudrama, 71–72
  of media and resources, 47
  of nonprint biographical materials, 65–71
  personal, 143–44
  of portfolios, 144–46
  of print biographical materials, 58–65
  of school library media specialist, 128–46
  of teaching, 132, 136–46
  teaching strategies for, 58–76
  through media production, 73–75
  types of, 129–30
  See also Assessment
Eyewitness Books, 53–54

Index

Focus, for research, 52–57

Gage, N. L., 142
Gender
   and education, 9–11
   and materials selection, 123–26
Geography studies, as model, 30–40
Goals, for education, 1, 18, 19
   See also Standards
The Graywolf Annual Five, 5

Helping Teachers Teach, 103
Herman, Joan, 143
Hirsch, E. D., Jr., 4, 5
Homework, issues in, 126
How Schools Shortchange Girls, 9
Hypercard, 57

Illustrators, biographical resources for, 67–71
In-service workshops, 104–26
Information Power, xiii, 19–20, 29, 42, 101, 130, 131
Information skills instruction, 42–50
Intellectual freedom, and selection, 114–19

Joyce, Bruce, 27, 28

Kozol, Jonathan, 18

Language arts, learning of, 12–13
Learning, aspects of, 11–15
Legislation, federal
   for disabilities, 6
   for gender, 10
Libraries for the National Goals, 1
Library cooperation, questionnaire on, 133–36
Literacy, parental, 126–27
Literature, different versions of, 120–23
Local control, and schools, 3

Magnet schools, 8
Mainstreaming, of children, 6
Management, school-based, 2
Mathematics materials, for selection, 113–14

Media
   evaluation of. *See* Evaluation
   production of, 73–75
Media center, and technology, 16–17
Models, of teaching, 27–32, 103–4
Models of Teaching, 27
Multiculturalism, issues in, 5–6

National Association for Sports and Physical Education, 3
National Council of Teachers of Mathematics, 3
National Council on Education Standards and Testing (NCEST), 2
NCEST. *See* National Council on Education Standards and Testing
New Standards Project (NSP), 3
Nonprint biographical materials, 65–71
NSP. *See* New Standards Project

OERI. *See* Office of Educational Research and Improvement
Office of Educational Research and Improvement (OERI), 10
Online databases, 56–57
"Outcomes of Quality Physical Education Programs," 3
Outline, for research, 51

Parents
   consultations with, 126–27
   literacy of, 126–27
   and school choice, 7–9
Photo-analysis, of teaching, 137–39
Portfolios, and evaluation, 144–46
A Practical Guide to Alternative Assessment, 143
Print biographical materials, evaluation of, 58–65
Production, of media, 73–75
Professionalization, definition of, 1–2
Project TAP (Time Allocation and Priorities), New Jersey, 130–32
   See also Appendix, 162
Public Law 94-142 (children with disabilities), 6

Index   171

Question log, 49–50
Questionnaire, on library cooperation, 133–36
Questions, for media specialist evaluation, 131

Readers' Guide, 56
Research, process of, 47–50
Research journal, use of, 49
Research topic, selection of, 50–57

Savage Inequalities, 18–19
Scheduling, issues in, 7
School library media specialist
  and evaluation, 128–46
  as instru[...]
  as resear[...]
  roles of, [...]
  as teache[...]
School-uni[...]
*The Scienti[...]
  142
Selection, [...]
  bibliogra[...]
  female v[...]
  intellectu[...]
  mathema[...]
  societal i[...]
  versions of literature, 120–23
Semantic webbing. *See* Webbing
Simonson, Rick, 5
Societal issues, and selection, 107–11
Staff development, 101–27
Standards, for education
  national, 1, 2–4
  teachers' role in, 2
  See also Goals, for education

TAP. *See* Project TAP (New Jersey);
  Teachers' Assessment Project (Stanford)
Taylor, William, 103
Teachers' Assessment Project (TAP), Stanford, 145
Teaching
  aspects of, 22–27
  evaluation of, 132, 136–46
  ideals for, 1–2
  models of, 27–30, 103–4
Technology, and media center, 16–17
Telecommunications, use of, 7
T.I.E. Model of Cooperative Instructional Development, 103–4
Time factor, and goals, 19
[...]ner, Philip, 103

[...]er, Harlow G., 4

[...]. *See* Vocational Education Act
[...]al interactions, analysis of, 137
[...]o analysis, of teaching, 139
[...]ocassettes, use of, 68–70
[...]ual reality, 17
[...]ational Education Act (VEA), 10

[...]ker, Scott, 5
[...]bing, semantic, 51, 77–100
Webs, semantic
  author, 83–85
  book, 85–99
  topic, 77–83
WEEA. *See* Women's Educational Equity Act of 1974
Weil, Marsha, 27, 28
What Did You Learn in School Today?, 4
Women's Educational Equity Act of 1974 (WEEA), 10